Environment and Economy

Environment and Economy
Essays on the Human Geography of Alberta

edited by
B. M. Barr
P. J. Smith

Pica Pica Press

First published by
The Pica Pica Press
(Textbook division of The University of Alberta Press)
Athabasca Hall
Edmonton, Alberta
Canada T6G 2E8

ISBN 0-88864-042-0

Canadian Cataloguing in Publication Data
Main entry under title:
Environment and economy
Bibliography: p.
ISBN 0-88864-042-0
1. Anthropo-geography - Alberta - Addresses,
essays, lectures. 2. Alberta - Economic conditions -
Addresses, essays, lectures. I. Barr, Brenton M.,
1940- II. Smith, P. J. (Peter John), 1931-
GF512.A4E58 1984   304.2'097123   C84-091034-7

Typesetting by The Typeworks, Vancouver, British Columbia
Printed by Hignell Printing Limited, Winnipeg, Manitoba, Canada

For Peggy, Elane, and John, for their contributions to the geography of Alberta.

B. M. B.

To the memory of Sidney Charles Smith, 1899–1984.

P. J. S.

Contents

Contributors

Dr. B. M. Barr	Professor, Department of Geography, University of Calgary, Calgary, Alberta.
Dr. P. G. Cadden	Research Officer, Alberta Municipal Affairs, Edmonton, Alberta.
Dr. L. D. Cordes	Associate Professor, Department of Geography, University of Calgary, Calgary, Alberta.
Mrs. A. D. Dhanani	Tripoli, Libya.
Dr. R. G. Ironside	Professor and Chairman, Department of Geography, University of Alberta, Edmonton, Alberta.
Dr. E. L. Jackson	Associate Professor, Department of Geography, University of Alberta, Edmonton, Alberta.
Dr. L. A. Kosiński	Professor, Department of Geography, University of Alberta, Edmonton, Alberta.
Mr. D. J. Pennock	Doctoral Candidate, Department of Geography, Queen's University, Kingston, Ontario.
Dr. P. J. Smith	Professor, Department of Geography, University of Alberta, Edmonton, Alberta.
Dr. R. Stamp	Educational Consultant, Toronto, Ontario.
Dr. E. S. Szplett	Lecturer, Department of Geography, University of Toronto, Toronto, Ontario.
Dr. N. M. Waters	Associate Professor, Department of Geography, University of Calgary, Calgary, Alberta.

Preface

The essays in this collection are all original, and all were written with one purpose in mind: to introduce the major characteristics of Alberta's economic geography to a wide audience. Although they are particularly designed for survey courses in the geography of Alberta at the college or university level, they are also intended as basic reading for anyone interested in the changes at work in Alberta's economic landscape. The authors address important topics in these essays: where people live and why; how they have organized this territory of theirs, the province of Alberta; and the influence of the host of factors by which the landscape is constantly being reshaped including relations between man and the physical environment, perceptions of natural resources, cultural attitudes and personal expectations, demographic trends, and economic and political conditions, both at home and abroad.

With this general end in view, the authors have aimed to present their ideas in a form that can be easily understood. Technical language has been kept to a minimum and special terms are always defined. There are many maps and tables, but we have tried to keep them clear and simple, and the text is not overburdened with statistical analyses. The authors have also forgone the usual trappings of scholarly writing. There are very few footnotes or quotations, and no citations or lengthy bibliographies or elaborate descriptions of research methods. All the essays are based on detailed, up-to-date research, and incorporate results that may have been presented elsewhere in theses or scientific papers, but the emphasis here is upon general insights and broad interpretations.

By the same token, all the essays had to be kept brief, and none of the contributors could develop their topics in the depth they would have liked. Suggestions for further reading are therefore appended to each chapter, although it is remarkable how little of general interest has been written about the geography of Alberta. Had it been otherwise, of course, the need for this book would have been less pressing. As it is, we hope our essays will open the door to the narrower and more specialized literature that certainly exists—in scientific journals, in research monographs, and in the reports of numerous government agencies. The Environment Council of Alberta (previously the Environment Conservation Authority) is a particularly valuable source, partly because its reports are intended to have a wide distribution, and partly because of the variety of man-environment relationships into which the Council has inquired.

There are also a number of useful reference works that should be available in most libraries. Two that have been drawn upon freely by the authors in this book are *Industry and Resources*, a regular publication of the Government of Alberta, and the *Atlas of Alberta*, which was compiled as a centennial project by the University of Alberta. *Industry and Resources* is a statistical handbook, but it also includes numerous maps and a straightforward text, and its contents are revised periodically. The *Atlas*, by contrast, is now outdated in much of its statistical information, though it continues to be an invaluable resource for all that. It lays out the basic geographical patterns of Alberta with a thoroughness and completeness that no book can rival. Indeed, only one book fits the needs of this list of general references. That is *Alberta: A Natural History*, edited by W. G. Hardy and first published in 1967. In its overview of the basic elements of the natural environment, and in its detailed descriptions of the regional ecosystems, this book is still the outstanding source on Alberta's physical geography.

Acknowledgments

The editors and authors wish to record their appreciation for the practical assistance and support which were so freely given by the departments of geography at the University of Alberta and the University of Calgary. Many people have contributed in many ways, but two deserve particular mention: Fran Metcalfe, who typed the complete manuscript more times than she would care to remember, and Inge Wilson, of the Cartography Laboratory at the University of Alberta, whose superb draftsmanship can be seen in every figure. The authors of Chapter 5 also wish to note their special thanks for the help given by Linda Jackson and Paul Precht.

Introduction
General Themes and Concepts

B. M. Barr

P. J. Smith

The people of Alberta are spread unevenly across the province's huge territory. At one extreme, three out of every five Albertans live in just two places, the cities of Edmonton and Calgary. At the other extreme, over thousands upon thousands of square kilometres, scarcely a person is to be found. In these simple facts rests the fundamental problem for human geographers: to explain how and why such variation can occur. Is it just a matter of physical environment? Are some areas naturally poor and inhospitable while others are full of richness and invitation? Is there some distinctive form or pattern in the way that Albertans have distributed themselves across the space that is Alberta? If there is a pattern, what organizing principles lie behind it? Are there general processes shaping the pattern, processes that affect a much larger stage than Alberta alone? Or is Alberta, in some vital sense, unique?

Directly or indirectly, these questions are addressed repeatedly throughout this book. They also relate back to a single geographical concept which underlies every essay—the concept of the *space-economy,* or the spatial organization of economic activity. The central idea is that all people in all places at all times practice some form of economic activity which provides them with their livelihood, or their means of maintaining life. This does not necessarily mean that they will labour on farms or in factories, or even that they will hold jobs in the conventional sense. But it does mean that everyone, everywhere, must have some kind of economic support, "economic" being defined in its broadest terms as the "production, distribution and use of income, wealth and commodities."

It also follows that all economic activities are set in geographical space, in two senses. First, each activity must use or occupy its own unique space; it has a *site* or absolute location. Second, and much more important to human geographers, all economic activities depend on complex interrelationships which cause them to be linked together in equally complex spatial systems. This idea of spatial relationships is conveyed by the terms *situation* and *relative location,* which refer to the location of a place in relation to all the other places with which it has a functional connection.

It should also be apparent that *distance* is the key geographical factor in these spatial relationships, although distance means much more than is suggested by a simple direct-line measurement. Indeed, other ways of thinking of distance hold much greater significance for the interpretation of the space-economy. To the geographer, distance really means ease of communication and it is best measured in terms of the cost, in both time and money, of communicating across space. From this perspective, space or distance is an obstacle that must be overcome; it is a source of *friction* within the space-economy. For some purposes today the friction is relatively weak, and space has collapsed into the cost of completing a phone call or some other electronically transmitted message. For other purposes, such as the shipment of bulky goods to their markets, the friction of distance is still strong; in cost terms, interdependent places remain far apart.

The effects of these different perceptions of distance on the space-economy of Alberta are confusing to say the least. In some respects, Alberta must still be considered to be relatively isolated, and that, in turn, is a source of economic disadvantage. Its location in the interior of a continental land mass, far removed from ocean ports and from large population concentrations, automatically excludes a broad range of economic activities. Manufacturing industry, in particular, continues to be weakly developed, and there is little reason to hope that the friction of high transport costs will soon be offset. For most types of manufacturing, the comparative advantage is likely to remain in the Canadian heartland of southern Ontario and the St. Lawrence lowland. Yet, for other economic activities, including some types of manufacturing, Alberta's location may not be a disadvantage at all. There is no geographical reason to prevent path-breaking research from being carried out in Alberta, or to prevent the successful establishment of sophisticated forms of manufacturing flowing from that research. Indeed, the very features of Alberta's location that make it uncompetitive for the large-scale development of conventional industry could work to the advantage of those economic activities for which the friction of distance is weak. From this perspective Alberta takes on characteristics not unlike those of the sun-belt states of the American southwest. The proximity of mountains and wilderness, the lack of congestion, the newness of the cities, and the youthfulness of the population make up a package of amenities that are powerfully attractive for some people and some activities. Many parallels can be drawn between the recent growth of Edmonton and Calgary, and cities like Denver and Phoenix.

This particular example also serves to emphasize the point that the char-

acteristic economic activities of any place are a result of the interplay
between the factors of site and situation. In general, the space-economy of
Alberta is conditioned by three main sets of influences: the relationship
between Alberta and the world outside; the relationships among all places
within Alberta; and the natural resource attributes of those places.

A *resource*, by definition, is anything valued by people for its contribution
to their economic, social, or psychological well-being. In Alberta's case, however, the resources of greatest note are those derived from its natural environment. The qualities of terrain, soil, and climate, and the use potential of land
and water, forests and minerals are the outstanding site features underlying
the economic activities that shape the pattern of Alberta's space-economy.
The reason that certain resources are valued in certain ways at certain times
is actually less a function of their inherent qualities than of their situation in
relation to the sources of demand. During the energy crises of the 1970s, for
example, Alberta's oil sands became a highly valued resource; the national
interest appeared to demand that they be developed at almost any cost.
Then, within a very short time, political and economic circumstances
changed drastically, and an acceptable cost became unacceptable. The resource had not changed in the meantime, but its value outside Alberta had
fallen markedly and development stalled. The growth prospects of towns like
Fort McMurray and Cold Lake evaporated, at least for a time; the viability of
proposed new refineries and processing plants was thrown into doubt, as
was the need for massive investments in transport facilities to serve them;
and even Edmonton and Calgary looked into futures that were suddenly
clouded.

Although this was an extreme instance, the dramatic change in growth expectations experienced in the early 1980s in Alberta demonstrates the control that factors external to the site of a resource exert over its actual use. The
point is surely an obvious one, yet must be emphasized, if only to avoid the
risk of deterministic explanations of the space-economy. It is all too easy to
assume that the natural characteristics of a site determine the use to which it
is put, because of simple associations that everyone can see. The location of
the oil sands processing industry, for example, is fixed by the location of the
sand deposits; there can be no forestry industry if there are no forests; the
type of agriculture varies with climatic and soil conditions; and so on. In
every case, however, the decision to use a particular natural resource in a
particular way at a particular time is influenced by a great variety of factors. It
goes without saying that the character of the resource or site has an important
bearing on the decisions that are made, but it is only one element in a complex equation that also includes economic, social, political, and psychological variables.

The role of site features in the organization of the space-economy is best
described in terms of opportunities and limitations. Some areas are extremely limited in their potential for human settlement; others may offer no

serious impediment at all. Limitations can always be overcome, of course, if there is sufficient will to do so, but that also depends on the pressure on alternative opportunities elsewhere. In Alberta, there is no incentive as yet to occupy vast tracts of wilderness, and perhaps there never will be; indeed, there are good reasons for resisting such pressures, should they ever arise. For the purpose of understanding the space-economy of Alberta, however, it is important to realise that nature has not determined that these lands can never be adapted to human use. Rather, other areas offer much greater ranges of more easily exploited opportunities that are still far from exhausted. As a consequence, the physically difficult lands are not well integrated into Alberta's systems of human activity; they are the most remote or peripheral areas within the space-economy, and their "distance" from the main population centres is an important factor in their local economies.

In summary, then, the natural environment *influences* patterns of economic activity but does not determine them, even in those areas that are most restricted in their opportunities for human settlement. Other, purely human factors will always come into play, emphasizing the point that the environment shaping space-economy decisions is much more than a matter of physical geography. *Environment* is literally everything that surrounds, so every outside influence upon the space-economy is part of its environment. Economic conditions in the rest of Canada and elsewhere in the world, social norms and popular attitudes, government policies and programs, laws and regulations of all kinds—whether alone or in combination—play their part in determining the economic activities by which Albertans support themselves. Geographical space is also a critical part of this decision-making environment. The friction of distance, whether real or imagined, limits the choice of livelihood as surely as the most difficult natural environment. Conversely, to reduce the friction is to expand the opportunities for economic support and, thus, to expand the range of activities that might be drawn to any site.

It must also be evident that the space-economy is a dynamic phenomenon, changing in response to changes in its environment. Of particular concern here are those long-term processes that produce major structural changes, such as the emergence of new economic activities and the new spatial arrangements of those activities, the development of new patterns of relationships among the different types of places, and the acceptance of fundamentally changed attitudes towards the natural attributes of site and place. In the span of 200 years, the space-economy of the territory that is now Alberta has evolved from a self-contained tribal society, dependent upon subsistence hunting and gathering for its livelihood, to a small element in the most complex system of global interdependence that human enterprise has so far been able to devise. In this evolutionary sense, Alberta now has one of the world's most advanced economies. Its systems of production are efficient, sophisticated, and highly productive. In normal circumstances, they are also prosperous, capable of generating an average level of personal affluence un-dreamed of even 40 or 50 years ago.

The historical process underlying these developments is commonly re-ferred to as *modernization*. Very briefly, modernization is defined as the pro-cess by which traditional subsistence societies are transformed into modern, commercial ones. Through an overlapping series of revolutions—agricul-tural, industrial, scientific, technological, and demographic—economic systems undergo radical structural changes which are simultaneously ex-pressed in the organization of the space-economy. Particularly important sequences of this process involve the evolution of rural agricultural societies into urban industrial ones, and the further evolution into a post-industrial stage at which Alberta is now arriving. In this stage, the production of goods is no longer the sole engine driving the economic system. Primary and secondary industries continue to be very important, in absolute terms, but they require a smaller and smaller share of the labour force, which is then freed to expand into other productive activities. At first, tertiary or service industries supplant the goods-producing industries as the employment growth sector, but this eventually leads to a stage in which the exchange of information and ideas is the most important condition for continued eco-nomic development.

In its general outlines, this evolutionary sequence is mirrored in the organ-ization of this book. It begins with the foundations of the modern space-economy in the period of agricultural colonization, and with the political events by which the distinctive territory of Alberta was forged. It ends with a first analysis of the new frontier of economic development in Alberta, in what are now coming to be known as the quaternary and quinary industries. But although the book ends at that point, the evolution of Alberta's space-economy will not; the current pattern is no more than the latest stage in a process of continuous change.

Finally, it must be emphasized that no moral connotation is attached to the idea of an evolving space-economy. Evolution does not necessarily mean that society has progressed or improved. Rather, the term is used here in the neutral scientific sense of a gradual adaptation to environment. Similarly, an advanced economy does not necessarily guarantee a better way of life; it may not even bring an end to long-standing structural problems. Alberta's economy in the 1980s is certainly advanced, but it also continues to be nar-rowly based; it is as vulnerable as ever to boom-and-bust fluctuations in response to external events. In addition, each new stage in the evolutionary sequence spawns its own problems, and they, in turn, generate their own pressures for further change. Great material benefits have obviously accrued from the economic developments of recent decades, but these benefits have not been equally distributed, nor have they been without cost. Some of the costs are now seen as critically important issues in their own right—pollu-tion, loss of farmland, destructive demands on the natural environment, regional disparities, deprivation of Native peoples, social and individual anomie, and on and on. Many of these problems are touched upon in the chapters that follow, and although we have not attempted to look into the future they can be taken as signposts of the need for continuing change. The recognition of problems, in itself, becomes part of the environment to which the space-economy adapts.

Part 1
People, Time, and Space

Part 1 of this book is concerned with changes in the settlement system and population characteristics of Alberta, through both time and space.

In little more than a century Alberta has progressed from a sparsely settled territory on the margin of the British Empire to one of Canada's most important urban-industrial regions. Robert Stamp in his essay, "The Emergence of Alberta as a Geopolitical Entity," reviews the historical events that have helped shape Alberta's human landscape, beginning with the transfer of territorial jurisdiction from the Hudson's Bay Company to Canada in 1869. Alberta was then opened to white settlement, and transportation arteries were developed to provide access to the outside world. A commercial economy was forged upon the exchange of primary commodities for manufactures produced abroad or in central Canada.

With the establishment of provincial government in 1905, Alberta began to engage in a series of accommodations with and reactions to the central government. These continue to the present. Some of the old points of friction have long since abated, but others have not. In particular, suggests Professor Stamp, the transfer of Crown lands and natural resource ownership from Ottawa in 1930 did not resolve the problems of Alberta's autonomy and legal rights. The two governments remain deeply divided about the disposition and pricing of raw materials, and the extent to which wealth gained by the sale of natural resources—particularly oil and gas—is exclusively within Alberta's control.

Alberta's role within Confederation has waxed and waned as a political issue throughout the province's history. The United Farmers of Alberta, the Social Credit League, and later the Progressive Conservative Party have all been associated with tides of protest over perceived inequalities and frustrations between residents of Alberta and other Canadian regions, particularly as made manifest by actions of the federal government. Although the specific issues have varied over time, as Robert Stamp points out, the themes of economic frustration and political alienation continue to underlie Alberta's human geography.

In addition to these historical and political factors, Alberta's settlement system is closely defined by the location and spatial form of the province's major economic sectors—agriculture and energy extraction—and by the transport facilities on which they depend. Peter Smith explores this topic in Chapter 2, "The Changing Structure of the Settlement System."

The evolution of Alberta's settlement system reflects the commercialization of the national and provincial economies. The initial concentration on subsistence agriculture or labour-intensive commercial farming has been superseded by energy-intensive corporate farming and the rise of urban-oriented service economies (augmented in the two metropolitan centres by manufacturing, commercial-tertiary, and quaternary pursuits). Although the rural farm population has declined, Professor Smith notes that improvements in personal mobility have permitted the rise of a large rural non-farm population and the growth of suburban communities. Over three-quarters of Alberta's people are now classed as urban; in less than a quarter century, the settlement system ceased to be predominantly rural and like other modern economic regions became organized around its urban places.

Alberta's population distribution is now dominated by the two metropolitan centres, and by other urban places that are accessible to agricultural and resource activities. Towns adjacent to the main highways and particularly to the "I"-shaped Edmonton-Calgary corridor, and towns serving as gateways to economic opportunity within the province or the Canadian north, have the most important roles in the settlement system.

This development pattern, in turn, is associated with highly uneven population growth rates. Nonetheless, as Leszek Kosiński describes in Chapter 3, "Population Characteristics and Trends," most areas of Alberta are now experiencing their greatest populations ever. The only exception is east-central Alberta where the effects of rural depopulation have not been offset by industrial expansion.

As well as varying largely in space, Alberta's population growth rates have been extremely variable over time. Fluctuations in migration have been especially pronounced, and Alberta's ability to attract and hold people has been conditioned by a large number of factors which are themselves extremely variable. At any particular time these factors come down to the comparative advantage or disadvantage that Alberta is seen to hold in relation to the rest of Canada and the rest of the world. With the economic growth and prosperity experienced since the Second World War Alberta has generally been in a positive position, but even so there have been short periods of net out-migration. The population growth trends have been further complicated by the changing effects of natural increase. Births have always exceeded deaths in Alberta and, on balance, natural increase has contributed more than migration to the province's population growth. But Alberta has also reached the advanced stage of the demographic transition, characterized by low fertility and low mortality and thus a low rate of natural increase. With the added effect of an aging population, the natural increase of Alberta's population must be expected to diminish still further in the foreseeable future.

A final feature of Alberta's population growth is its long association with a diversity of cultures and ethnic groups, notably from non-English and non-French European countries. Yet English is the preferred language for most Albertans today, and the 1981 census has confirmed the trend to linguistic assimilation. There are variations among the different ethnic groups, related to such factors as recency of immigration, degree of urbanization, intermarriage, education, and the strength of ancestral ties, but the drift towards cultural homogeneity is unmistakable. This trend holds as well for the native peoples of Alberta who, like everybody else, are increasingly being absorbed into an urban English-speaking milieu. At the same time, natives comprise a disproportionately large segment of the population of the poorest peripheral areas of Alberta. Whichever environment they choose, and whether they opt for cultural integration or for a unique identity, the future of the native peoples poses Alberta with one of its greatest challenges.

1 The Emergence of Alberta as a Geopolitical Entity

Robert Stamp

The purpose of this chapter is to sketch the historical dimensions of Alberta's human landscape by focusing on its evolution as a geopolitical entity. The treatment is in three parts: the period of territorial status between 1870 and 1905; the political issues surrounding the achievement of provincial autonomy in 1905; and Alberta's political development as a province since 1905. While the chief concern is with political history, mention is made of the social and economic background that shaped political events. A context is therefore set for the major development themes, such as urbanization and industrialization, to be treated more fully in later chapters.

The Territorial Period to 1905

Prior to becoming part of Canada in 1869, the 660,000 km² of the future Alberta, along with the much greater area of the rest of the Canadian West and North, were the exclusive domain of the Hudson's Bay Company. All who entered came under the political sovereignty of the Company, which was then managed partly by a governor and committee in England and partly by the Council of the Northern Department of Rupert's Land, a body that comprised a second, Canadian governor and the chief factors from the principal trading posts. This council met annually at York Factory, the company's overseas headquarters on Hudson Bay, and there passed regulations for its entire North American domain. Apart from limited local government in the District of Assiniboia (around present-day Winnipeg), company rule over the region was absolute.

The sparse, seminomadic population between the Red River and the

Rocky Mountains must always have been small, though their numbers cannot be estimated. Once the home of the Cree and Blackfoot nations, the region had been steadily drawn into the fur trading orbit of the Hudson's Bay Company. First came the exploratory forays of company men, Anthony Henday in 1754, and David Thompson in 1787. Then, before the end of the eighteenth century, company posts were established at Fort Chipewyan, Edmonton House, and Rocky Mountain House. From 1823 to 1854 Chief Factor John Rowand administered this vast territory from Fort Edmonton. But even by the mid-point of the nineteenth century, the white and mixed-blood population remained few in numbers, and clustered mainly around the fur trade posts, leaving the remainder of this "Great Lone Land" to its native population.

The Canadian Confederation of 1867 soon brought an end to political rule by the Hudson's Bay Company and an economy based solely on the fur trade. Canadian expansionists, centred mostly in Toronto, had for some years eyed the western prairies as a potential hinterland of their own. Did not the fertile soil of the West promise farmland for surplus Ontario population? Would not an agricultural West and an industrial East provide reciprocal markets for each other's goods? After some period of negotiation, the Canadian government on November 1, 1869, purchased the entire Hudson's Bay Territory for £300,000. While the company retained ownership of some 2,800,000 ha of land, it surrendered political control to Ottawa.

The end of company rule did not lead automatically or quickly to complete self-rule for the prairie region within Canada. Granted, the Assiniboia or Red River region, thanks to the push for self-government from Louis Riel and his followers, became the tiny province of Manitoba in 1870. But the empty lands between the Red River and the Rockies were granted territorial rather than provincial status as the North-West Territories. For administrative purposes, the lieutenant-governor of Manitoba, from his official residence in Winnipeg, served also as lieutenant-governor of the Territories.

Despite slow population growth and the absence of local government, the machinery of constituted law and order was not absent from the North-West Territories. Here, perhaps, is the most fundamental difference between the opening of the American West, with its tradition of rough, frontier justice, and the much quieter Canadian West. North of the 49th parallel, law and order preceded settlement. Security was provided initially by the Hudson's Bay Company and the Christian missionaries. Then came the Dominion Lands Act of 1872 which laid the basis for the quarter-section homestead survey. The following year saw the creation of the North West Mounted Police; their march west from Fort Dufferin in Manitoba to Fort Macleod in present-day southern Alberta chased the American whisky traders from the region. The signing of Treaty No. 7 with the Blackfoot Indian nation in 1876 further lessened the possibility of conflict between the native population and the future white settlers of the area. Even the Canadian Pacific Railway had crossed the southern prairies by 1883, prior to the mass migration of people westward.

The federal government's North-West Territories Act of 1875 was one more attempt to avoid the unorganized, somewhat lawless example of the American West. This statute gave the region between Manitoba and the Rockies its own capital at Battleford (which was later moved to Regina); its own lieutenant-governor, David Laird; and its own legislature, initially an appointed council that was gradually replaced by elected members. Even at an early stage in development, the institutions of the white man's civilization were present in the Canadian West. There was no place for the revolutionary frontier tradition of the American West.

By 1881 some 1,000 white settlers resided within the boundaries of the present province of Alberta. All they had established was the bridgehead of three villages—Edmonton, Calgary, and Fort Macleod—with a single line of communication connecting them. As yet this line, the Old North Trail, was but a crude track running north from Montana to Edmonton and then northeast to the Athabasca River. Edmonton, the oldest and largest settlement, boasted some 700 people, both white and native. Fort Macleod, its only real rival, could muster another 500 people of mixed background around its mounted police post. In between lay tiny Calgary, a hamlet of some 75 people clustered by another police outpost.

Partially due to the rise of these three future Alberta centres, but more because of the pressure of settlement in the region that would later become Saskatchewan, it became advisable to divide the prairie portion of the Northwest Territories into four administrative areas. By a federal order-in-council on May 8, 1882, the provisional districts of Assiniboia, Saskatchewan, Athabasca, and Alberta were established (Figure 1–1). Officially, this was said to be for "the convenience of settlers and for postal purposes," but there was also the implication that the new districts might form the bases of future provinces.

Assiniboia, Saskatchewan, and Athabasca were logical names for three of the areas, rooted as they were in the native languages of the West, and already in casual usage by fur traders and settlers. But the fourth district presented more of a problem. With vice-regal and royal concurrence, however, it was given the third name of Princess Louise Caroline Alberta, daughter of Queen Victoria and wife of the Marquis of Lorne, Canada's Governor General. While this district stretched no further north than Lesser Slave Lake and no further east than the confluence of the Bow and Oldman rivers (thus excluding Medicine Hat), it was the beginning of the geo-political entity known as Alberta.

In the years after 1882 a distinct district consciousness developed. This became apparent when the territorial legislature and the federal parliament both defined constituencies as and within the four provisional districts. The belief that Alberta was a distinct entity was evidenced by the formation of a

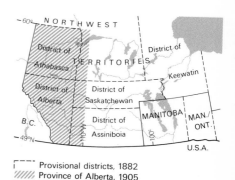

- - - - Provisional districts, 1882

///// Province of Alberta, 1905

Figure 1–1   Major administrative units of western Canada showing how the province of Alberta was related to the provisional districts into which the Northwest Territories were divided in 1882.

special committee of the Alberta members of the territorial assembly to deal with matters affecting their own district. Indeed, by the fall of 1890 the Calgary *Herald* was calling for the creation of an entirely separate Territory of Alberta, with Calgary as its capital.

Such boosterism was a reflection of general population growth within the provisional district of Alberta, as well as a southward shift in the concentration of that population. In 1891, in addition to some 9,000 Indians, the total white and Métis population of the future Alberta was estimated at 17,500. In Edmonton and its surrounding district there were 3,800 people, 700 of whom lived within the townsite. The remaining 13,700 were concentrated in the southern region, where settlement had been accelerated by the arrival of the Canadian Pacific Railway in 1883. The town of Calgary alone boasted 3,800 people in 1891.

Meanwhile, constitutional development continued within the Northwest Territories. By 1888 elected representatives had replaced appointed members, and the legislative council became a legislative assembly. In 1897, after years of disagreement between Ottawa and the territorial government in Regina, full responsible government was attained. This meant a territorial executive committee (or cabinet) dependent for its continued existence on majority support in the legislature. In less than three decades, the region had evolved from the most rudimentary government structure to a full-fledged parliamentary system with the civil service apparatus needed to provide effective service within its sphere of authority. The only remaining step for the district was to attain full provincial status.

The Creation of the Province in 1905

The censuses of 1901 and 1906 revealed that the Northwest Territories had a population base that would warrant serious consideration of provincehood. In 1901 there were already 165,555 people in the territories, 73,022 of whom lived within the district of Alberta. But the settlement wave, prompted by the federal government's immigration policies, was just beginning. The census of 1906 recorded 417,956 residents in the Northwest Territories and 185,412 in Alberta. Calgary had grown to a city of over 13,000 people, while the combined populations of Edmonton and Strathcona (the latter a separate town on the south bank of the North Saskatchewan River, across from Edmonton) were just over 14,000. Medicine Hat totalled 3,000 people and Lethbridge 2,900, while Wetaskiwin, with 1,600 residents, was the largest of six towns with populations greater than 1,000.

The campaign for provincial autonomy became heated in the opening years of the new century. Its acknowledged leader was Frederick Haultain, a Fort Macleod lawyer who was also chairman of the legislature's executive committee—in effect, the territorial premier. Adhering to a position of nonpartisan politics, Haultain had the support of both Liberals and Conservatives. But the creation of new provinces was a federal responsibility. It came under Section 146 of the British North America Act, and although the Liberal administration of Prime Minister Wilfrid Laurier was known to favour provincial rights there were some contentious issues to be resolved first.

Chief of these, at least from a national perspective, was the school question, or the determination of those rights, if any, that would be granted to denominational schools of the Roman Catholic minority. Section 93 of the British North America Act guaranteed such rights, as and if they existed in law in the particular province at the time it joined Confederation. The first territorial school legislation in 1884 had established the dual confessional school approach used in Quebec, whereby Protestant and Catholic school systems functioned independently of each other. This soon lost favour, however, because of growing Protestant strength combined with Haultain's declared preference for one national school system. The school ordinance that was passed in 1901 provided for an approach similar to Ontario's, in which the local Catholic separate school boards enjoyed limited rights within a single provincial educational system.

The school clause presented in the first draft of the provincial autonomy bill, introduced by Laurier in the House of Commons in February 1905, was interpreted by many Protestants as opening the door to a return to the dual confessional system of 1884. It was certainly seen in this light by Clifford Sifton, Minister of the Interior and spokesman for the west in the federal cabinet. He promptly resigned his cabinet seat in protest. When the bill came back to the Commons for a second reading later in the spring, the objectionable clause was reworded to conform to the 1901 ordinance. The immediate effect of the controversy was that Alberta's official inauguration was delayed from July 1 to September 1, 1905; the long-range effect was to leave many westerners feeling that Ottawa had meddled unduly in an area of local responsibility.

Ottawa's decision to retain control of crown lands and natural resources proved in later years to be far more irritating to Albertans than the school question. Laurier argued the case for national government ownership on two grounds. First, the original provinces of 1867 had been crown colonies with their own crown lands, whereas the lands in the Northwest Territories had been the property of the government of Canada since 1870. Second, provincial control of resources might lead to regional policies regarding the disposal of public lands that would clash with the national government's efforts to increase immigration. It was not for another quarter of a century that Ottawa, in 1930, transferred control of crown lands and other natural resources to the province of Alberta. A half-century later, Premier Peter Lougheed reminded Albertans that while 1980 marked the seventy-fifth anniversary of provincehood, it marked only the fiftieth anniversary of complete autonomy.

Still another decision of Ottawa's in 1905 concerned the number of provinces to be created out of the Northwest Territories. Premier Haultain stood for one large province, presumably with its capital remaining in Regina. But Alberta separatists argued that size and population demanded the creation of two provinces running north and south from latitude 49 to latitude 60. Ultimately, the federal government did decide on two provinces, probably less in response to Alberta separatism than out of a desire to reduce Haultain's own power base.

But where would the boundary run? If there was to be anything approaching equality of size for the new Alberta and the new Saskatchewan, then it must lie east of the old 1882 boundary of the provisional district of Alberta. But how far east? Sentiment in the Calgary ranching community was for the 107th meridian, since that would have incorporated the Maple Creek rangelands into Alberta. But that was too far east for a balanced division of the territory. The federal government therefore chose the 110th meridian, giving Alberta 660,000 km² and Saskatchewan 650,000 (Figure 1–1). Medicine Hat was in but Maple Creek was out.

For all the importance of separate schools, natural resources, and provincial boundaries, the average resident of Edmonton and Calgary in early 1905 was more excited about the selection of the capital city for the new province. The prestige, business, and government activity which would accrue to a capital made the decision an important one to the municipalities involved. Red Deer, Banff, and Vegreville each advanced claims, but the main contenders were Calgary and Edmonton. Calgary claimed superior railway connections and proximity to the population centre of the province, while Edmonton argued it was closer to the geographic centre. But politics were all-important in the eventual choice. While Calgary had voted Conservative in the 1904 federal election, Edmonton had re-elected its sitting Liberal member, Frank Oliver, who was soon to succeed Clifford Sifton as Minister of the Interior. It was not surprising, then, that Prime Minister Laurier announced Edmonton as the provisional capital in February 1905.

The decision about the permanent capital was left to the new provincial government. Again, politics played the decisive role. An interim provincial administration had to be formed prior to the official inaugural ceremonies in Edmonton on September 1. Naturally, the federal Liberals named a territorial Liberal, G. H. V. Bulyea, as Alberta's first lieutenant-governor. Bulyea in turn called on a fellow Liberal, Alexander Rutherford, to form the first cabinet. Rutherford and the Liberals subsequently won a landslide victory in the first provincial election in November 1905. Their strength in the northern half of the province, plus the fact that Rutherford himself was an Edmonton lawyer, guaranteed that Edmonton would be confirmed as the permanent capital city during the first session of the provincial legislature in the spring of 1906.

Edmonton had won the capital, but Calgary still hoped to be selected as the site for the proposed provincial university. After all, the sister province of Saskatchewan had split its two prizes between the rival centres of Regina and

Saskatoon. But that was not to be in Alberta. Premier Rutherford made sure the new University of Alberta stayed close to his home base. The chosen site was in Strathcona, the still-independent city across the North Saskatchewan River from Edmonton. As consolation prizes, Calgary was given the first provincial normal school for the training of teachers (1906) and the first provincial institute of technology (1915), but the southern city had to wait until 1966 for its own autonomous university.

Fortune smiled on Premier Rutherford and his Liberals during their early years of office. During the first decade of the twentieth century, Alberta and Saskatchewan were the major beneficiaries of Clifford Sifton's vigorous immigration policies. Tens of thousands of settlers from Great Britain, the United States, continental Europe, and eastern Canada poured into the new provinces each year. Among them, Mormons from the United States contributed new irrigation techniques and dryland farming methods in the southern part of the province; Scandinavian and German settlers moved into the fertile wheat belt of central Alberta; and Poles and Ukrainians wrested their livings from the less fertile parkland belt further north.

Provincial Administrations After 1905

By the outbreak of the First World War in 1914, most of the available good land was taken; future homesteading would have to move further north into the Peace River region (Figure 1–2). At the same time, marginal lands also came under cultivation—lands that would defeat many of their second generation families in the dry years of the 1930s. But in 1914, the future was bright. Towns and cities grew as well, since an agricultural countryside needed wholesale and retail collection and distribution centres. By 1914 Calgary and Edmonton (now amalgamated with Strathcona) each had populations between 50 and 60 thousand.

Railway construction also proceeded apace (Figure 1–3). The transcontinental line of the Canadian Northern Railway reached Edmonton in 1905; the Grand Trunk Pacific would soon follow. These two national systems, plus the older Canadian Pacific, pushed branch lines across the southern half of the province. Caught up by the enthusiasm for railway construction, the provincial government chartered various private lines and guaranteed their bonds. The furore over what was thought to be an all-too-close relationship between the government and the Alberta and Great Waterways Railway (to Fort McMurray) led to Premier Rutherford's resignation in 1910. Yet his Liberal successors, A. L. Sifton and Charles Stewart, continued these prodevelopment policies, restrained only by the emergency of the First World War.

Rutherford and the Liberal government set a pattern for Alberta politics that lasted well beyond their years in office. It was essentially a pattern of one-

Figure 1–2 Expansion of the land area surveyed for homesteads and agricultural settlement between 1880 and 1965. Source: *Atlas of Alberta*, p. 47.

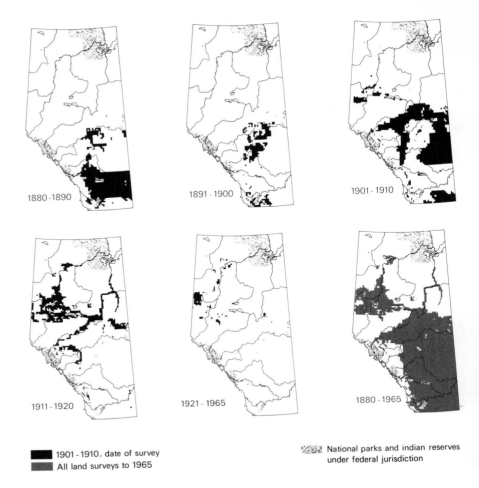

1880 - 1890

1891 - 1900

1901 - 1910

1911 - 1920

1921 - 1965

1880 - 1965

■ 1901 - 1910, date of survey
■ All land surveys to 1965

National parks and indian reserves under federal jurisdiction

Figure 1–3 Railway networks of Alberta in 1900, 1915, 1923, and 1977. Source: P. J. Smith and Denis B. Johnson, *The Edmonton-Calgary Corridor*, pp. 24–25.

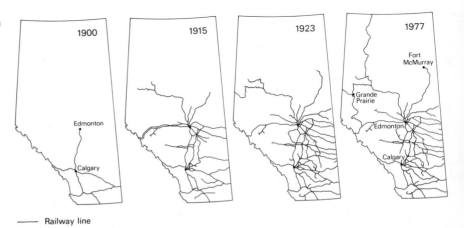

1900

1915

1923

1977

Fort McMurray

Grande Prairie

Edmonton

Calgary

—— Railway line

party politics, in which the party in power commanded huge majorities in the legislature (23–2 after the 1905 election, 37–4 after 1909); remained in power for a considerable number of years (1905–1921); was decisively beaten at the end of its appointed time by a new political force, the United Farmers of Alberta (UFA); and never recovered its original strength.

The rise of the United Farmers of Alberta as a political force was symptomatic of the widespread unrest in Canada in the years immediately following the First World War. Labour militancy, which culminated in the Winnipeg General Strike of 1919, was fuelled by low wages and poor working conditions, and ignited by sparks of socialist rhetoric. Agrarian unrest, on the other hand, was motivated by the desire to restore the individual farmer to the status of independent entrepreneur, by freeing him from the control of such external forces as banks and grain elevator companies. When these farmers' movements entered partisan politics, they did so at two levels—nationally as the Progressive Party, and provincially as the United Farmers of Alberta. The origins of the UFA can be traced back to 1909 but its surge to power came after 1916, under the leadership of Henry Wise Wood, when it capitalized on a general feeling of discontent in the post-war period to defeat the Liberals in the 1921 provincial election.

The United Farmers spoke often of group government rather than party government during their fourteen years in office (1921–1935). They leaned toward the theory of direct, as opposed to representative, democracy, and stressed the responsibility of each elected member of the legislature to his local constituency UFA organization. It was therefore difficult for the cabinet to enforce party discipline in the legislature. Equally constricting was the division of leadership between the UFA president, who remained outside the legislature, and the successive party premiers. Thus, the administrations of Herbert Greenfield, John Brownlee (after 1925), and R. G. Reid (after 1934) were not characterized by vigorous government initiatives in response to social and economic change.

The provincial economy was not as strong during the 1920s as it had been in the boom years prior to the First World War. Wheat prices fluctuated, denying farmers the almost guaranteed annual increase in prosperity they had once enjoyed. Poor crops and minor recessions in the less-fertile districts of the Palliser Triangle further darkened the picture. Meanwhile, the once-important coal mining industry declined seriously after 1919, and the infant oil industry was many years away from its spectacular post-1947 boom. The Great Depression of the 1930s, accompanied by drought, soil-drifting, and grasshopper plagues, simply accelerated the economic decline that had begun a decade earlier.

By 1935 the United Farmers government was in serious trouble. Plagued by scandal and unwilling to adopt the radical monetary theories of social credit, its leaders watched helplessly as William Aberhart mobilized the forces of evangelical religion and economic reform into the Social Credit

League. Aberhart's diagnosis of the economic problem was simple: there was not enough money in circulation to purchase the amount of goods being produced. His solution was simplistic: give every Albertan a "social credit" of $25.00 a month, so that the provincial economy would be stimulated by increased individual purchases. In the absence of any real-world test, these radical economic theories had to be taken on faith, but their appeal was compelling. In the 1935 election, Alberta voters gave Aberhart and Social Credit a majority of 56–7.

William Aberhart added two new ingredients to Alberta provincial politics during his eight years as premier. The first was an authoritarian style of leadership. Gone was the constituency power of the UFA years; it was Premier Aberhart who exercised tight control over cabinet and legislature. No matter that theoretical Social Credit monetary policies were not put into practice; any dissidents were squelched by the premier's forceful personality. As his second contribution, Aberhart introduced an anti-Ottawa bias into Alberta political life. Such a stance had been latent in the pre-1905 territorial period, and implicit in the UFA reformist thrust of 1921. But now it blossomed as Aberhart blamed the province's economic problems on national government policies, chafed at Ottawa's disallowance of a number of pieces of radical provincial economic legislation, and refused to co-operate with the Royal Commission on Dominion-Provincial Relations (1937–1940).

Aberhart's death in 1943 restored a measure of stability to provincial and federal-provincial relations. His successor was Ernest Manning, an equally religious but much more temperate politician, who occupied the premier's chair for the next quarter of a century. Manning and his cabinets abandoned many of the original Social Credit theories, and provided the province with stable, conservative government from the 1940s through the 1960s. Their task was eased by the fortuitous discovery of oil at Leduc in 1947, since the resulting economic boom brought prosperity to most of the province and a steady flow of oil royalties to augment the government's revenues. Even on Manning's retirement in 1968, there seemed to be few clouds on the Social Credit horizon.

Yet, just as in 1921 and 1935, political forces were developing that would sweep out the old party and bring in a fresh new team to manage provincial affairs. Through their appeal to an increasingly urban-oriented Alberta, which had become less sympathetic to the social conservatism of Social Credit, Peter Lougheed and the Progressive Conservative Party won 49 of 75 seats in the 1971 provincial election. Even larger majorities of 69–6, 70–5, and 75–4 in the elections of 1975, 1979, and 1982 confirmed the long-established tradition of one-party government in Alberta. The OPEC-inspired, world-wide oil-pricing crisis of 1973 also promised the Lougheed government a still greater level of prosperity than the Leduc discovery of 1947 had done for Ernest Manning's government. Controversies over oil pricing and resource control also increased throughout the decade of the

1970s, and resurrected an anti-Ottawa posture in Alberta politics. The national energy policy of 1980 made it clear that Alberta's rights in its most valued natural resource were appreciably less than the government of Alberta considered them to be.

Constitutional disputes of this kind are a fact of life in a democratic federation. In geopolitical terms they represent a conflict in the needs of the modern state at two widely different areal scales. At one level, Alberta is an independent unit of government with sovereign powers over a distinctive territory. Alberta's geographical reality is founded, first and foremost, in its jurisdictional autonomy. Yet Alberta is also part of Canada, a small piece of an extremely large mosaic. It is really not surprising that it should sometimes be difficult to separate the loyalties and interests applying to such different scales of spatial organization.

Supplemental Readings

Barr, J. *The Dynasty: The Rise and Fall of Social Credit in Alberta.* Toronto: McClelland and Stewart, 1974.

Hanson, E. *Dynamic Decade: The Evolution and Effects of the Oil Industry in Alberta.* Toronto: McClelland and Stewart, 1958.

Macpherson, C.B. *Democracy in Alberta: Social Credit and the Party System.* Toronto: University of Toronto Press, 1953 and 1962.

MacGregor, J. *A History of Alberta.* Edmonton: Hurtig, 1972.

Owram, D., ed. *The Formation of Alberta: A Documentary History.* Calgary: Historical Society of Alberta, 1979.

Thomas, L. H. *The Struggle for Responsible Government in the North-West Territories 1870–97.* Toronto: University of Toronto Press, 1956.

Watkins, E. *The Golden Province: Political Alberta.* Calgary: Sandstone Publishing, 1980.

2 The Changing Structure of the Settlement System

P. J. Smith

*From the broad historical overview of the settlement **process** in Alberta, and the sequence of events by which a distinctive territorial unit was forged, we turn now to an equally broad view of the geographical consequences, as expressed in the forms and functions of the contemporary settlement **system**. Of all geographical phenomena, settlements are of fundamental importance because they tie people and their activities to particular places. It is through the spatial patterning of the different kinds of settlements and their organization into a functional system, that the basic structure of the human geography of Alberta can best be displayed. The picture will be fleshed out in subsequent chapters but here we are concerned with general trends and overall patterns, with particular emphasis on the period of massive cultural change since the Second World War. All facets of life in Alberta have been transformed, and the settlement system has been restructured in the process. Since this is a process that shows no sign of coming to an end, the theme of society in transition is probably more vital to this chapter than to any other part of the book.*

General Characteristics of the Settlement System

To speak of a "settlement system" is a convenient way of describing the complete array of human habitation in any region. To be properly identified as a system, however, the settlements must be related in some way. From the most remote homestead to the largest city, they must be linked together by the special functions they each perform, for it is from this pattern of relationships among the settlements that the system gains its distinctive unity—the unity that defines it as a system.

This general idea can be illustrated most graphically from a map of highway traffic volumes (Figure 2–1). Since almost all Albertans have access to some kind of motor vehicle, and since Alberta highways are used overwhelmingly for movement within the province, highway traffic patterns are an excellent indicator of the patterns of relationships that unify the whole system. The geographical organization or spatial form of the system also stands out in bold relief. There is, to begin, the obvious dominance of Edmonton and Calgary as nodes on which the major routes converge. It is also clear that Edmonton and Calgary have a special relationship with each other, since the corridor between them carries the heaviest volume of highway traffic in the province. There is also a strong suggestion of the hierarchical organization of the urban settlement system. Lethbridge, Medicine Hat, and Grande Prairie, for example, show up as secondary nodes. The lesser points of convergence in the traffic flow patterns then indicate the locations of the many small service centres, all comparatively unspecialized (meaning that their functions are common to many places), that rural Alberta is dotted with. Finally, within the interstices of the main highway network, and most peripheral to the organization of the communications-settlement system, is the sparsely distributed rural population with its own distinctive settlement forms—dispersed farmsteads, Métis or Hutterite colonies, Indian reserves, tourist resorts, lumber camps and the like.

A close relationship between highway traffic and the distribution of different kinds of settlements is obviously to be expected. A larger, if simple, principle is also demonstrated in Figure 2–1: given the requirements for trade and exchange in a modern commercial economy, functional relationships imply the large-scale movement of people, goods, and information. All places are linked by transport and communication networks which are as much part of the settlement system as the settlements themselves. Neither could exist without the other, and change in one leads inevitably to change in the other. Any increase in economic activity at any place in the system immediately increases the need to communicate with other places. It may also result, eventually, in the need to construct new transportation and communication facilities. But these same facilities, once in operation, may stimulate yet more development at certain favoured locations. Edmonton and Calgary are notable examples, able to capitalize on their historical advantages to become accessible to larger numbers of people than any other cities in Alberta. As the modern web of highways, railways, airways, pipelines, and telecommunications developed, it was always Edmonton and Calgary that stood out as the hubs of the networks. Every improvement in facilities and services enhanced their positions and so contributed to their further growth. But as they grew and became more specialized in their functions, pressure to improve their transport and communications connections continued, causing further changes in their relationships with all other places in the settlement system. This is a classic illustration of positive feedback, the process by which change within a system breeds yet more change.

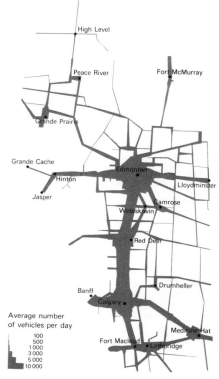

Figure 2–1   Diagrammatic representation of average daily highway traffic volumes in Alberta in 1981.
Source: Government of Alberta.

- spacial patterns reflected in highway movements
- positive feedback: improved linkages leads to special and improvement, which in turn increase pressure to improve linkages

Settlement systems, then, are highly dynamic, but positive feedback is by no means the only explanation. Settlement systems are also open systems, which means that they are exposed to a constant barrage of external demands and forces. These, in turn, are subject to their own pressures for change. In response to new economic circumstances, often determined on national or international levels, population growth and investment are concentrated at some places but avoid others; technological changes in industry, in transportation, and in communication bring new opportunities to some communities while condemning others to obsolescence; changes in lifestyle preferences bring different qualities of residential environment into favour, and can cause the forms of cities to be reshaped; and so on. The settlement system is constantly striving to reach an equilibrium condition. But equilibrium can never be reached, because the stream of stimuli for change is constant, and the system is constantly adapting to these stimuli.

It also follows that if the external environment is changing in some systematic way, the settlement system will display a parallel evolution. For this

Figure 2–2 A general view of the evolution of the Alberta settlement and transport systems by stages in the modernization of the space-economy. Source: P. J. Smith, "Alberta Since 1945: The Maturing Settlement System". In *A Geography of Canada: Heartland and Hinterland,* edited by L. D. McCann, p. 305. Scarborough: Prentice-Hall Canada, 1982.

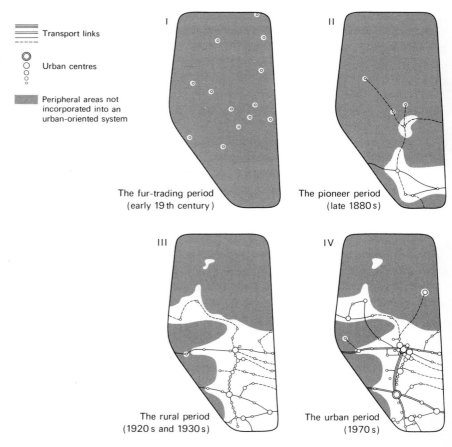

reason the concept of economic modernization is particularly important, since it implies a regular sequence of stages of development as illustrated in Figure 2–2. Initially, during the fur trade era, the European settlements in the territory that became Alberta were tied to the natural transport routes, the waterways. The settlements all performed the same function and communicated directly with the major collection centres at York Factory and Fort Garry. Gradually, however, a separate trading system developed in the western plains, and Edmonton House became its central point. The first overland routes also were focused there—the Carleton Trail from Winnipeg and the Old North Trail from Fort Benton, the major supply post on the upper Missouri River.

Edmonton never entirely lost the locational advantage bestowed by its situation in these primitive transport networks. Yet, for a time, after 1883 it yielded pride of place to Calgary, which became the principal point of entry to the western plains region following the construction of the Canadian Pacific Railway. The intersection of the railway and the Old North Trail was obviously destined to be of prime importance in the evolving settlement system, and possible competitors, such as Medicine Hat and Lethbridge, were essentially doomed to subordinate roles. As rural settlement was stimulated, Calgary was immediately established as the dominant trade and service centre of southern Alberta. From the outset it was the regional capital, the largest and most specialized place in the region—"most specialized" in the sense that some of its services were available nowhere else.

Edmonton, meanwhile, was overshadowed, even after it was linked to Calgary by a branch railway in 1891. But as the pressures for agricultural colonization strengthened in the late 1890s and early 1900s, Edmonton began to assume a similar character of regional capital for central and northern Alberta. The watershed year was 1905, the year of provincehood and of the construction of a new transcontinental railway, the Canadian Northern, through Edmonton. From then on, the Alberta settlement system was binodal, organized around two primary centres of approximately equal size and comparable functions. The point is strikingly demonstrated in the pattern of expansion of the railway network between 1900 and 1923. (See Figure 1–3 from Chapter 1.) As the pioneering phase waned and the agricultural economy became fully commercialized, a mesh of small service towns and branch railways spread across the Alberta plains. Ultimately, however, towns and farms looked to Edmonton and Calgary as their principal supply and collection centres. The railways radiated from these cities, and so, too, did the highways as they began their modern development in the 1920s.

It is clear, when the early evolution of the Alberta settlement system is interpreted in these terms, that inertia is an important system characteristic. The basic structural features tend to be extremely persistent, and may well be reinforced through successive stages of development. Even if their original rationale disappears, it is still difficult to break completely with the initial structural order, as Edmonton's experience demonstrates so well. The estab-

Edmonton became core of a hinterland

lished form of a settlement system is thus a major influence on the direction of the system's further evolution; it is a stabilizing force, always tempering, in some degree, the effects of pressures for change.

Rural Settlement Trends Since the 1930s

In Alberta, the nearest approach to equilibrium since agricultural settlement began late in the nineteenth century, was probably experienced during the 1930s. There was little growth in Alberta or anywhere else, and even the natural increase of the population was depressed. It was also a time when rural population was at its climax. In 1931, about two-thirds of Alberta's people were classed as rural and most of those lived on farms. The detached farmstead was the predominant settlement type, and the urban system was organized largely to provide services to the agricultural economy and to farm families. The towns and cities were rural service centres (or central places) and their small size was a direct reflection of that limited function; even Edmonton and Calgary had populations of around 80,000 for much of the 1930s, while Lethbridge had a mere 13,000. As economic conditions improved in the late 1930s, a small growth impulse began to be experienced, particularly in the largest cities. This accelerated during the war years, because of Alberta's new strategic importance in relation to the construction of the Alaska Highway, the development of petroleum resources in the Mackenzie Valley, and the acceleration of oil exploration within Alberta.

All this, of course, was but the prelude to the new boom years that followed the petroleum discoveries of the late 1940s. Their significance for the structure of the settlement system could be summed up in one word—urbanization—for it was urbanization (or the increasing concentration of the population in urban places) that marked the course of Alberta's progression from a rural agricultural society to an urban industrial one. Agriculture has not become less important in Alberta, in an absolute sense, on the contrary, agricultural production has increased greatly since the 1930s. But agriculture has contributed proportionately less and less to the total provincial income, as Alberta's economy has broadened and strengthened. A smaller and smaller farm labour force has also been able to produce an ever-expanding output.

As a direct consequence of these trends, the rural population of Alberta was at its peak, absolutely and relatively, in the late 1930s. On the basis of the 1951 Census of Canada (when the definitions of rural and urban were made more precise), the rural population of Alberta stood at 530,000 in 1941, and its share of the total population then was exactly two-thirds. Ten years later, by the same definition, the rural total had fallen to 490,000 and the proportion to 52 per cent. By 1981, only 23 per cent of Alberta's population was technically classed as rural, and even that overstated the case, since it included urban commuters who lived in the countryside beyond the census metropolitan areas and the incorporated urban places. Even more revealingly, the farm population dropped from 340,000 in 1951 (the first time that rural population was divided into farm and non-farm) to 190,000 in 1981, or from 36 per cent of the Alberta population to 8.5 per cent.

But while the farm population has occupied a rapidly diminishing place in the Alberta settlement system, the total rural population has not experienced a comparable decline; in fact, it increased by 80,000 between 1971 and 1981. The explanation lies in what happened to the non-farm population, those people who live outside the towns and cities but are not farmers. In 1951 there were already 150,000 rural non-farm residents, reflecting a well-established pattern of living that had gained strength during the 1930s, as people sought cheap land and cheap houses away from the batteries of regulations and taxes they found in the urban centres. The expansion of the petroleum and forestry industries after the Second World War also contributed to this tendency, because it created jobs that were not tied to particular towns but required workers who could move across far-flung districts. Then came the increasing popularity of a new style of urban living, the country residence, a high-quality home on a large lot in a planned subdivision within commuting distance of a city.

The effect of these different behaviours on population numbers is not completely clear. Between 1951 and 1971 the censuses record a fluctuating rural non-farm population, but that could probably be explained by urban annexations and by changes in the definition of Edmonton's census metropolitan area (in both cases, once-rural people were being counted as urban). In more recent years, however, there has been a clear upward trend in rural non-farm population, from 180,000 in 1966 to 320,000 in 1981.

Urban Settlement Trends

Even though the rural non-farm population continues to grow, its share of the the Alberta total is comparatively modest, particularly when set against the more than three-quarters of the population who now live in urban settlements of one kind or another. In the span of a generation, between the 1940s and the 1970s, the settlement system shifted from rural dominance to urban dominance. By the 1980s, Alberta's population was as thoroughly urbanized as that of any part of the modern world. The implications are profound, affecting the way of life of all Albertans, not just those who live in urban places.

Urban Growth

Since the 1940s, most of Alberta's population growth has been urban growth. Between 1946 and 1981 the provincial population increased from

46-81 :
all urban growth ;
 # urban settlements
↑ by 3 times

803,000 to 2,238,000, for a total gain of 1,435,000. The urban gain in the same period was only slightly less, at 1,374,000. It was therefore inevitable that Alberta's urban settlements would become substantially larger, but it is not so well known that growth also brought an increase in the number of urban settlements. A population of 1,000 is often used as a crude breakpoint between urban and rural; by this criterion there were only 38 urban places in Alberta in 1946, as compared with 114 thirty-five years later (Table 2–1).

Table 2-1
Numbers of urban places by size classes, 1946–76

Minimum population	1946	1956	1966	1976	1981
100,000	2	2	2	2	2
25,000	0	1	3	4	6
10,000	2	3	1	5	6
5,000	0	4	5	8	16
2,500	4	15	29	32	35
1,000	30	39	39	47	49
Total urban places	38	64	79	98	114
Total population (in thousands)	301	631	1,004	1,413	1,757
Percentage of Alberta population	37	56	69	79	79

Source: Canadian census data.

Hierarchical Expansion Table 2–1 also shows that there were more places in most of the urban size classes in 1981 than in 1946. As the larger places became even larger, and moved up the scale, the group of smallest places (1,000–2,500 people) was being replenished by villages growing into towns or by the creation of new towns.

A better impression of the expansion of the Alberta urban system, and of the upward movement of most places, is provided by Figure 2–3. This figure also illustrates that the system is roughly organized into a pyramidal hierarchy, with Edmonton and Calgary as its twin summits. The class intervals in Table 2–1 and Figure 2–3 are entirely arbitrary, but they do establish the system's general tendency to narrow upwards from a broad base. It is also evident that the pyramid was more balanced in 1981 than it had ever been before. As Alberta's population urbanized, and the economy became more diversified and urban-centred, the urban system became more finely structured and it filled out at every level.

	1946	1956	1966	1976	1981
500 000 +					Calgary Edmonton
100 000 +	Edmonton Calgary	Edmonton Calgary	Edmonton Calgary	Calgary Edmonton	
25 000 +		Lethbridge	Lethbridge Red Deer Medicine Hat	Lethbridge Medicine Hat Red Deer Sherwood Park	Lethbridge Red Deer Medicine Hat St. Albert Fort McMurray Sherwood Park
10 000 +	Lethbridge Medicine Hat	Medicine Hat Jasper Place Red Deer	Grande Prairie	St. Albert Grande Prairie Fort McMurray Lloydminster Camrose	Grande Prairie Lloydminster Camrose Leduc Fort Saskatchewan Spruce Grove
5 000 +		Grande Prairie Bowness Camrose Lloydminster	St. Albert Camrose Lloydminster Sherwood Park Wetaskiwin	Leduc Fort Saskatchewan Spruce Grove Wetaskiwin Hinton Brooks Drumheller Taber	Wetaskiwin Brooks Airdrie Hinton Crowsnest Pass Drumheller Taber Peace River Edson Lacombe Whitecourt Vegreville Innisfail Ponoka Stettler Drayton Valley
2 500 +	Red Deer Camrose Drumheller Wetaskiwin	Beverly Wetaskiwin Taber Ponoka Stettler Forest Lawn Lacombe Wainwright Drumheller Cardston Drayton Valley Fort Saskatchewan Vegreville Edson Banff	Taber Ponoka Hinton Fort Saskatchewan Peace River Stettler Wainwright Edson Vegreville Drumheller St. Paul Brooks Drayton Valley Lacombe Olds Banff Pincher Creek Leduc Cardston Fort Macleod Vermilion Westlock Hanna Fort McMurray Barrhead Claresholm Coaldale Innisfail Jasper	Peace River Ponoka St. Paul Drayton Valley Stettler Vegreville Grande Cache Edson Wainwright Lacombe Whitecourt Banff Westlock Olds Coaldale Jasper High River Slave Lake Pincher Creek Rocky Mtn. House Claresholm Vermilion Fort Macleod Cardston Redcliff Barrhead Innisfail Bonnyville Devon Grand Centre Stony Plain Hanna	St. Paul Stony Plain Olds High River Rocky Mtn. House Morinville Banff Coaldale Grande Cache Slave Lake Bonnyville Westlock Wainwright Devon Redcliff Okotoks Sylvan Lake Vermilion Pincher Creek Barrhead Cochrane Claresholm Canmore Jasper Cardston Grand Centre Fort Macleod Didsbury Strathmore Fairview Raymond Hanna Beaumont High Prairie Swan Hills

Note: (i) Sherwood Park, Banff and Jasper have never been incorporated but their size requires them to be included.
(ii) Lloydminster's ranking is based on its total population, including residents of Saskatchewan.

Figure 2–3 The expansion of the urban hierarchy of Alberta from 1946 to 1981. In each of the five years (1946, 1956, 1966, 1976, and 1981) all incorporated urban places with more than 2,500 people are ranked in order of their population sizes. Source: Canadian census data.

The explanation of hierarchical organization lies in the functions performed by places of different sizes, and particularly in their roles as central places. These places exist to provide services to tributary regions. The hierarchy of service centres is therefore built upon a parallel hierarchy of service needs and trade areas. At the bottom of the pyramid are those services, such as grain storage, bulk fuel delivery, and mail pick-up, that have to be immediately accessible. These services, and sometimes no others, are available in hundreds of hamlets across the province. They are also available in larger centres, but in those places more specialized services are available as well. Although these services are needed less frequently, the larger population base makes them viable. Obviously, the cities at the top of the hierarchy provide the most specialized services. The difference between a Bashaw and a Stettler, and between a Stettler and a Red Deer, rests essentially in the size of territory served and the variety of services offered.

Centralization   In 1946, at the end of the rural period, the Alberta urban system was a simple central-place system. Even Edmonton and Calgary were little more than country towns, still best described as regional capitals. They were the most important service centres in Alberta, providing the greatest array of services and not just to the rural population but to the people who lived in all the smaller and less specialized cities and towns. In addition, they were the chief points of contact between Alberta and the outside world. As a result, Edmonton and Calgary were the major transport centres in the province, the chief entrepôts or distribution centres, and the largest manufacturing cities, particularly for the processing of agricultural produce, notably meat packing and brewing and distilling. The cities lower in the hierarchy filled similar roles, but on a lesser scale. They acted as capitals for much smaller regions with much smaller populations. Even their characteristic industries, for example creameries and cheese factories, were tied to highly localized service areas. Indeed, only one of the eight urban places with more than 2,500 people in 1946 had a special industrial function; this was Drumheller, the centre of coal mining activity in the Red Deer River valley.

As the urban system expanded after 1946, much of the growth was concentrated in the established network of rural service centres. This had two consequences: the major central places in 1946 (Lethbridge to Wetaskiwin) all moved up in the system; and many smaller central places crossed the population threshold of 2,500 people and so appeared for the first time in Figure 2–3. Some cities, notably Grand Prairie and Lloydminster, emerged as strong subregional capitals, serving the same sort of role for northwestern and east-central Alberta (and the adjoining part of Saskatchewan) that Lethbridge and Medicine Hat had long served in the south (Figure 2–4). Other centres profited from the expansion of farming and agricultural processing industries in their vicinities. But the main point is that some rural service centres are still able to grow, despite the steep decline in farm population.

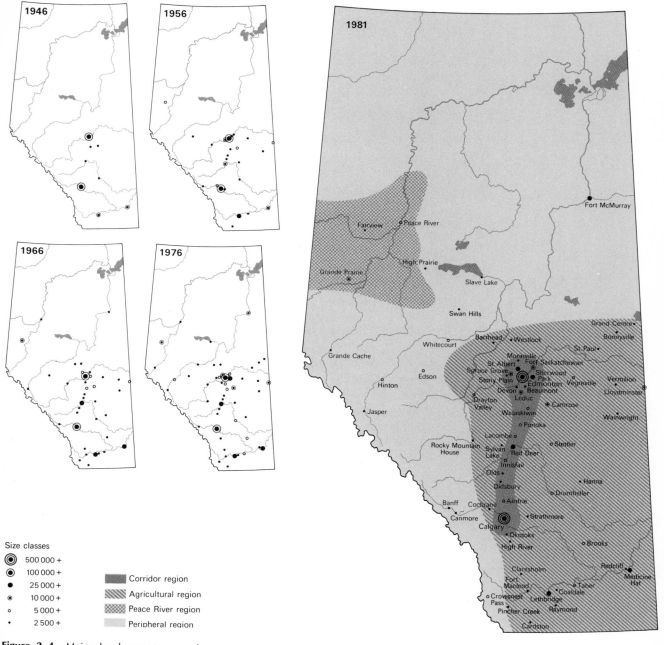

Figure 2–4 Major development zones of Alberta and the spatial distribution of the expanding urban hierarchy, 1946–1981. The mapped centres are the same as those listed in Figure 2–3.

At first sight this conclusion may seem contradictory, but it can be explained, in part, by a process of centralization. This refers to the tendency for service functions to be concentrated in fewer, larger, and more widely spaced urban centres. Just as the hierarchical order of central places is based on their degree of centrality, from most central (Edmonton and Calgary) to least central (the smallest hamlets), so it is possible for places to become more central or less central over time. Some places grow while others stagnate, decline, or disappear.

The key to understanding the selective growth in a central place system is accessibility. Better highways, better cars, and cheap gasoline, all of which have been available in Alberta since 1946, have diminished the barrier of distance. Farm families today can travel further in less time and more comfort than those of 40 or 60 years ago. Instead of being tied to the nearest centre no matter how small or limited in its services, they can look to larger, more distant centres where they can enjoy the same quality and choice of services that city residents take for granted. The smallest places come to be bypassed by the rural consumers, and their trade areas are captured by their larger neighbours. As a result, the more central places grow at the expense of the less central ones, and are then able to increase their attractiveness and their growth potential by offering still greater arrays of services.

Inevitably, it is the smallest central places that are least able to compete in the centralization process. The consequences for the urban system between 1951 and 1971 are illustrated in Table 2–2, which has been compiled from census data on the populations of Alberta's smallest incorporated places, its villages and small towns. Two-thirds of the communities with fewer than 1,000 people were clearly growing in the 1950s but only one-third (generally the largest) continued to grow in the 1960s. Conversely, no more than 9 per cent of these communities were strongly decreasing in the 1950s,

Table 2-2
Population change in small urban places by ten-year intervals, 1951–81

Type of population change	Numbers of incorporated towns and villages with populations less than 1,000 at the beginning of each period			Numbers of incorporated towns and villages with populations between 1,000 and 2,500 at the beginning of each period		
	1951–61	1961–71	1971–81	1951–61	1961–71	1971–81
Increase of 10% or greater	98	53	138	31	27	33
Increase or decrease of less than 10%	40	53	35	6	15	10
Decrease of 10% or greater	14	63	12	2	1	0
Total	152	169	185	39	43	43

as compared with 37 per cent in the 1960s. Even the group of slightly larger places (1,000–2,500) showed some retarding of growth in the 1960s, whereas the next group in the hierarchy (2,500–5,000) almost uniformly continued to grow. Meanwhile, at the absolute bottom of the central place hierarchy—the unincorporated hamlets and elevator sidings—many communities were simply disappearing. In one study of the Red Deer trade area, for example, it was found that 30 places were lost from the system between 1941 and 1971.

The larger implication of these trends is that Alberta's central place system has undergone a process of structural rationalization as it adapted to cultural and technological changes. The cultural change is best described as the rising expectations syndrome. Prosperity, mobility, and the pervasive spread of urban attitudes towards personal comfort and well-being all affect the way in which rural people approach their service delivery system. That system, in turn, is strongly influenced by a variety of technological changes which are closely intertwined with the cultural ones. Highway improvements, for instance, do more than facilitate travel; they also help to change people's attitudes toward their service needs and lifestyle. Similarly, universal access to television advertising, supermarkets and, more recently, suburban-style shopping centres, are powerful shapers of attitudes and behaviour. Among other things, they contribute to yet more demands for highways to be upgraded, so that the accessibility of the most central places can be enhanced still further. It is entirely predictable, therefore, that the expansion of the Alberta urban system since 1946 should have been closely related to the provincial network of major highways, as can be seen in the alignment along the Yellowhead Highway, in the Calgary-Lethbridge-Medicine Hat triangle and, above all, in the Edmonton-Calgary corridor (Figure 2–4).

cars + higher expectations = centralization

Resource Exploitation

Despite the continuing importance of central place functions in the Alberta urban system, centralization is by no means the only reason for the growth of certain urban places. Rather, it is chiefly characteristic of those parts of the province where rural service is still the mainstay of the urban population (Figure 2–4). Even in the southern agricultural region, other growth factors have supervened, making it impossible to isolate the specific effects of centralization with any confidence.

The most obvious of these other factors, given the natural-resource orientation of Alberta's economic development since 1946, is the growth that has been generated by the oil and natural gas industry and, to a lesser extent, by forestry and coal mining. Most of the largest central places—Medicine Hat, Red Deer, Grande Prairie, Lloydminster, and Camrose—have benefited in some degree from new roles as service, processing, and manufacturing centres for the resource industries. Many smaller places have also profited, sporadically, from the opening of new oil and gas fields, and from the con-

boomy places w/o
ag. benefit most
from resources

struction of gas processing plants. As with the centralization of conventional rural services, services for the resource industries gravitate toward the most accessible centres within their service regions.

This trend is even more evident on the margins of agricultural settlement, where the resource industries have had a particularly large impact on the established service centres. The growth potential of towns like Rocky Mountain House and Edson was limited by their peripheral situations and the marginal condition of agriculture. (This is discussed more fully in Chapter 4.) These towns were given new life when resource exploitation shifted into the largely unpopulated forest zone, because they were the obvious gateways and service points for much of the resource frontier.

The next stage of development, which was accompanied by deeper and deeper penetration of the forest, saw the building of new resource towns. New or upgraded transport facilities were also required to provide these towns with physical links into the Alberta settlement system. It is particularly striking, for example, that the only recent additions to the railway network have been the Great Slave Lake Railway, reaching north to Hay River and Pine Point, and the Alberta Resources Railway, connecting Hinton and Grande Prairie. Both were built in the 1960s. (See Figure 1–3 in Chapter 1.) The construction of all-weather highways into communities like Fort McMurray and Grande Cache, and the development of northern airfields to the standards required for commercial mainline service, are other features of the opening of the resource frontier.

The first of the new resource towns to reach the upper levels of the urban system was Drayton Valley, the service centre for the Pembina oilfield. Although it was on the agricultural margin, and secured some further growth by becoming a new central place, it was more notable as the vanguard of the advancing urban frontier. Drayton Valley was followed by such new towns as Hinton and Fort McMurray, which appeared in Figure 2–3 for the first time in 1966, and by Grande Cache, Whitecourt, and Slave Lake, which reached the critical population level of 2,500 before 1976. By then, Fort McMurray and Hinton were the seventh and eleventh largest towns in Alberta (if Edmonton's various satellites are not counted separately).

The expansion of the agricultural and resource frontiers has also been an important factor in the relative patterns of growth and decline among Alberta's smaller urban places (Table 2–2). Between 1961 and 1971, a total of 80 towns and villages with populations of less than 2,500 can be said to have grown appreciably (that is, by more than 10 per cent). Almost half of these communities were in the frontier zone, including the Peace River region. At the same time, very few frontier towns and villages experienced an appreciable loss of population. In all, 64 communities declined by more than 10 per cent between 1961 and 1971, but only 3 were in the frontier zone; 59 were in the long-developed agricultural zone, where centralization was then making its strongest imprint. In the frontier zone, by contrast, urban growth was widespread but fitful, in consequence of the sporadic nature of resource investment. The opening of a new gas field or a new tract of forest land usually is accompanied by a spurt of development in nearby communities, but is likely to be followed by a period of little population change (defined in Table 2–2 as an increase or decrease of less than 10 per cent). In a way, urban development trends are just as selective on the frontier as they are in the agricultural south of Alberta, though the cause is different and the effects are localized. Growth at one point is not the result of a competitive process that is simultaneously causing other places to decline.

In the decade following 1971, with the great upsurge in resource-based industries, a strong growth trend again asserted itself. Indeed, the impact was even greater than Table 2–2 suggests, since 75 per cent of the villages and small towns in the growing category experienced population increases greater than 25 per cent. The growth effects were also widely spread, in keeping with the distribution of the natural resources. (This topic is discussed in Chapter 5.) Only the agricultural regions were not able to share fully in this resurgence. All twelve of the incorporated places that decreased by more than 10 per cent in 1971–81, and 80 per cent of those that were essentially stable, were in the southeastern quarter of the province; the rest were in the Peace River region.

Rapid population growth, and the processes of urbanization, centralization, and natural resource exploitation, have had profound effects on Alberta's urban system. Yet these are all dwarfed in comparison with the changes that have occurred in Edmonton and Calgary. Alberta's population distribution has become not merely urban but metropolitan. Table 2–3 makes the point simply: in 1946, 27 per cent of Alberta's population lived in the two largest cities; by 1976 their share had increased to 56 per cent. Over that 30-year period, 78 per cent of Alberta's entire population increase was accounted for by the growth of Edmonton and Calgary. There was also a pattern of increasing concentration of population increase in the two cities (Table 2–4), peaking in 1966–71 when the rest of the province actually experienced a slight decrease.

An inevitable corollary of this concentration of population growth is that Edmonton and Calgary also increased their dominance over the Alberta urban system. This trend can be traced back to the beginnings of agricultural settlement and so effectively demonstrates the influence that the form of the urban system exerts on the relative growth potential of the places within it. In 1901, when Edmonton (including Strathcona) and Calgary had only 4,000 people each, they were just twice as large as Lethbridge. By 1921 they were already five times larger, and in 1946, after the relative stability of the 1930s,

Metropolitanization = Ed. & Calg. growing faster than anyone else

Table 2-3

Population of Calgary and Edmonton census metropolitan areas, 1946–81

	1946	1956	1966	1976	1981
Calgary	100,044	200,449	330,575	469,917	592,743
Edmonton	113,116	251,004	401,299	554,228	657,057
Total	213,160	451,453	731,874	1,024,145	1,249,800
Percentage of Alberta population	27	40	50	56	56

Source: Canadian census data.

Table 2-4

Population increase in Alberta and the combined census metropolitan areas by five-year periods, 1946–81

	Alberta increase	Metropolitan increase	Metropolitan share of the Alberta increase (%)
1946–51	136,171	99,020	73
1951–56	183,615	139,273	76
1956–61	208,828	165,177	79
1961–66	131,259	115,214	88
1966–71	164,671	167,137	101
1971–76	210,163	125,134	60
1976–81	399,687	225,655	56
1946–81	1,434,724	1,036,640	72

Source: Canadian census data.

they were between six and seven times larger. Over the next 30 years the ratio increased regularly, to 10 to 1 in Calgary's case and to 12 to 1 for Edmonton.

The concentration of population in a few large or metropolitan centres is more than an Albertan phenomenon of course. It is associated with the structural transformation of advanced economies, as manifested in the great expansion of quaternary and quinary activities and the emergence of the post-industrial age. (These trends are discussed in more detail in Chapters 8 and 10.) Simultaneously, though, metropolitanization is a reflection of the increasing maturity and self-sufficiency of Alberta's own economy, through the growth of residentiary industries. These exist to provide goods and services to a local market that has become more demanding and affluent through a generation of conspicuous consumption. On top of all that,

Metrop effects
Satellites

Alberta has been a growth region within the Canadian space-economy due to the growing national importance of its resource-based industries. Inevitably, these various urban growth trends have had their largest effects on the leading places in the Alberta system. As a result, by 1981 the combined population of the metropolitan areas of Edmonton and Calgary was one-and-a-quarter million, which was the population of all Alberta in 1956.

Metropolitanization has also been important as another factor in the expansion of the urban system. This is illustrated in Figures 2–3 and 2–4 through the addition of towns and cities whose growth is explained solely by their satellite relationship with Edmonton and Calgary. As early as 1956 there were five of these towns. The four largest, Jasper Place, Bowness, Beverly, and Forest Lawn, were dormitory suburbs on the cities' boundaries. But they were amalgamated with Edmonton and Calgary between 1960 and 1963. As a portent for the future, the fifth town, Fort Saskatchewan was most significant. It was well separated from Edmonton, and has managed to retain its independence. It was also a small, rural service centre that suddenly experienced the effects of industrial dispersal within Edmonton's newly emerging metropolitan region. By 1981, five of Alberta's twelve urban places with populations between 10,000 and 100,000 were satellites of Edmonton. In a sense, then, the filling-out of the urban hierarchy was less than it appears from Table 2–1, because it owed so much to the metropolitan constellation that Edmonton had become (Figure 2–5).

Calgary did not experience a comparable pattern of development after it absorbed its original dormitories. It had fewer towns in its vicinity than Edmonton, and because they were more distant, there was not the same opportunity for dispersal to occur. Regional planning policy has also been directed at keeping urban development within Calgary's boundaries, whereas the policy in the Edmonton region has been to encourage dispersal—despite the objections of the City of Edmonton. One practical consequence is that Calgary's census metropolitan area is identical with the city area, which also explains why Calgary moved ahead of Edmonton in Figure 2–3 in 1976. On the basis of its census metropolitan population Edmonton was still the larger; in 1981 it had 657,000 people to Calgary's 593,000.

Yet, even those official statistics understated the reality. In Calgary's case, no allowance was made for the increasing popularity of country residences, nor for the fact that the nearest small towns, such as Airdrie and Okotoks, have begun to show suburban characteristics. In the Edmonton region, the formula for census metropolitan areas caused the eastern portions of the counties of Parkland and Leduc to be omitted (Figure 2–5), so that Edmonton's metropolitan population was undercounted by about 50,000, equivalent to the population of Lethbridge. One revised definition has produced 1981 metropolitan populations of 762,000 for Edmonton and 659,000 for Calgary.

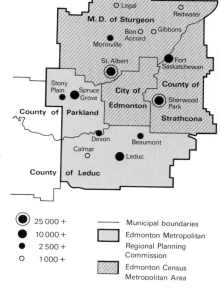

Figure 2–5 Main units of local government and administration in the Edmonton metropolitan region. The size distribution of the satellite towns and the boundary of the census metropolitan area are derived from the 1981 census. The area covered by the Edmonton Metropolitan Regional Planning Commission, which was established on 1 January 1982, is the best approximation of the actual metropolitan area.

Corridor Spread Effects

driving factor =
highways (accessibility)

The idiosyncracies of the census aside, it is notoriously difficult to define metropolitan regions, if only because they are constantly expanding. Growth at the centre is accompanied by spread effects, carrying the metropolitan influence to an ever-greater distance. There are signs, for example, that the cities of Camrose and Wetaskiwin are coming into Edmonton's orbit. Both offer services, such as a radio station, and automobile sales, that are directed at the Edmonton market. As well, they have their own small commuter populations.

The distribution of spread effects is directly influenced by the pattern of transport facilities and, above all, by highways, from which it can be expected that the effects will spread in all directions from a metropolitan node. In Alberta, however, there are two nodes, which means that there is also a special channelling effect into the corridor between them (Figure 2–6).

Figure 2–6 The theory and reality of corridor organization.
(a) Hypothetical structure of a binodal corridor system with a four-level hierarchy of urban places. The arrows indicate the directions of major and minor spread effects.
(b) Actual development pattern in the Edmonton-Calgary corridor based on the 1981 census.

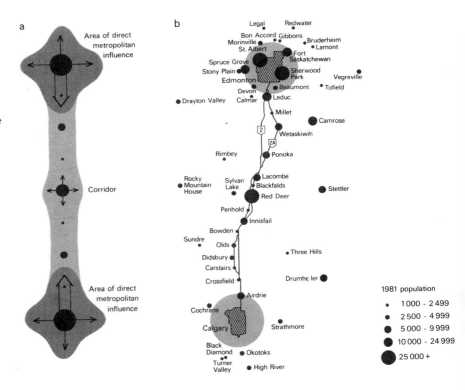

In essence, the Edmonton-Calgary corridor serves two functions. It is, first, a transportation corridor between the terminal nodes, a channel of communication or interaction between Edmonton and Calgary, and the busiest channel in the province. This is a comparatively modern development. In the 1920s and 1930s, Edmonton and Calgary were essentially independent; they served almost identical roles as the capitals of distinctive regions. Despite some functional specialization, for example the concentration of government services and university education in Edmonton, their similarities were incomparably stronger, and the need for interaction was weak. With the population growth and economic changes of the past 40 years, however, combined with a great improvement in transport technology, it has been possible for more complementary specializations to emerge. In other words, at the highest level of service the two cities are beginning to function as one, although they are 275 km apart. Thus, Calgary has gained strength as the financial centre of Alberta and, perhaps, of western Canada, whereas the large employment increases generated by public service are more heavily concentrated in Edmonton. Another example can be drawn from the petroleum industry, with Calgary increasingly specialized in its head office role while Edmonton is the chief centre for manufacturing and processing industries. (Chapters 9 and 10 explore these topics further.)

complementary specializations, allowed by good linkage

At one and the same time, then, the interdependence of Edmonton and Calgary has increased the demand for better communications between the two cities, while improvements in transportation, such as short-haul jet aircraft, and a non-stop divided highway, have facilitated still higher levels of interaction and specialization—the fourth stage of development illustrated in Figure 2–2. Concomitantly, though, the accessibility of other places in the corridor has also been improved. When the modern Highway 2 was built, the towns along its route were by-passed, leading to the fear that they would go into economic decline. It is now clear that they have a special growth advantage. The corridor contains the most intensive concentration of large, growing urban places in Alberta (Figure 2–4), and a corridor location is yet another factor in the expansion of the urban system since 1946 (Figure 2–3). Thus, the corridor's second function is to accommodate the spread of development from the metropolitan nodes. The process is still in an early stage, but it is by no means too soon to speak of an Edmonton-Calgary region as the dominant feature of the Alberta settlement system.

Counter-urbanization

While it is logical to expect that spread effects will be amplified in a corridor linking two large cities, the reasons for the spread of growth are by no means as clear. They can best be associated with a new North American phenomenon which has come to be known, rather misleadingly, as counter-urbanization. This does not mean that the population is becoming less urban in either distribution or attitudes, but rather that the growth impetus is shifting away from the largest cities to smaller cities and towns. Through the 1970s this trend was widespread in Canada, and in Alberta it was marked by a sharp decrease in Edmonton and Calgary's growth rates and in their share of the total provincial increase (Table 2–4). Between 1971 and 1976, for instance, their combined increase was only 14 per cent, the lowest it had been since the 1930s. There was a modest rise to 22 per cent in 1976–81 during the short-lived boom brought on by the international energy crisis, but the increase for the full census decade was still only 39 per cent, as compared with 46 per cent in 1961–71 and the high point of the modern period, 98 per cent, in 1951–61. Meanwhile, the corridor towns and cities as a group showed a marked increase in their growth rate, from 34 per cent in 1961–71 to 87 per cent in 1971–81. Similarly, the whole group of cities with more than 10,000 people in 1981 (excluding Edmonton's satellites) increased their rate of increase from 27 per cent to 69 per cent for the same two decades. Even towns lower in the hierarchy experienced the same kind of shift, though in a lesser degree. Thus, the group of places with populations between 2,500 and 10,000 in 1981 (again excluding the metropolitan satellites) recorded rates of increase that jumped from 27 per cent in 1961–71 to 46 per cent in 1971–81.

Admittedly, these are no more than tentative signs that a new pattern of structural change may be at work in the Alberta settlement system, and their significance is masked by the special growth effects of the resource industries. Insofar as the Alberta experience is representative of a larger tendency, however, it can be assumed that the negative aspects of concentrated development are beginning to encourage some people to seek alternative places to live or to operate their businesses. The difficulty of moving around in large and increasingly congested cities, for example, may more than offset their central situations in the transport network; for some businesses, a location like Red Deer or Wetaskiwin may come to provide more convenient access to clients. Large size brings benefits, too, in the sense of the critical mass of population that is needed to support the most specialized services and amenities, but not everyone wants these things. Those people whose lifestyle preferences can be satisfied in smaller places will therefore tend to be concentrated in the outer parts of the metropolitan regions, in the corridor communities, and even further afield. There was evidence, as shown in Table 2–2, that many of Alberta's agricultural service centres were taking on new vigour in the 1970s, irrespective of the effects of centralization. They were providing retirement homes for neighbouring farmers, bases for part-time and suit-case farmers, and increasingly, a refuge for disgruntled urbanites.

The process of small town rehabilitation is now a vital part of the Alberta scene. It has derived support from a number of community programs such as the Regional Resources Project in the Hanna area, east of Calgary, and the Main Street Alberta program of the Devonian Foundation. The renewed interest in the opportunities of small town life also gives credence to the Alberta government's desire to encourage some decentralization of growth from Edmonton and Calgary, with the twin aims of keeping the cities manageable and liveable while restoring the smaller places to a more prominent position in the urban system. If, in a small way, the adjustments are already occurring, there will be a spontaneous momentum that can be capitalized upon through government assistance. But whatever the effects of this intervention may be in the future, it is clear that the Alberta settlement system continues to be in flux; the drive towards equilibrium may be in vain but it is also inexorable.

Supplemental Readings

Barr, B.M., ed. *Calgary: Metropolitan Structure and Influence.* Victoria: Western Geographical Series, Vol. 11, 1975.

Bettison, D.G., Kenward, J.K. and Taylor, L. *Urban Affairs in Alberta.* Edmonton: The University of Alberta Press, 1975.

Jankunis, F. and Sadler, B., eds. *The Viability and Livability of Small Urban Centres.* Edmonton: Environment Council of Alberta, 1979.

Sheehan, P. *Social Change in the Alberta Foothills.* Toronto: McClelland and Stewart, 1975.

Smith, P.J., ed. *Edmonton: The Emerging Metropolitan Pattern.* Victoria: Western Geographical Series, Vol. 15, 1978.

Smith, P.J. "Alberta Since 1945: The Maturing Settlement System." In *A Geography of Canada: Heartland and Hinterland,* edited by L.D.McCann, 295–337. Scarborough: Prentice-Hall Canada, 1982.

Smith, P.J. and Johnson, D.B. *The Edmonton-Calgary Corridor.* Edmonton: University of Alberta, Department of Geography, 1978.

3 Population Characteristics and Trends

Leszek A. Kosiński

The population of any region can best be described in terms of its dynamic and cross-sectional characteristics. These sets of characteristics are also closely interrelated; for example, age composition has a direct bearing on the number of births, and, conversely, average family size, which reflects past fertility, influences the age structure in the community. To understand the demographic reality of a region, then, it is necessary to analyse the relationships between the structural and the dynamic characteristics of population.

Demographic processes are not autonomous, but vary in relation to numerous economic, social, and political factors operating within and without the community. It appears, however, that the most general causal factor explaining a long-term evolution of demographic trends is the process of modernization, which implies changes in personal attitudes and social mores caused by modifications in employment, residence patterns, educational standards, and the like. As a consequence, the accepted theory of demographic change attempts to explain the shift from one demographic regime to another in terms of a process of transition. This means also that the extent and rate of modernization and its accompanying social change can be inferred from the evidence of a demographic transition. Furthermore, transition usually starts first in some favoured location, from which it is diffused wavelike through both time and space. An analysis of the areal differentiation of demographic trends can therefore help to identify the nodes of change in demographic behaviour. Finally, the concept of transition can be applied to cultural characteristics of population, such as language. The process of modernization implies closer contacts and more intensive interaction and this, in turn, favours greater cultural integration.

As emphasized in the preceding chapters, Albertan society has undergone considerable changes during the last several decades. Diversification of the economy, an advanced degree of urbanization, and the expansion of tertiary and quaternary services are all features of the modernization process. All have influenced the evolution of demographic patterns. Nor was Alberta immune from what was happening in other parts of Canada and, indeed, other parts of the world. Some of the changes in Alberta, particularly migratory trends, can be explained only if distant but nonetheless related developments are taken into consideration.

The basic patterns of population change relatively slowly, but there are also short term trends which may occasionally go counter to the long term tendencies without reversing them. For example, the percentage of foreign-born Albertans has been on the decline throughout the twentieth century, but in some periods of heavy immigration it has increased for a short time. As well, local developments can differ from the overall provincial trends, so that the interpretation of population is not independent of the spatial scale of inquiry.

The following analysis is concentrated on the patterns of change in selected characteristics of the population of Alberta. The emphasis is on developments of the recent past, but some projections for the future and likely consequences of the expected changes are also included.

Population Change

The present population of Alberta—some 2 million—may not seem large, particularly in relation to the large territory of the province, but its size and composition is the result of an amazingly dynamic and diversified process of growth which took place within a relatively short period. The rapidity and extent of the changes, decade by decade, are shown in Table 3–1. Throughout the twentieth century, Alberta has normally experienced a rate of growth well above the Canadian average, with the result that its share of the national population has increased substantially. Yet the growth was also uneven; the decennial increases varied a great deal. After the great increase prior to the First World War, based mainly on overseas immigration, the subsequent decades witnessed gradually declining increments, to the point of almost no increase in the difficult 1930s. After the Second World War, however, the decennial additions to Alberta's population again reached several hundred thousands and the province once more ranked high in the nation in terms of provincial rates of change.

The total growth can be disaggregated into two major components, natural (or demographic) and migrational. When analysed separately, the changing nature of Alberta's population is thrown into a clearer light (Table 3–2).

Table 3-1
Population change in Alberta, 1901–81

	Population (in thousands)	National population (%)	Intercensal change		
			Change (in thousands)	Change (%)	Rank of Alberta according to the provincial rates of change
1901	73	1.4			
			301	413	2
1911	374	5.2			
			215	57	1
1921	589	6.7			
			143	24	2
1931	732	7.1			
			64	9	6
1941	796	6.9			
			144	18	4
1951	940	6.7			
			392	42	1
1961	1,332	7.3			
			296	22	3
1971	1,628	7.6			
			610	37	1
1981	2,238	9.2			

Source: Canadian census data.
Note: Data for Newfoundland included in comparisons beginning in 1951.

Table 3-2
Components of population change in Alberta, 1931–81

		Total change	Natural increase	Estimated net migration
1931–41	Thousands	65	106	− 42
	%	100	165	− 65
1941–51	Thousands	143	150	− 7
	%	100	105	− 5
1951–61	Thousands	392	265	127
	%	100	68	32
1961–71	Thousands	296	240	56
	%	100	81	19
1971–81	Thousands	610	213	396
	%	100	35	65

Source: Canadian census data except for 1981.

The total number of births and deaths has increased as the population increased. In the late 1970s, approximately 35,000 persons were born and 12,000 died each year in Alberta. This resulted in a difference (or natural increase) amounting on average to 23,000 per annum. For the analysis of long term trends, however, it is necessary to convert the actual vital statistics into rates, by relating them to the total population of a given area.

At first glance, it appears that death rates in Alberta have been remarkably stable in the long run, while birth rates have fluctuated a great deal (Figure 3–1). In fact, death rates declined from 9 to 6 per thousand population, and the annual oscillations almost disappeared as medical services became more widely available and improved living conditions led to an increase in health standards. This, in turn, led to a greater probability of survival; according to the 1975–77 life table, newly-born female Albertans could look forward to 77.9 years of future life and males to 71.0 years. These were among the highest values in Canada at that time; only males in Saskatchewan and females in Saksatchewan, Prince Edward Island, and British Columbia were marginally better off than Albertans. Judging by the experience of other societies, however, the process of aging, which will inevitably affect Alberta's population, resulting in a higher proportion of old people, will bring an increase of overall mortality rates in the future, even if the situation improves for each age category.

Birth rates declined through the 1920s and reached a low of 20 per thou-

Demographic Change

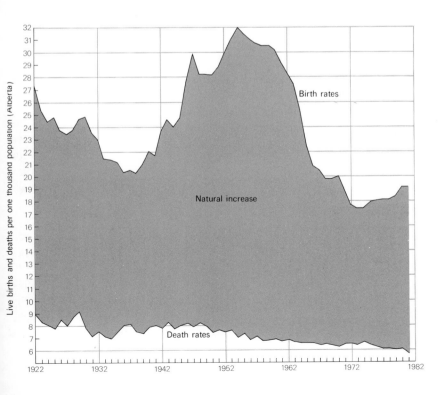

Figure 3–1 Birth rates, death rates, and rates of natural increase for Alberta in every year from 1922 to 1981.
Source: Statistics Canada.

sand in the late 1930s. The economic depression and environmental problems of the "dirty thirties" had obviously discouraged some potential parents from having families. The situation changed in the following decade due to post-war prosperity, and the influx of large numbers of young immigrants. An atmosphere favouring high levels of fertility was created. The 1950s produced the famous "baby boom," with annual birth rates soaring to 30 per thousand. The increasing employment of women, and other changes in lifestyle, resulted in another decline in birth rate. By the late 1970s, it had dropped considerably below the interwar minimum. These drastic changes in fertility level created a series of demographic waves which, in turn, imposed transitional pressures upon the labour market and upon various types of social services, including education.

As a result of these changes in vital processes, the natural increase of population has varied in time. In the 1950s it was nearly twice as high as in previous decades, but it declined considerably thereafter (Table 3–2). It has always been positive, though. Alberta has never experienced an excess of deaths over births. In terms of the demographic transition, Alberta has now reached the post-transitional stage of relatively low fertility, very low mortality, and modest natural increase.

Migration   The role of the second component of change—migration—has varied even more dramatically than that of natural increase. Not only has the volume of change been variable, but the direction of migration has also varied. For example, there have been periods when the outflow of people from Alberta has exceeded the inflow. During the 1930s, in particular, there was a net loss of more than 40,000, or about two-fifths of the natural increase of that decade. In the 1940s, by contrast, the net migrational loss was very slight and the overall growth of population was nearly equal to the natural increase of 150,000. In the 1950s the situation changed yet again, and the net migration gain exceeded 100,000. This represented roughly one-third of the overall growth. During the subsequent decade the net migration gain was much more modest, but in the 1970s migration gain was once more an important component of growth. It was even more important than the natural increase which accounted for only one-third of the overall increase.

In Alberta's early days, newcomers were attracted by the availability of land. Now, however, nearly all new arrivals settle in urban areas and particularly in the two metropolitan centres. Migration has been a major factor in the urbanization trend discussed in detail in Chapter 2.

During the last two decades, annual estimates of both internal (within Canada) and international migration have been made available by Statistics Canada. These data clearly show a much greater importance of interprovincial migration as compared with international flows. The two types of flow have also been subject to different trends.

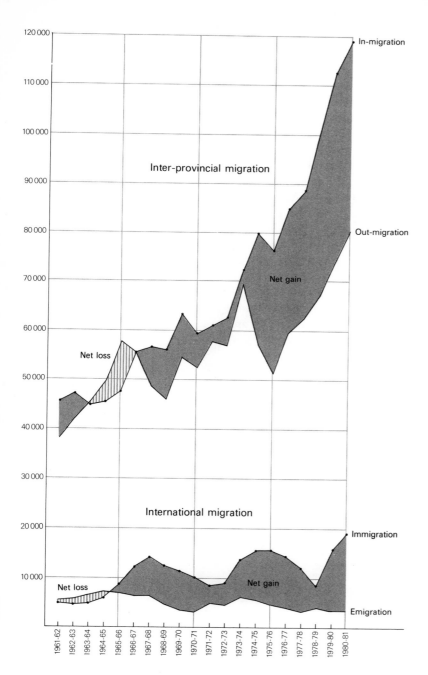

Figure 3–2 International and inter-provincial migration to and from Alberta in every year from 1961–62 to 1980–81. Source: Statistics Canada.

Between 1961 and 1981, some 221,000 international migrants chose Alberta as their destination in Canada, while 97,000 people emigrated from the province. However, the net gain of 124,000 was far from evenly distributed (Figure 3–2). Immigration fluctuated greatly—from a low of less than 5,000 per annum in the early 1960s (when there was actually a net loss of population through internation migration), through a series of peaks and troughs to a high of 19,000 in 1980–81. Emigration, by contrast, has recorded a general downward trend since the mid-sixties, so that the annual net gains have tended to reflect the variations in immigration. The sharp increase in the late 1970s is especially striking.

Analysis of the immigration data by country of origin reveals an important new trend. This is a consequence of changes in Canada's immigration regulations, combined with economic conditions in various parts of the world. Thus, between the mid-fifties and the mid-seventies the proportion of immigrants from traditional sources—Europe and the United States—declined from 97 per cent to 52 per cent, while the proportion from Latin America, Africa, and Asia increased from 2 per cent to 45 per cent. Nearly one-half of all immigrants now originate from new source areas in which population pressure is mounting and which are no longer ineligible because of a selective Canadian immigration policy.

The numbers of people involved in interprovincial migration have been much greater than those coming from other countries. They also increased continuously in an obvious response to Alberta's economic prosperity (Figure 3–2). In the period between 1961 and 1981 the annual number of

Figure 3–3 Total net migration between Alberta and other Canadian provinces for the period 1971–72 to 1980–81. Source: Statistics Canada.

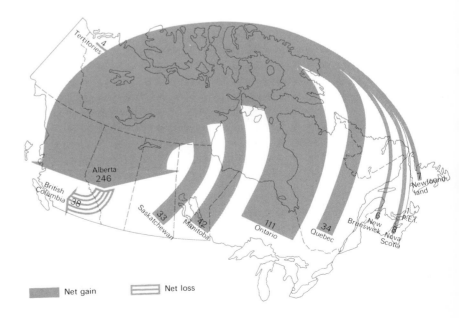

Net gain   Net loss

in-migrants nearly tripled, while the out-migrants doubled; the net losses of the mid-1960s were replaced by net gains, reaching particularly high levels in the second half of the 1970s. Over the full two decades, the total numbers of arrivals (1,350,000) and departures (1,110,000) are quite staggering; the difference (240,000) represents Alberta's net gain from interprovincial migration. It is noteworthy that most of that gain (210,000) accrued in the 1970s.

The directions of interprovincial flows for the period 1971–81 are presented in Figure 3–3. It appears that Alberta enjoyed net gains from all provinces and territories (to a total of 246,000), except British Columbia (a loss of 38,000). It was also with British Columbia that Alberta shared the greatest interchange of people; some 286,000 left Alberta for the western province while the reverse flow was only 248,000. Second-ranking Ontario sent 232,000 and received 121,000, resulting in a net gain for Alberta of 111,000. Then followed Manitoba, Quebec, and Saskatchewan, in that order, while the Atlantic provinces played a relatively insignificant role.

In conclusion, it is worth repeating that the actual population increase that results from these large movements is but a small fraction of the total arrivals and departures. This proportion (known as efficiency of migration) is higher among international migrants (39 per cent) than it is among interprovincial ones (10 per cent). In other words, the former have been more stable migrants; they have been more likely to stay in Alberta once they have settled here. The efficiency of interprovincial migration has varied considerably as well, with Quebec having the highest value.

Future Population Growth

According to Statistics Canada forecasters, the population of Alberta should climb to the range of 2.5–2.9 million in 1991 and to 2.8–3.5 million in 2001, subject to future variations in the rate of natural increase and migrational trends. Provincial forecasters expect even faster growth, to 2.6–3.1 million in 1991 and 3.0–3.9 million in 2001. Obviously, only time will tell which is the better prediction. But in the meantime, Alberta will likely continue to increase its share of the national population, possibly reaching 11 per cent before the end of the century. If that occurs, Alberta will maintain its position as the fourth most populous province and may well come to rival British Columbia for third place.

Spatial Patterns of Population Change

Just as population change in Alberta has varied over time, so, too, has it varied geographically. Different areas of the province have experienced different patterns of growth and decline, with the result that the overall pattern of population distribution is constantly shifting. The phenomena of rural-urban migration and the increasing concentration of population in

Figure 3–4 Population growth and decline by census division for each census decade from 1901 to 1981. In two decades (1931–41 and 1941–51) the mean provincial population growth rate was lower than the rate of natural increase, implying a *net loss* through migration. The most rapidly growing divisions in this period were those with growth rates greater than the provincial rate of natural increase; the slowest growth was experienced in those divisions that fell below the average growth rate for Alberta. In the six remaining decades, the provincial growth rate was greater than the rate of natural increase, implying a *net gain* through migration. In this situation the highest rates of growth accrued to census divisions above the average growth rate, while those divisions that fell below the rate of natural increase had the lowest rates of increase. In the legend, the symbols on the left refer to the decades of net migration gain; the symbols on the right refer to the decades of net migration loss.
Source: Statistics Canada.

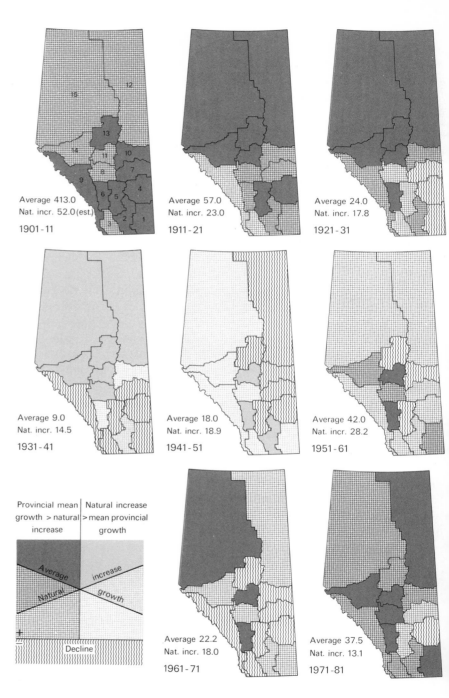

urban and, more specifically, metropolitan centres, are an important part of this process. Since they have already been discussed in Chapter 2, however, attention will be focused here on the long-term adjustment that can be observed at the census division scale (Figure 3–4).

In the first decade of this century, the population of Alberta increased five times, but in the southern part of the province the rates of growth were generally higher than average. During the next three decades, this situation was reversed as agricultural land settlement shifted northward. As early as the 1920s, the three census divisions in the extreme southeastern corner of Alberta declined in population. In three other divisions, growth was less than should have been provided by natural increase, so that an outflow of people can be inferred.

In the 1930s, when the overall growth of Alberta's population was less than the natural increase, the area of population losses expanded into most southern divisions. Even the Calgary census division suffered migration losses, although its population increased somewhat. This pattern extended into the 1940s, as most divisions either declined in population or grew at a very slow rate. The only exceptions were the three divisions centred on Calgary (CD6), Edmonton (CD11), and Lethbridge (CD2). For the first time, the primacy of the two metropolitan areas was clearly established; it has been maintained ever since.

In the 1950s, when the provincial mean growth exceeded the natural increase again, only three census divisions suffered absolute population losses. Yet the increase in several others was less than the natural increase—again implying out-migration. The highest growth was concentrated along the Calgary–Edmonton axis, including Red Deer and extending towards Hinton. The Medicine Hat area, which had suffered losses for three previous decades, also recorded high growth related to resource development. The dominant position of the main metropolitan axis was maintained in the 1960s, although migration losses were experienced in the Red Deer area. The Hinton and, even more strikingly, the Medicine Hat divisions were also in a low growth category again, together with the northeastern part of the province. Indeed, absolute population losses occurred in seven divisions surrounding the central core. On the other hand, resource developments around Grande Prairie brought spectacular growth to CD15.

The pattern changed yet again in the 1970s. Only the peripheral, rural Hanna division (CD4) experienced an actual decline of population, and two neighbouring areas grew by less than their natural increase. In the remaining 12 divisions, growth was equal to or higher than the natural increase for this period (signifying net in-migration). Five of these divisions had growth rates exceeding the provincial average. The five divisions were the two metropolitan divisions, Calgary (CD6) and Edmonton (CD11); the booming Medicine Hat district (CD1); the recreation and resource-based Hinton area (CD14); and Fort McMurray (CD12) which had the highest growth rate in the province.

Most areas of Alberta have reached their highest populations at the present time. The only exceptions are four rural divisions in the east-central part of the province, which experienced their maximum populations in 1941 (CD10), 1931 (CD5), and 1921 (CDs 4 and 7), respectively. Their maxima were 13 to 27 per cent higher than the present population, except for the Hanna division (CD4) whose 1921 population was more than twice the present level. This is a further reflection of the spatial adjustments that were first mentioned in Chapter 2.

Recent and anticipated trends indicate that the rapid growth of provincial population experienced during the 1970s will continue into the foreseeable future. That growth is also likely to continue to be concentrated in the metropolitan areas and it is expected that census divisions 6 and 11 will account for 33 and 36 per cent of the provincial population respectively by 1991. That will leave only 31 per cent to be spread unevenly among the remaining thirteen divisions.

The increasing dominance of Edmonton and Calgary in Alberta's population trends has another important effect. This analysis of the spatial pattern of change has been based on the assumption that demographic trends were similar across the province. However, when attention is focused separately on fertility and mortality, critical differences among areas are revealed. These are caused by variations in age/sex composition, the cultural and social backgrounds of the local population, residence patterns, and accessibility of social services. A detailed analysis of these differences over time is beyond the scope of this survey, but a brief look at the recent situation will show the range and pattern of vital rates.

In 1976 crude birth rates ranged from 14 to 21 per thousand, but the two metropolitan divisions were relatively close to the provincial average of 18 per thousand (Edmonton 18.2 and Calgary 16.8). The lowest birth rates were registered in rural, peripheral divisions with older populations depleted by a long-lasting outflow of people. On the other hand, areas with large inflows related to resource development, or a relatively high proportion of Native Indian population, were at the high end of the range. The highest birth rates occurred in census divisions 3, 14, and 15. In the same year, crude mortality rates ranged from less than 6 per thousand in the metropolitan divisions and the youthful northern division of Grand Prairie (CD15) to as much as 9 or 10 in rural central and southern divisions, such as Pincher Creek (CD3), Drumheller (CD5), Stettler (CD7), and Camrose (CD10). The natural increase also varied correspondingly. But, because of the dominance of Edmonton and Calgary in the total population, the average values for the province are increasingly influenced by the levels of mortality and fertility in the two metropolitan centres.

Cultural Characteristics

The cultural background of the Alberta population is far from uniform, but the long-term trends point to an increasing degree of integration. It is possible to analyse changes in various cultural characteristics because of the long series of census data pertaining to birthplace, ethnicity, and language.

In the early part of this century, the majority of Alberta residents were not born within the province. That changed as the population stabilized and increased. The proportion of Alberta-born residents rose steadily from 20 per cent in 1911 to 62 per cent in 1971, but then it dropped sharply to 51 per cent in 1981. Because of the massive influx of migrants through the 1970s, the proportion of Alberta's population actually born in Alberta had returned to its 1951 level. It can also be noted that the long-term adjustments have been mainly at the expense of the foreign-born population, whose share of the Alberta total dropped substantially between 1911 and 1981—from 56 per cent to 16 per cent. By contrast, the proportion born elsewhere in Canada declined from 24 per cent in 1911 to 15 per cent in 1941. It then climbed again, reaching 21 per cent in 1971 and almost 30 per cent a decade later.

The majority of Alberta-born Canadian residents (only residents are covered by Canadian censuses) live in Alberta—nearly 80 per cent in 1981. The only sizeable concentration outside the province was in British Columbia, where there was a total of 205,000 native Albertans in 1981, or 13 per cent of the Alberta-born population in Canada.

The population of British origin (including English, Scottish, Welsh, and Irish) has always constituted the largest group in Alberta. Its share was as high as 60 per cent in the first quarter of this century but it has drifted downwards since. In the 1981 census 43 per cent of the population declared that they were descended solely from British stock and a further 9 per cent claimed some British ancestry (Figure 3–5). The remainder of Alberta's pop-

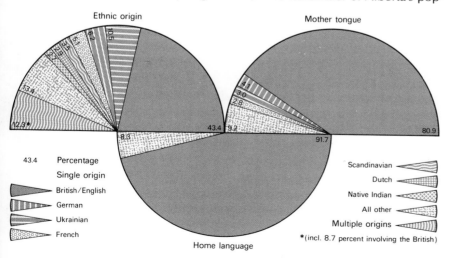

Figure 3–5 Ethnic and linguistic characteristics of Alberta's population in 1981. "Ethnic origin" refers to the nationality or race of the original immigrants from whom the present population is descended; "mother tongue" is the language first learned and still understood; and "home language" is the language most commonly used, regardless of mother tongue. In the 1981 census it was possible, for the first time, to declare more than one ethnic origin and 12 per cent of the Alberta population did so. Source: Statistics Canada.

ulation consists mainly of various European ethnic groups, while Native Indians and other non-Europeans account for no more than one-eleventh of the total. People of German, Ukrainian, and French origin follow the British, in that order. In contrast to some other groups, notably the Scandinavians who were prominent in Alberta's early years but have been displaced by subsequent migrations, the relative position of the French has improved markedly in recent years.

The geographical distribution of the various ethnic groups reflects the time of their arrival and initial settlement, as well as their subsequent mobility in Canada. For example, apart from the metropolitan centres, which tend to concentrate the largest numbers of all groups, most people of German origin can be found in the south, centre, and northwest, Scandinavians in the central and southeastern parts of the province, Ukrainians in the central and eastern areas, and French in the west and north. An examination of the relative positions of the various ethnic groups in individual census divisions suggests that seven different types of ethnic patterns can be distinguished. These patterns are identified by ranking the ethnic groups in descending order (an equal sign [=] signifies approximately equal shares):

1. British/German/Scandinavian in five census divisions in the southern and eastern part of the province. In total these divisions (CDs 1, 4, 5, 7, and 8) account for 12 per cent of Alberta's population. In the case of Drumheller (CD5) the Native Indian population is almost as large as the Scandinavian ethnic group.
2. British/German/Dutch in CD2 (Lethbridge), 5 per cent of the provincial population.
3. British/Native Indian/German in two widely separated areas. In the first, CD3 (Pincher Creek), the three groups are followed by people of Dutch and Scandinavian descent; in the second, CD15 (Grande Prairie), French, Ukrainian and Scandinavian groups follow. These two CDs represent 7 per cent of the Alberta population.
4. British/Ukrainian/German in CD10 (Camrose) which has 3 per cent of Alberta's population.
5. British/German/Ukrainian in CD11 (Edmonton) and CD13 (Whitecourt), adjoining central divisions where 37 per cent of the population is concentrated.
6. British/German/French/Ukrainian, a combination found in three western divisions (CD6 - Calgary, CD9 - Banff, and CD14 - Hinton) with 32 per cent of the population.
7. British/Native Indian = French/Ukrainian in CD12 (Fort McMurray) which accommodated only 4 per cent of the provincial population in 1981.

Some clearly distinguishable cultural-religious groups, such as Mennonites and Hutterites, are included in the German ethnic category, and Métis are often counted as French.

While ethnic diversity might persist in Alberta, the process of assimilation leads to a considerable and increasing cultural unity. This is revealed most strikingly by data on language.

In 1981 four-fifths of the Alberta population declared English to be their mother tongue (defined as the language first learned and still understood) and over 90 per cent used English at home (Figure 3–5). The degree of linguistic shift can be seen from the following comparison. In 1981 there were 1,156,000 people of British background in Alberta, including 193,500 who declared partial British origin. In the same year 1,264,000 declared English to be their mother tongue, 1,478,000 spoke English at home, and 1,606,000 understood English. This indicates the considerable expansion of English as a unifying cultural factor. By contrast, amongst the 233,000 people of German background, who formed the second largest ethnic group in Alberta, only 91,500 declared German to be their mother tongue, no more than 27,500 spoke it at home, and nearly all could speak English. This is indicative of the linguistic erosion experienced by all the smaller ethnic groups.

Table 3–3 depicts the two stages of the process of language transfer for the ten largest cultural groups in Alberta. The first two columns present the shift between ethnic origin and mother tongue (in other words, assimilation in previous generations); the second pair of columns illustrates the change from

Table 3-3

Language transfer and retention amongst Alberta's population in 1981

Ethnic/ linguistic group	$\dfrac{\text{Mother tongue}}{\text{Ethnic origin}} \times 100$		$\dfrac{\text{Home language}}{\text{Mother tongue}} \times 100$	
	Canada	Alberta	Canada	Alberta
English (British Isles)	154	188	110	112
German	46	39	31	30
Ukrainian	55	50	32	25
French	97	56	95	48
Scandinavian	24	18	11	9
Dutch	55	35	17	17
Native Indian	35	44	63	60
Polish	50	35	44	36
Chinese	78	79	84	84
Italian	71	61	69	51

Note: The groups are ranked from largest to smallest on the basis of ethnic origin as declared to the census. Only those groups exceeding 1 per cent of the population in 1981 were included, and only single ethnic origins were taken into consideration. MT/EO index therefore tends to overestimate both the transfer to English and the losses to every other language.

mother tongue to the language most often used at home (or linguistic assimilation of the persons enumerated). Values above 100 indicate those groups that have gained from the language transfer; values below 100 indicate the groups that have lost.

Retention of language varied among the ethnic groups but it was lower in Alberta than in Canada as a whole, particularly for the French. One-half or more of the Chinese, Italians, French, and Ukrainians declared a mother tongue that corresponded to their ethnic background, but for Germans, Dutch, Poles, and Scandinavians the proportion was much lower. It also seems that the process of linguistic assimilation has accelerated in the present generation. People who still speak a given language represent only a fraction of those who spoke it in their childhood. Again, the Chinese had the highest retention ratio in 1981, followed by Native Indians; Dutch and Scandinavians were at the bottom of the list. About half of Italian and French mother-tongue speakers continued to use their language at home, as compared with about one-third of Poles and Germans and one-quarter of Ukrainians.

Recency of immigration, degree of concentration in urban and metropolitan areas, intermarriage, access to education, and concern with the ancestral culture are among the factors explaining the differing degrees of assimilation of various ethnic groups. At the same time, the transition from a multilingual to a unilingual society does not mean that all differences between ethnic groups disappear. A family study conducted in Alberta in 1973–74 indicates that current and expected family size differ among various ethnic groups. While the average family size of those included in the survey was 1.70, the range was from 1.49 to 2.08, with British as the lowest, Germans and east Europeans in general below the average, and Ukrainians, other western Europeans, Irish, and French as the highest, above the average.

Native peoples represent a unique component in the ethnic mosaic of Alberta. At the 1901 census 13,400 Native Indians were enumerated. They accounted for 18.4 per cent of the total population of Alberta. The total did not change very much until 1941, when it started to increase. According to the 1981 census 72,055 people (3.3 per cent of Alberta's population) declared native ancestry, including 12,045 with mixed origin. Status Indians made up the largest group, outnumering non-status Indians by four to one (35,810 to 8,595). Métis people formed the second largest group, although their census total of 27,135 is much lower than earlier estimates which have ranged as high as 100,000. A small number of Inuit (510) were also enumerated in 1981.

More than two-thirds of the Native population (including Métis) live in the two northern census divisions (CDs 12 and 15) where they were the second largest ethnic group, after people of British origin, in 1981. Relatively large numbers are also to be found in the two metropolitan census divisions and in the Red Deer and Pincher Creek areas (Figure 3–6). This distribution pattern

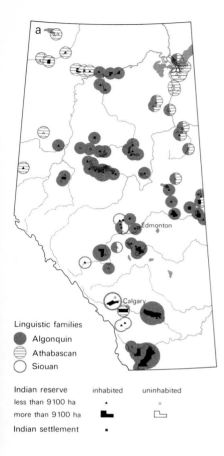

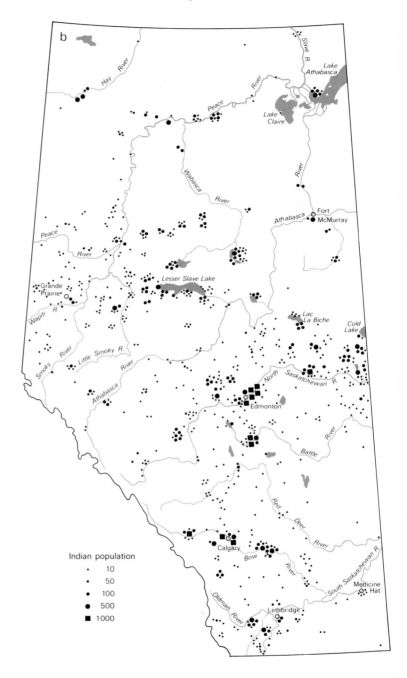

Figure 3–6 The distribution of the Native Indian population of Alberta in 1976. Map (a) shows the locations of reserves classified by size and by linguistic family. Map (b) shows the actual numbers of Native Indians. Source: *National Atlas of Canada*.

is strongly influenced by the locations of reserves, even though the right to live on reserves is restricted to status Indians. According to information from government agencies, 41 bands were registered in Alberta in 1977. Their combined membership was 35,300 of whom 25,400 lived on reserves, 7,700 off reserves, and 2,200 on Crown land. The greatest concentrations of reserves are around Fort Vermilion, Slave Lake, Fort Chipewyan, Cold Lake, and Edmonton, but the largest reserves are in the south, around Calgary and Pincher Creek.

In 1981, 26,600 Albertans declared one of the various Amerindian languages as their mother tongue (Figure 3–6). The Algonkian or Algonquin languages accounted for 22,600 of this total, with Cree speakers (17,200) as the single largest sub-category. The remaining 4,000 people were equally divided between the Siouan and Athapaskan (Athabascan) languages. As with other ethnic groups, the number of Albertans who continue to use Amerindian languages at home is lower still (Table 3–3). In 1981 there were only 15,900 people in this situation, including 13,770 Algonkian speakers, of whom 10,640 spoke Cree, and 1,500 Athapaskan speakers.

The comparison of numbers of people of native origin with Amerindian speakers shows that the process of assimilation has reached an advanced stage. Those who resist are mostly to be found outside the cities of Alberta. According to the 1981 census over 80 per cent of people declaring an Amerindian mother tongue resided in rural areas and nearly all of them were classed as rural non-farm population. Nevertheless, the drift of native people into urban centres continues to gain strength. The resultant problems of adjustment and cultural change, which are already severe, can only be expected to increase in the future.

Changing Age Composition

As a consequence of past variation in both vital processes and age/sex selective migration, the age composition of Alberta's population is far from regular. The so-called population pyramid for Alberta in 1981 shows many deviations from its ideal triangular shape (Figure 3–7). The sizeable bulge between roughly 17 and 25 years of age is a result of the postwar baby boom and the in-migration of young population. The narrower base reflects the declining fertility of recent years. A surplus of males exists in most age groups and it is only above the age of 56 that females assume numerical domination. Although future migration will undoubtedly modify the existing population composition, the basic structure is already given and forecasts of future developments based on the knowledge of existing trends can be attempted. Those forecasts are particularly important for the planning of social services and labour force management.

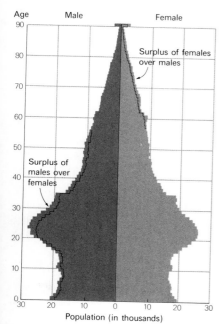

Figure 3–7 The Alberta population pyramid, 1981.
Source: Statistics Canada.

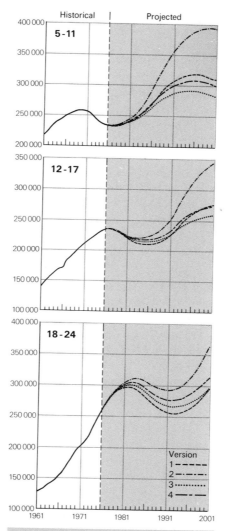

Figure 3–8 Past and projected size of selected school-age population groups in Alberta, 1961–2001.
Source: Statistics Canada.

The four versions of the projection, prepared by Statistics Canada, differ in their basic assumptions. Version 1 assumes low and declining migration gains, version 2 very high and stable gains, versions 3 and 4 declining intermediate gains. Fertility level is expected to be higher in versions 1 and 2 than in 3 and 4. Of the four versions number 2 is closest to the forecast prepared by the Alberta Bureau of Statistics.

An example of what can happen with school-age population is presented in Figure 3–8. It is derived from a projection prepared by Statistics Canada, and illustrates different alternatives based on varying assumptions about future fertility and migration. From this, it appears that the elementary school age group (5–11 years) will be increasing through the 1980s and by 1991 will reach between 285,000 and 355,000, compared with less than 240,000 in 1981. For the secondary level (12–17 years), the decline of the late 1970s will be reversed and the 1977 level (236,000) will be approached again by the early 1990s (224,000–252,000).

Since nearly everyone in these two age groups attends school, the future demand for services can be predicted on the basis of the population forecast. It appears that the short-term future for primary school teachers is bright, but secondary school teachers are likely to be faced with a temporary decline of demand, followed by a strong improvement. The situation is more complicated at post-secondary level, since the demand depends not only on the size of the appropriate age group but also the enrollment rate. The demographic forecast for the 18–24 age group suggests that the peak will be reached in the early 1980s (its exact timing and level can vary somewhat), followed by a limited or considerable decline extending into the early 1990s. The effect of this demographic trend is likely to be aggravated because the proportion of those 18–24 years old who enrolled in post-secondary institutions declined in Alberta throughout the 1970s. It increased slightly in 1981–82 but even then the participation rate was considerably lower than it had been a decade earlier and about 30 per cent below the national average. Against this, the decline could be moderated somewhat by the enrollment of older persons, an increasingly noticeable tendency.

Thus, the size and share of all school-age groups of the population will fluctuate in the near future. On the other hand, the proportion of population above 24 will increase continuously, providing a substantial supply of manpower. According to the projections of Statistics Canada, the population of 25–44 year olds will increase from half a million in 1975 to between 840,000 and 1,020,00 in 1991 and up to 1,100,00 in 2001. Its share of the total population should be particularly high in 1991 (33–36 per cent), but will probably drop to about 30 per cent ten years later. The older middle-age group (45–64 years) seems destined to increase faster in the 1990s than in the 1980s, but in any case it will reach at least 440,000 in 1991 and 615,000–760,000 in 2001. Its share of the total population is likely to be 23 per cent by the end of the century, as compared with 17.3 per cent in 1976.

The oldest age group is likely to double in size, at least, by the end of the century (280,000–300,000 in 2001 compared with 140,000 in 1976), but its proportion should increase only slightly from 7.5 per cent in 1976 to 8 or 9 per cent in 1991 and 8.5–10 per cent ten years later. In comparison with other provinces it will be a modest growth, and Alberta is likely to retain its fourth lowest rank insofar as the proportion of senior citizens is concerned. Nevertheless, there will be a considerable aging of the provincial population. In 1976 the median age was 26.1 years, but is likely to reach 31 by 1991 and 33–35 by the turn of the century.

In the long run the changes in the sex/age composition of provincial population indicate that there has been a transition from a youthful and demographically unbalanced society to a more mature and balanced one. Periodically, this process has been modified and delayed by the impact of immigration, but it has worked its course, nevertheless.

Conclusion

During the last 80 years Alberta's population has increased about 30 times. It has also spread over the territory of the province and changed in many ways in the process. Differences still exist but they tend to be less remarkable than in the past. The shift from a rural and agricultural economy to an urban and industrial one has done more than affect the composition of the population; it has been a mark of fundamental changes in social behaviour. That has been reflected, in turn, in the process of demographic transition, the late stage of which is reflected in the continuous decline of mortality and the more recent decline of fertility. Yet, fertility and mortality levels continue to differ across the province due to cultural, economic, and social variations, as well as to differences in age/sex composition and the accessibility of social services. Further convergence of demographic trends in space is to be expected, though some differences are bound to remain.

The long term trends in population change by census divisions show great differences between areas and frequent reversals of trends. Sometimes, early settlement created sound bases for further development. In other cases, the early optimism could not be sustained and population levels that were reached 60 or 50 years ago turned out to be a maxima, as yet not reached again. However, in the last 40 years or so, as the province became more urbanized a more stable system emerged. This system is based on the two metropolitan centres of Edmonton and Calgary, which have shown a consistently high growth quite unlike the boom or bust pattern of other parts of the province. It is to be expected that more stable economic conditions in an urbanized society will reduce the differences and shifts in the spatial patterns of population change.

Since its early days, Alberta has relied on immigration, both from abroad and from other parts of Canada. The movements have always been reciprocal but, more often than not, Alberta has gained from the exchange of people. In extreme periods, such as the 1970s, the effects of migration have been so large that all the patterns of population change have been distorted.

Over the long term, however, it is more significant to observe the increase in the proportion of Alberta-born residents in the Alberta population. This is another indication of an increasing stability of population.

Similarly, although the cultural diversity of Alberta's population is still an outstanding characteristic, there is a very strong tendency towards linguistic consolidation. English is clearly replacing all other languages. This cultural transition need not lead to full homogenization of the society, but the prime differences in the future are likely to be based on educational, occupational, and residence characteristics rather than on ethnic or linguistic background.

Supplemental Readings

Alberta Treasury, Bureau of Statistics. Statistical reviews and other reports, as issued periodically.

Cuff, D.J. "Statistical Surfaces for Populations: The Alberta Case." *The Albertan Geographer*, no. 11 (1975): 42–50.

Kosiński, L.A. and Frascara, J. *Population of Alberta*. Edmonton: Government of Alberta, Advanced Education and Manpower, 1980. Loose-leaf folder.

Laatsch, W.G. "Hutterite Colonization in Alberta." *The Journal of Geography* 70 (1971): 347–359.

Lamont, G.R. and Proudfoot, V.B. "Migration and Changing Settlement Patterns in Alberta." In *People on the Move: Studies on Internal Migration*, edited by L. A. Kosiński and R. M. Prothero, 223–235. London: Methuen, 1975.

Lehr, J.C. "The Sequence of Mormon Settlement in Southern Alberta." *The Albertan Geographer*, no. 10 (1974): 20–29.

McVey, W.W. *Population Trends in Alberta: Historical Review and Assessment for the Future*. Edmonton: Government of Alberta, Advanced Education and Manpower, 1977. Multilithed in two volumes.

Part 2
Environment, Land, and Resources

Part 2 of this book examines the meaning of the natural environment for people, and geographical variations in the problems and dilemmas caused by the human use of resources in mining, forestry, agriculture, and recreation.

The natural environment has had a pervasive influence throughout Alberta's modern development. Many of the human and economic dimensions of Alberta's geography can be understood only through their interrelationships with the province's biophysical systems and the regional patterns of environmental limitations to which they give rise. This underlying natural framework is described in Chapter 4, "Biophysical Constraints of the Natural Environment on Settlement," by Larry Cordes and Dan Pennock.

Prior to the transformation of the space-economy following the development of Alberta's petroleum deposits, the predominant influence on land-using activities was the natural productivity of the land. Productivity, in turn, is a function of a number of factors including physiography, climate, soils, natural vegetation, and technology. Across the southern half of Alberta, where the majority of the population is concentrated, these factors are in generally favourable combination. The physiography of the Alberta plains is suited, for the most part, to crop and livestock production, so regional variations are in response mainly to climatic and soil patterns. Above all, the availability of water is crucially important. But agriculture is increasingly being forced to compete with urban and industrial demands for water, and the prospect of large-scale diversions from the rivers of northern Alberta continues to excite attention.

Northern Alberta, except for the Peace River region, has an aqueous moisture regime, poor thermal budget, saturated soils, and a low natural productivity for crop growth. The region's future therefore appears to lie with energy extraction and timber harvesting. Although the biophysical environment also constrains the growth of timber, the major obstacle to the economic viability of resource-based activites in northern Alberta is the extent to which forestry and mining practices are compatible.

To permit a more sensitive appraisal of relations between human and economic activity and the natural environment, Cordes and Pennock have devised a classification scheme that allows Alberta to be divided into seven distinctive biophysical regions. Two of these regions, the mixed-grass prairie and the aspen parklands, dominate Alberta's space-economy. They contain almost all the agriculture, the greater part of the energy industry, and most of the urban settlement. A third region, the boreal forest, has a severe thermal deficit constraining agricultural settlement and forest regeneration, but it is underlaid by sufficient mineral resources to ensure that it can make a vital contribution to the province's economy.

When the inherent economic and locational attributes of the province's natural environment are combined with Alberta's geographic, economic, political, and social structure, conflicts rise in the use of resources. These are discussed by Edgar Jackson and Anne Dhanani in their chapter, "Resources and Resource-Use Conflict." Energy, forestry, and recreation are three major examples of resource-use conflicts in Alberta. They are exacerbated by a) concentration of settlement, b) rapid but localized population growth and urbanization, c) province-wide economic reliance on primary industry (including resource extraction), d) the plethora of governmental jurisdictions charged with environmental responsibility, and e) divergent objectives among governments and private owners in the goals associated with land use. Such conflicts basically stem from competitive users, environmental degradation, and spatial incompatibility.

Resource use sustains Alberta but resource uses coincide spatially over much of the province and cause conflict at many locations. The primary coal, oil, and gas industries consume large tracts of forest land without making effective use of the timber removed or compensating the forest industry for taking land out of the cycle of productive regeneration. Land associated with energy and forestry activities often loses its appeal as a scenic and recreational amenity. Extensive land clearing in fragile environments generates soil erosion and stream pollution, destroys fish and wildlife habitats, and hinders the natural regeneration of forest cover.

Jackson and Dhanani suggest that resolving resource-use conflicts requires co-operation among many different agencies and a fundamental reinterpretation of goals. Unfortunately, these conflicts are likely to persist as long as the province depends so heavily and extensively on resource extraction for its economic, and hence human, patterns of activity.

In the brief period of its existence, Alberta has undergone rapid agricultural colonization, development, depopulation, abandonment, and retreat. In Chapter 6, "Rural Alberta: Elements of Change," Geoff Ironside considers some of the impacts that a period of rapid social and economic change has brought to rural communities.

Farm numbers are declining in Alberta, and with that has come a decrease in the number of farm residents. The pattern of decline is most apparent in those census divisions outside the main population concentrations where the biophysical limitations are most severe, where non-farm employment opportunities are sporadic in both space and time, and where social and educational infrastructures are limited. The agricultural community throughout the province has also been affected by technological change, rising capital expenditures, the expansion and acquisition of farm holdings, fluctuations in profitable lines of production, and uncertainty in national and international markets.

Many other changes in rural Alberta are non-agricultural in origin, though impinging on agriculture. The growing demand for recreational land and exurban residential development, the expansion of the province's major urban places, and the reservation of service corridors conspire to remove land from agriculture. Farming units are dislocated, and pressure increases for the development of marginal lands in northern districts. In some cases human activities associated with non-agricultural rural land uses lead to environmental damage, water and land pollution, and vehicular congestion. Changing uses of rural land are also accompanied by rising service and maintenance costs, and a demand for more comprehensive services, the costs of which must be met from taxes and other government revenues.

As well, changes in rural Alberta are associated with regional disparity and inequality of opportunity. This leads Professor Ironside to foresee a need for improvements to the regional planning system. Greater public intervention may also be demanded in agriculture, industry, and settlement, and there is a need for more accurate monitoring of the impacts of change on the physical, human, and economic environments—particularly the abrupt, sporadic change associated with large-scale or mega projects. There are many signs that rural Alberta will remain in a state of flux for the foreseeable future.

4 Biophysical Constraints of the Natural Environment on Settlement

L. D. Cordes
D. J. Pennock

Before the discovery of oil at Leduc in 1947 and the subsequent transformation of the economy, the major land-using activities of Alberta were determined by the natural productivity of the land. This fixed the general level of economic sustenance that could be derived from employment in agriculture and forestry, and hence the number of people who could be supported in any area. In its turn, however, productivity depends on the natural environment—that combination of physiography, climate, soils, and vegetation which varies through time and space and which, through the complex interactions among its major elements, imposes intricate sets of limitations on the productive capability of land.

In this chapter, these environmental interrelationships are described, in a general way, as a basis for establishing the biological and physical framework of Alberta. That framework, in turn, is basic to the development of a set of biophysical regions, each of which is characterized by a distinctive array of limiting environmental factors which have controlled, in some way, the historical pattern of settlement. The scope of this survey is necessarily broad. Interesting anomalies in the overall pattern, such as the Cypress Hills, receive little or no attention. The geology of Alberta receives little mention either, although its influence on oil and gas development has become, and will probably remain, a major factor in Alberta's development.

Alberta has four major physiographic regions with distinctive patterns of land-form and geology (Figure 4–1). The dominant feature is the heavily folded and faulted limestones of the front and central ranges of the Rocky

Physiography

Figure 4–1 Physiographic regions of Alberta. The four major regions from southwest to northeast are the Western Cordillera, the Rocky Mountain foothills, the Alberta plains, and the Canadian Shield. Source: *Atlas of Alberta,* p. 9.

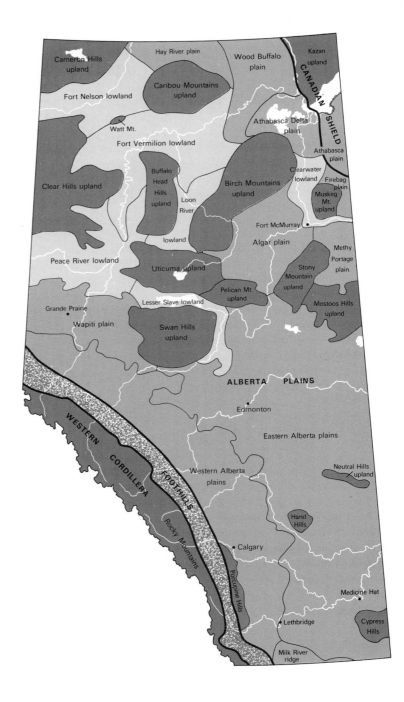

Mountains, formed when the process of continental drift pressed the oceanic plate of the Pacific against the North American continental plate, causing it to lift and fracture. Rocks were raised as high as 4,000 m above sea level in what are now the highest summits of the Western Cordillera. The zone immediately east of the Rockies, by contrast, was subjected to much less pressure, with less fracturing of the rock. The result is displayed in the long narrow ridges of the foothills belt.

The largest physiographic unit, occupying almost all the remaining area of the province, is the plains of Alberta, with its numerous upland remnants. Here, the standstones and shales have retained a flat appearance since little stress was applied to them during the mountain-building period. These huge, undisturbed rock beds originated as marine sediments and it is commonly believed that the plant and animal life of the ancient seas is the source of hydrocarbons from which so much of Alberta's contemporary wealth is derived. The extensive coal deposits are certainly of vegetable origin, as an abundance of fossil evidence testifies, but their quality is directly influenced by the amount of pressure which they have had to sustain. In the Alberta case, this means that the shallow, weakly compressed coals of the plains are chiefly classed as sub-bituminous and lignite, whereas the high quality thermal and coking coals are found in the foothills and front ranges of the Rocky Mountains. (See Figure 5–7 in Chapter 5.) Similarly, there seems to be a connection between mountain-building activity (orogenesis) and the occurrence of oil and natural gas. (See Figures 5–2 and 5–5 in Chapter 5.) The exact nature of the connection is still in dispute but, when the world's known petroleum fields are mapped, a most striking pattern emerges; all are associated with zones where tectonic plates have converged in the remote past or are still converging, as they are in western Canada.

On the surface of the Alberta plains there is a variety of landforms caused by Pleistocene ice sheets. At the height of glaciation, when the ice reached a maximum thickness of 1800 m, most of Alberta lay beneath the Laurentide ice sheet centred on Hudson Bay. The chief exception was a narrow zone in western Alberta which was covered by glaciers originating in the Western Cordillera; their remnants can still be seen in the Columbia Icefields.

The retreat of the ice began about 13,000 years B.P. (before present) but Laurentide ice lingered in northeastern Alberta until about 8,000 years B.P. It left a complex residue behind, in the various forms of glacial deposition which account for most of the surface irregularities on the Alberta plains (Figure 4–2). These deposits also make up the substrate upon which soil processes and the growth of vegetation have occurred, and they therefore have a vital role in determining local variations in soil capability for agriculture. The most extensive group of deposits is comprised of till or ground moraine, the material which results from the grinding action of ice on the underlying rock. It varies in composition from fine clay to large boulders (the so-called "field stone," a popular building material), and its surface appear-

Figure 4–2 Surface geology of Alberta.
Source: *Atlas of Alberta,* p. 8.

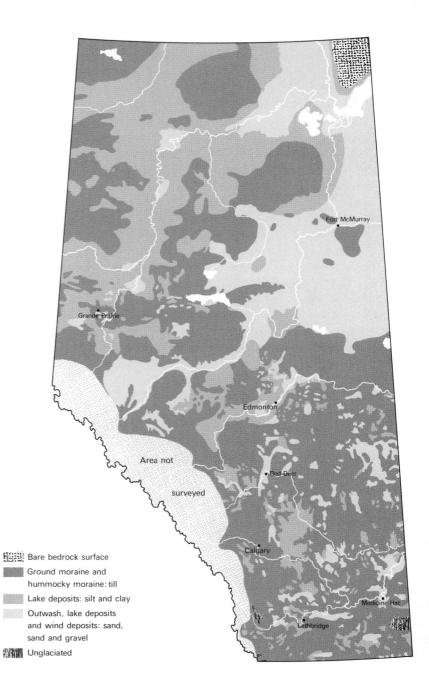

ance ranges from smooth and gentle undulations to rough hummocks, sometimes of considerable local relief. These are in marked contrast with the flat beds of the huge meltwater lakes that formed at various stages during the ice retreat. They have left a surface mantle of clay and silt which is at its most notorious in the gumbo of Lake Edmonton and Lake Peace. Elsewhere, however, where there was active transport of the glacial materials by wind and water, the fine particles were removed completely, leaving the coarse beds of sand and gravel which characterize the third group of glacial deposits in Alberta.

The major river systems of the province were formed during late glacial times. Wide channels were needed to accommodate the large amounts of glacier melt-water, but as their flows diminished the rivers cut down through the underlying material to produce the steep-walled valleys so characteristic of central and southern Alberta rivers. In northeastern Alberta, however, the longer duration of the ice and the more resistant rock of the Canadian Shield prevented the formation of complex drainage networks. Instead, there are vast areas of deranged drainage, where the streams lack sufficient outlets and large ponded areas have been created. It has been calculated that 40 per cent of Alberta's forested land (which accounts for 60 per cent of the province's area) is in terrain unsuitable for any kind of commercial production; the muskeg swamps of the northern half of Alberta are responsible for the major part of this huge limitation on human settlement.

The rivers of Alberta can be grouped into two major natural systems. Those in the northern half of the province belong to the Mackenzie River Basin, while those in the south form the upper part of the Saskatchewan-Nelson Basin (Figure 4–3). The two longest rivers in the province, the Peace and Athabasca, both have heavy flows northward into the Mackenzie River. In contrast, the major rivers in the southern portion of the province, the North Saskatchewan, Bow, and Oldman, have considerably smaller mean annual flows with somewhat greater year-to-year variability.

Because the majority of Alberta's population is located in the southern half of the province, considerable pressure has been placed on the rivers of the Saskatchewan-Nelson Basin, particularly in years of low flows. The most intense utilization of water resources occurs in the Bow and Oldman River basins, where the annual variability in precipitation has led to the development of irrigation projects on large tracts of high quality agricultural land (Figures 4–3 and 4–4). Future increases in urban population in this region will undoubtedly compete with expanding irrigation projects and with other major users, for example, petrochemical industries, for the limited supply of water. This prospect explains the recurrent popularity of schemes to transfer water from the large, relatively stable rivers of the north to the smaller, less dependable rivers of the south. For example, a plan proposed by the Saskatchewan-Nelson Basin Board would divert water from the North Saskatchewan River to the Bow River, to increase its flow by 85 m³ per second. The

Figure 4–3 Drainage basins and major rivers of Alberta. The average river flows and main irrigated areas are also shown. Source: Government of Alberta.

North Saskatchewan River would then be compensated with water from the Peace and Athabasca Rivers. The outcome would be a substantial increase in the amount of water available in southern Alberta, particularly during years of low precipitation. However, the cost would be high, certainly in financial terms and perhaps also in adverse environmental effects.

Figure 4–4 Average variability of precipitation across Alberta for the whole year and for the growing season. Source: *Atlas of Alberta*, p. 16.

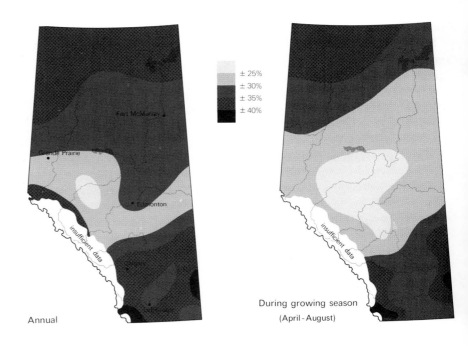

± 25%
± 30%
± 35%
± 40%

Annual

During growing season
(April - August)

The Regional Climates of Alberta

Initially, the navigable waterways and the mountain passes to which they led exercised the major control over the penetration of the Alberta region by white interests. The fur traders and, later, the railway builders turned to the river valleys for their routeways and their settlement sites. With the onset of effective colonization by agricultural settlers, however, the region's climates came to assume a dominant influence on population distribution and the settlement pattern, at least within those sections of the Alberta plains physiographically suited to crop and livestock production.

The simplest way of explaining this influence is to take a regional view, organized around those climatic factors which have biological significance. It must be understood, however, that this view is a static one, based on average conditions over the past thirty years. It therefore ignores the accumulating evidence of on-going climatic change, most strikingly in southeastern Alberta, where it appears that the climate is gradually becoming moister.

The dominant factors controlling temperatures and precipitation in Alberta are the height and width of the Rocky Mountains, and the origin and direction of movement of the major prevailing air masses. The orographic (mountain) barrier of the Western Cordillera causes a rain shadow effect over much of Alberta. As the Pacific Maritime air mass rises to pass over the mountains, it is cooled, its ability to hold moisture is reduced, and precipitation falls on the Pacific side of the Cordillera. Then, as the air mass descends into Alberta, it gains heat again and produces the warm, dry Chinook wind. Only the western, mountainous areas of Alberta come regularly under the influence of the remnants of the mild, moist Pacific air mass, producing considerable amounts of snow but relatively mild temperatures (Figure 4–5).

The influence of the weakened Pacific air mass east of the mountains is minimal, which means that the seasonal fluctuations of the climate of the greater part of Alberta are largely controlled by continental air masses originating in the Arctic and in the midwestern United States. In the north and central districts of Alberta, the moist, cold Polar Maritime air mass and the cold, dry Arctic air mass are dominant in January. Their interaction produces moderate amounts of snow but uniformly low temperatures over the area. Southeastern Alberta, by contrast, is dominated by the continental air mass from the central United States. This causes temperatures to be 10–15°C higher than in the north, while the snowfall is much less than in the north and west. The transition between winter and summer is characterized by larger amounts of precipitation in the south because of frontal precipitation.

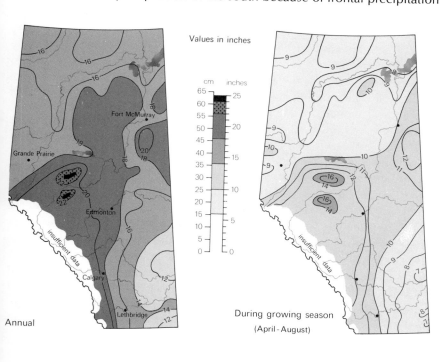

Values in inches

Annual

During growing season
(April-August)

Figure 4–5 Distribution of mean annual precipitation across Alberta for the whole year and for the growing season. Source: *Atlas of Alberta*, p. 16.

Not until July do the air masses reach a relatively stable position which persists until late fall.

In the northern half of Alberta in July, the dominant Polar Maritime air mass brings low precipitation and cool temperatures everywhere except the Peace River area, which is influenced then by a warmer, moist Pacific air mass. The mountains come under a similar influence, and the higher altitudes and remnants of the orographic rainfall create cool, moist summer conditions. In central and southern Alberta, on the other hand, air from the central United States dominates. Its passage through the Midwest causes it to gain heat and lose moisture, and to bring dry heat to southern and central Alberta. Normally, only localized summer storms occur when this air mass prevails.

Climatic Factors of Biological Significance

The climatic factors important to crop production are not the total amounts of heat and moisture but the proportions available for plant growth. Accordingly, the limitations of the climate for settlement may be best defined by using thermal and moisture criteria which can be directly related to the productivity of the land. Plants produce vegetative matter by combining radiation, heat, water, and nutrients during photosynthesis. The growing season begins when the soil is no longer frozen, and moisture and nutrients can enter the plant. It is therefore the thermal and moisture regime of the soil, derived from, but lagging behind, the atmosphere, which dominates an area's productive potential.

Growth cannot occur until the soil and air temperatures reach a threshold which averages around 5°C. This means that the thermal characteristics important to production are the length and intensity of the period after the threshold temperature is reached. The length of the growing season refers to the period when the mean daily temperature is above 5°C. The intensity of the thermal regime during the growing season is measured by the number of accumulated degree-days. This is calculated by subtracting the threshold temperature for growth, 5°C, from the mean daily temperature for each day in the growing season, and then summing the daily values over the length of the growing season. Although it is a generalized measurement, the degree-day provides a useful index for gauging thermal differences among areas.

The proportion of the total precipitation available for plant growth is largely controlled by two interactions between the moisture regime and the temperature regime. The higher the temperature of the air, the greater its ability to evaporate water from the soil. Moisture is also released from the leaves of plants during photosynthesis, through the process known as transpiration. The loss of the moisture provided by precipitation is compounded by the soil itself, which may bind water so tightly that it cannot be absorbed by plants. The amount of precipitation actually available to plants is governed, therefore, by the combination of evaporation, transpiration, and soil-moisture storage.

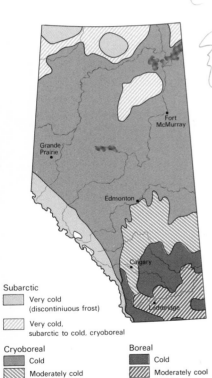

Subarctic
- Very cold (discontiniuous frost)
- Very cold, subarctic to cold, cryoboreal

Cryoboreal
- Cold
- Moderately cold

Boreal
- Cold
- Moderately cool

Figure 4–6 Soil climates of Alberta.
Source: J. S. Clayton et al., *Soils of Canada.*

The relationships among these factors can be analysed using the concept of potential evapotranspiration. After a certain amount of moisture (10 cm) is allocated to storage by the soil, the capacity of the atmosphere to remove water by transpiration and evaporation can be measured on the basis of its thermal regime. The significance of this for Alberta is that, over most of the southern and central areas of the province, the capacity of the atmosphere to remove water is greater than the amount of water available to be removed. Once the available water has been removed, and a water deficit results, plant growth cannot occur. The length of the water deficit period thus reduces the total thermal growing season to that time when both water and heat are available.

Regional climates important to settlement are identified according to these thermal and moisture characteristics of the soil because they control the land's productivity. Hence the classification of soil climates developed by the Canadian Department of Agriculture, rather than a classification related to atmospheric conditions, is used here (Figure 4–6).

The soil temperature regime of southeastern Alberta imposes the fewest limitations on crop variety. This area has a "moderately cool-cool boreal" regime, with a growing season of between 170 and 220 days and 2,500–3,100 accumulated degree days. The western and central parts of Alberta are classified as having a "moderately cold cryoboreal" thermal climate with relatively cool summers. Central Alberta has a growing season of fewer than 220 days and between 2,000 and 2,250 degree days, a regime which imposes moderately severe limitations on crop types and forest productivity. The northern half of Alberta has a "cold cryoboreal" regime with a small area of "very cold subarctic" in the northeast. The dominant thermal regime has a growing season of only 120–180 days and a total number of degree days of only 1,000–2,000; this imposes severe restrictions on both crop and forest production.

Soil Temperature Regimes of Alberta

Although the southeast is the warmest area of Alberta, it also has the greatest moisture deficit. The subarid zone has severe deficits and the soil is dry during most of the growing season. The semiarid zone is slightly less limited, but still has moderately severe deficits throughout most of the growing season. The subhumid zones in central Alberta and the Peace River area have significant, but not debilitating, moisture deficits in the growing season. Much of central and western Alberta has a humid moisture regime and only slight deficits. With the exception of the Peace River area, the northern half of Alberta has an aqueous regime in which the soil is saturated for long periods, due to the thermal budget's inability to remove sufficient water by

Moisture Regimes of Alberta

evapotranspiration. This saturated soil regime, like the low thermal regime, imposes such constraints on crop growth that the area is unproductive.

Regional Climates for Plant Growth

When these climatic influences on plant growth are synthesized, the regional climates of Alberta can be generalized into three categories (Figure 4–7). The north, with the exception of the Peace River area, has both a thermal deficit and a moisture excess, so that its productivity is severely limited. Central and western Alberta comprise a transitional climatic zone in which the thermal and moisture regimes are balanced. The two remaining regions, southeastern Alberta and the Peace River area, have a thermal excess that leads to a moisture deficit.

Soil-Climate Relationships

For all the importance of the broad pattern of regional climates, it is not sufficient, on its own, to describe the regional variety of the biophysical limitations on the productivity of land in Alberta. The capacity of the soil to provide nutrients that are essential for plant growth is also extremely important. The nutrient status of a soil is largely controlled by regional soil-forming processes, and can be determined by examining the presence, type, and depth of distinctive layers or horizons in the soil. The layer closest to the surface, the A horizon, consists of finely-divided organic matter derived from the breakdown of plant tissue. Within the A horizon, various chemical elements, such as sodium, calcium, iron, aluminum, and silica, are released from glacial residue during the process of weathering. These elements, in turn, may be carried downward by water and deposited in the B horizon, below which lies the unaltered glacial residue, the parent material of the soil, the C horizon.

The presence of the B horizon is directly related to climate because it provides water for plant growth and weathering. Thus, the three climatic zones of Alberta vary in the ways their climates affect the development of soils.

Zone 1: Thermal Excess and Moisture Deficit

Lack of soil moisture causes the soils of Zone 1 to be dominated by the surface accumulation of organic matter. As leaves and roots of the predominantly grass vegetation are broken down or decomposed, the stored nutrients are released to form a nutrient-rich Ah horizon which is the topmost layer of the A horizon. Its depth increases as the moisture deficit decreases, because greater amounts of organic matter are added to the soil than are removed through leaching. Similarly, the lack of moisture causes the calcium and sodium released by weathering to remain in the soil. Accumulations of these elements occur near the surface in very dry areas within Zone 1, but are found deeper in the soil as moisture increases to the north and west.

Figure 4–7 The three regional climates of Alberta.

Zone 1 ▨ Thermal excess and moisture deficit

Zone 2 ▨ Thermal and moisture balance

Zone 3 ▦ Thermal deficit and moisture excess

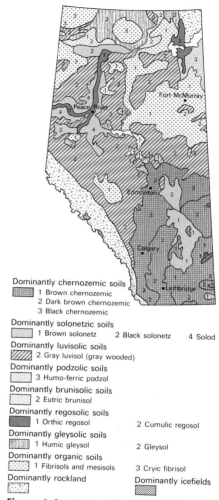

Dominantly chernozemic soils
▦ 1 Brown chernozemic
2 Dark brown chernozemic
3 Black chernozemic
Dominantly solonetzic soils
☐ 1 Brown solonetz   2 Black solonetz   4 Solod
Dominantly luvisolic soils
▨ 2 Gray luvisol (gray wooded)
Dominantly podzolic soils
☐ 3 Humo-ferric podzol
Dominantly brunisolic soils
☐ 2 Eutric brunisol
Dominantly regosolic soils
■ 1 Orthic regosol   2 Cumulic regosol
Dominantly gleysolic soils
▦ 1 Humic gleysol   2 Gleysol
Dominantly organic soils
☐ 1 Fibrisols and mesisols   3 Cryic fibrisol
Dominantly rockland   Dominantly icefields
▨   ▨

Figure 4–8 Major soil groups of Alberta.
Source: J. S. Clayton, et al., *Soils of Canada.*

The characteristics of high amounts of organic matter and calcium accumulation at depth identify chernozemic soils (Figure 4–8). The chernozemic order is further divided into brown, dark brown, and black great groups, depending on the color and depth of the surface organic layer. Where sodium replaces calcium as the dominant chemical ion, the soils are classified as solonetzic (alkali).

High sodium and calcium concentrations at the surface of the soil cause other nutrients to be unavailable to plants, creating areas of low productivity. Where they occur at depth, however, in moister areas of Zone 1, the thick Ah horizons provide more nutrients than any other soil of Alberta. In other words, within Zone 1, the black soil group is the most productive while the brown soil group is the least productive.

Water passing through the A horizon removes chemicals and deposits them in the underlying stratum to form the B horizon. When iron, aluminum, or humus are deposited in the B horizon, the soil is classified as podzolic. But when chemical elements are carried to the B horizon in a combined particle known as clay, the result is luvisolic soil. Water has a major role in the formation of podzolic soils, often carrying vital plant nutrients out of the soil completely. The nutrients in luvisolic soils, on the other hand, are concentrated with clay in the B horizon, and are largely unavailable for use by

Zone 2: Thermal and Moisture Balance

plants. In both soil types, therefore, the lack of available nutrients constrains productivity and large amounts of chemical fertilizer must be added if the deficiency is to be corrected.

Zone 3: Thermal Deficit and Moisture Excess

The influence of local topography in northern Alberta is important to the formation of soils. The B horizon forms on the sloped areas of well-drained sites, although it has a lower intensity than in Zone 2 because less energy is available for weathering. This reduction in intensity, coupled with the relative youth of the soils, produces a poorly-developed soil known as brunisol.

Elsewhere, the deranged drainage network of the north, and the ponding of low-lying areas, leads to the saturation of the associated soils. Decomposition of dead plant material is retarded and the annual additions cause a thick fibrous mat of organic material to accumulate. In these organic soils, nutrients contained in plant material are not released for subsequent use, and that, coupled with their saturated condition, means that they are totally unproductive.

Regional Implications

The nutrient status of soils modifies the generalizations about productivity which can be made from climatic data. Because nutrients are unavailable, Zone 3 has a lower productivity than the climatic data suggest, while the climatically optimal Zone 2 has its productivity limited by the loss of nutrients through the soil. Conversely, in the driest areas of Zone 1, the ineffectiveness of leaching inhibits productivity due to the excessive amounts of sodium and calcium in the soil. The upshot is that optimum soil productivity in Alberta is associated with those areas of Zone 1 that have moderate water deficit regimes and deep calcium and sodium concentrations. They occur, most notably, in the great arc of black chernozemic soils from Lloydminster to Edmonton and Calgary.

Vegetation-Climate Relationships

The major plant species dominating each area have adapted over many thousands of years to be most productive, or competitive, in a specific range of climatic and soil conditions. The distribution of these major plant species throughout Alberta therefore reveals the natural productivity of each area. Again, the regional climate framework (Figure 4–7) can be used to present the analysis, although two additional variables, fire and man, must also be considered. It has to be realized, too, that the vegetation pattern of Alberta is far more complex than is outlined here and there are large transitional areas between the major vegetation types.

The dominant plant species of Zone 1 have adapted their growth patterns to long periods of the growing season when insufficient moisture is available. Their entire growth cycle occurs in spring, when moisture is available; for the rest of the thermal growing season they are dormant.

Zone 1: Thermal Excess and Moisture Deficit

The driest areas of southeastern Alberta have short, drought-resistant grasses; blue gramma grass (*Bouteloua gracilis*) is common. In areas of smaller moisture deficit, greater vegetative matter (or biomass) can be sustained, and mixed grasses such as spear grass (*Stipa comata*), june grass (*Koeleria cristata*), and western wheatgrass (*Agropyron smithii*) are dominant.

The dominant deciduous tree in Alberta, the aspen (*Populus tremuloides*), occurs in areas of Zone 1 with moderate moisture deficits because of its ability to survive in periodic droughts. It sends up young shoots from its root system, thereby obviating the need for moist surface conditions during reproduction. The dominant grass in the aspen area is rough fescue (*Festuca scabrella*).

Moist, cool Zone 2 is dominated by coniferous forests. The species that would be most prevalent in the absence of fire, white spruce (*Picea glauca*), can live in a wide range of climatic and soil conditions. It can also sustain growth in shaded or low light conditions, which the other major tree species of Zone 2, lodgepole pine (*Pinus contorta*) and aspen, cannot. When fires are controlled, white spruce overtops the initially faster-growing lodgepole pine and aspen, forcing them to die out. Because of frequent fires, the lodgepole pine and aspen are currently dominant. Both regrow quickly, the pine because its cones release their seeds after intense heating, and the aspen because its roots survive to send up new shoots in burned areas.

Zone 2: Thermal and Moisture Balance

As with soils, topographical differences within Zone 3 are the major variable controlling plant distribution. The well-drained upland sites have a thick cover of jackpine (*Pinus banksiana*), which is very similar to lodgepole pine except that it is more competitive in colder conditions. Moister, but not saturated, sites are occupied by white spruce, yielding to black spruce (*Picea mariana*) in areas that are too wet for any other tree species. On the most saturated organic soils, only moss species such as sphagnum moss can survive.

Zone 3: Thermal Deficit and Moisture Excess

Biophysical Regions of Alberta

The physiographic, climatic, soil, and vegetative environments interact to form regions of varying influence on the patterns of settlement. For the purposes of this chapter, a seven-region system has been developed. It is based on climatic limitations to productivity, although the regional names reflect the most visible manifestation of their environment, the vegetation (Figure 4–9).

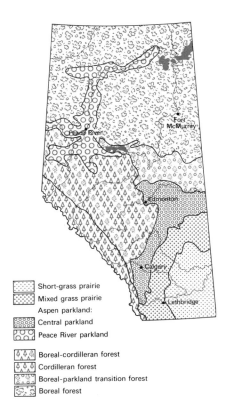

Figure 4–9 Biophysical regions of Alberta.

Legend:

- Short-grass prairie
- Mixed grass prairie
- Aspen parkland:
- Central parkland
- Peace River parkland
- Boreal-cordilleran forest
- Cordilleran forest
- Boreal-parkland transition forest
- Boreal forest

Region 1: Short-Grass Prairie

The short-grass prairie region has the most severe annual water deficits in the province, or between 30 and 40 cm. Soils range between brown chernozemic and solonetzic but are limited by high calcium or sodium values. The natural vegetation comprises short, drought-resistant grasses such as blue gramma.

Much of this region was settled in the late nineteenth and early twentieth centuries and up to 1,620,000 ha were cultivated. In the dry period after 1928, the naturally low productivity of the area came to be better understood, and a government relocation program was implemented to help farmers move away. The amount of cultivated land was halved, and the abandoned land was converted to pasture for domestic cattle, although its carrying capacity still is low. The generally low productivity also causes the relatively fertile areas to be heavily used; natural species are then liable to be removed by overgrazing. Wind erosion of the thin Ah threatens to reproduce the problems of the 1930s.

In some parts of the short-grass region, the severe water deficit has been offset by irrigation. Over 162,000 ha have had their productivity increased in this way already (Figure 4–3), and the development of additional irrigation systems may further offset the environmental limitations for agriculture. As already mentioned, the amount of water available for irrigation is itself limited.

Region 2: Mixed-Grass Prairie

The water deficit in this area (20–30 cm in the growing season) is less severe than in Region 1 but is still the major factor limiting productivity. The soil type, dark brown chernozem, is more fertile. Western wheat grass and other taller grasses form the vegetation type.

The moderate moisture deficits mean that greater sustained yields from agriculture can be achieved here than in Region 1; 1,620,000 ha are cultivated, out of a possible total of 3,650,000 ha. The productivity of the area and its range of crops have been greatly increased through widespread irrigation practices. Once again, though, the water supply is limited.

Region 3: Aspen Parklands

The aspen parkland occurs in two areas of Alberta. The first is in south-central Alberta; the second is the large area of the Peace River drainage network where the moist, warm summer air masses create conditions different from those prevailing over the rest of northern Alberta. The general implications of this regional environment have been the same in both areas of Region 3, although the responses of man to the environment have often differed.

The central parkland area has a moderate water deficiency (between 5 and 15 cm), which, when coupled with a warm growing season and fertile black chernozemic soil, cause it to have the greatest potential productivity in Alberta. It has naturally followed that it has been more heavily utilized than any other region of Alberta, with approximately 75 per cent of its land area in agricultural production. The seasonal precipitation is great enough for the most successful dryland production of cereal grains in Alberta.

The Peace River parkland has the same climatic and vegetation regime as central Alberta, though the vegetation is thought to be a left-over, or relic, from a warmer period following deglaciation. The soil also differs somewhat, in that it has a high sodium content. Solonetzic soils are therefore common, but there are fewer constraints on their use for agriculture than in the solonetzic areas of southern Alberta.

With heavy development occurring as late as the 1930s, the Peace River area was the last great agricultural region to be opened in Alberta. (See Figure 1–2 in Chapter 1.) The aspen parkland has been largely cleared for cereal crops, but their range and yield tend to be more limited than in the south-central zone of Region 3, because of the somewhat cooler climate.

Region 4: Boreal-Cordilleran Transition Forest

Region 4, although having a favourable moisture regime, has a cooler and shorter growing season than the first three regions. Temperature constrains productivity everywhere, but the deficiency of nutrients is an even greater constraint in the luvisolic and podzolic soils. Moist, cool conditions allow tree species (white spruce, lodgepole pine, and aspen) to occur throughout, though the two conifers predominate to the north and in the higher elevations of the west.

Region 4 has been characterized by a retreat of the agricultural frontier. Cultivation was originally successful, because the initial churning-up of the clay-rich B horizon of the luvisols released sufficient nutrients for crop growth. The nutrients were rapidly depleted and the large areas that became relatively unproductive were abandoned. Timber has since taken over as the key renewable resource in this area, reflecting the climatic advantage for tree growth which this region has over the forests further north or west.

Region 5: The Sub-Alpine Forest

In this cordilleran region, physiography is the overwhelming constraint to settlement. Only the small area of valley bottoms has any settlement potential. The climate, vegetation, and soils also vary extremely, in relation to the physiography. The limited amount of settlement has largely depended on the transportation arteries through the mountain passes or on the location of major coal seams, supporting sporadic linear communities in some accessible valleys.

Region 6: Boreal-Parkland Transition

Region 6 contains environmental elements which are characteristic of the regions to both north and south. Aspen is dominant on higher, well-drained sites, although spruce is important in northern districts. The soil is luvisolic, but displays poorer development than in Region 4. The low thermal regime has produced many areas of moisture saturation with organic soil deposits and black spruce-moss communities.

The range of vegetation and soil types, and the mild thermal deficit, create poor conditions for agriculture. Forestry is limited by the 130-year period that is needed for the satisfactory regrowth of trees. Settlement has therefore been slow, and native people have comprised most of the population, up until the recent oil and gas exploration and development in the region.

The thermal deficit is the dominant constraint to settlement in the boreal forest and leads to large, saturated organic soil areas of black spruce and sphagnum moss. The mixed wood communities on the well-drained sites are impoverished in comparison with their southern counterparts. The climatic regime has created conditions of very low productivity throughout the region, and forest regeneration is severely limited by slow growth rates. Mineral resources offer the only promise of permanent white settlement, and even the native population is sparse.

Region 7: The Boreal Forest

This analysis has been focused primarily on the role of the natural environment in the agricultural settlement of Alberta. On a broad scale the location of the major urban centres and the pattern of service settlements can also be seen as partly a response to the environment's control of the land's productivity, though two factors have tended to reduce the direct environmental role. The first is the exploitation of fossil energy sources, leading to settlements in areas of low productivity and severe climate, such as Fort McMurray in the boreal forest. The second is man's increasing ability to mitigate the adverse effects of climate, as demonstrated, for example, in the increase in agricultural productivity which irrigation has brought to southeastern Alberta.

These two factors affect a small proportion of the existing primary and related settlements. The role of the environment in Alberta's human and economic geography during the first 120 years of settlement has been pervasive and directly underlies the distribution of many of the economic activities examined in this book. As the economic base of Alberta's settlement matures and deepens in quaternary and quinary industry, the direct spatial relationships between the location of settlement and the characteristics of the natural environment diminish, but the influence of earlier and more direct biophysical constraints on Alberta's settlement patterns persists through the great spatial inertia of existing investment in the human landscape.

Conclusion

Clayton, J.S., Ehrlich, W.A., Cann, D.B., Day, J.H., and Marshall, I.B. *Soils of Canada.* Ottawa: Canada Department of Agriculture, 1977.
Hardy, W.G., ed. *Alberta: A Natural History.* Edmonton: Hurtig Publishers, 1967.
Longley, R.W. *The Climate of the Prairie Provinces.* Ottawa: Environment Canada, Atmospheric Environment Service, Climatological Studies 13, 1972.

Supplemental Readings

Moss, E. H. "The Vegetation of Alberta." *Botanical Review,* 21 (1955): 493–567.

North, M. E. A. *A Plant Geography of Alberta.* Edmonton: University of Alberta, Department of Geography, 1976.

Strahler, A. N. and Strahler, A. H. *Modern Physical Geography.* New York: John Wiley & Sons, 1978.

5 Resources and Resource-Use Conflict

Edgar L. Jackson

Anne D. Dhanani

In Alberta, in recent decades, the traditional resource uses of agriculture and forestry have been supplemented by large-scale uses of land for water storage, recreation, mineral extraction, and the exploitation of energy resources (oil, coal, natural gas, and hydro-electricity). The present mosaic of resource uses in Alberta represents the influence of such factors as land productivity, historical trends in settlement and population, the physical location of mineral resources, efficiency of techniques for resource exploitation, and the evolution of governmental land use management practices.

While resource uses have permitted a high standard of living in Alberta, a number of conflicts have begun to emerge, despite the province's size of approximately 654,000 km², its rich endowment of natural resources, and its sparse population distribution of fewer than 1.4 persons per square kilometre outside Edmonton and Calgary. The geographic, economic, political, and social characteristics of the province, and the inherent attributes of the resource uses themselves, all combine to create the potential for resource use conflicts. The following factors are particularly pertinent to their analysis: the concentration of settlement, rapid population growth, and urbanization in the southern portion of the province; the resource-based nature of the economy; and the diversity and fragmentation of governmental jurisdictions.[1] Forces external to the province, in the form of Canadian and foreign demands for Alberta's resources, exacerbate the internal population-resource conflicts.

The range of resource uses and conflicts in Alberta is wide and complex. Because the whole spectrum cannot be covered in the space of this chapter, only three categories of resources—energy, forestry, and recreation—are dealt with here to provide an introduction to the general problem.

Land Use Zones

figures {

general {

After 1869, when the Hudson's Bay Company surrendered its rights to Rupert's Land, almost all the land in what is now Alberta was owned by the Government of Canada. As settlement progressed, the best of this land was transferred to private ownership, either through the homesteading system or through block grants, notably to the CPR. Yet, when the Crown lands and other resource rights were surrendered to the Government of Alberta in 1930, no more than one-third of the total had been alienated. Today, the provincial government owns 54 per cent of Alberta's land area, and the federal government 10 per cent (mainly in national parks, but also including Indian reserves and military bases); 1 per cent, spread among many owners, is given up to highways and urban settlements; and the remaining 35 per cent is privately owned, although rights to the associated minerals are normally held by the provincial government.

In 1948, Alberta was divided into three land use zones—the "white," the "yellow," and the "green"—for resource management and the allocation of Crown land (Figure 5–1). These zones are generally well adapted to spatial variations in the biophysical environment, since their boundaries roughly correspond with the climatic and vegetational regions defined in Chapter 4.

The so-called "white area" includes both prairie zones, the central parkland, the south-eastern portion of the boreal-cordilleran forest, and much of the boreal-parkland transition forest. (See Figure 4–9 in Chapter 4.) Most of the land is owned privately, with exceptions such as the "special areas," the provincial parks, and Elk Island National Park. Agriculture is the predominant land use, although major deposits of coal, oil, and gas are also exploited. This area contains most of Alberta's population.

The "yellow area" corresponds closely with the Peace River parkland region. Settlement here has a mixed basis, related chiefly to forestry and agriculture. As a management zone, however, the "yellow area" is chiefly distinguished by the availability of small amounts of land for homesteading under strictly regulated conditions.

The "green area" consists of that part of the cordilleran forest outside the mountain national parks, combined with the boreal forest of northern Alberta and the remainder of the transitional boreal-cordilleran forest zone. It takes up nearly 50 per cent of the province and is predominantly Crown land, permanently excluded from sale or settlement. The area is to remain essentially in a wildland state, though forestry, recreation, and grazing are permitted. Agriculture, however, is not allowed.

Energy, Forestry, and Recreation Resources
Energy

Energy resources are by far the most important of the three main resource categories discussed in this chapter because of the revenues they bring to the province and the prominent role played by Alberta in the national energy system. The economic and political importance of Alberta's energy resources

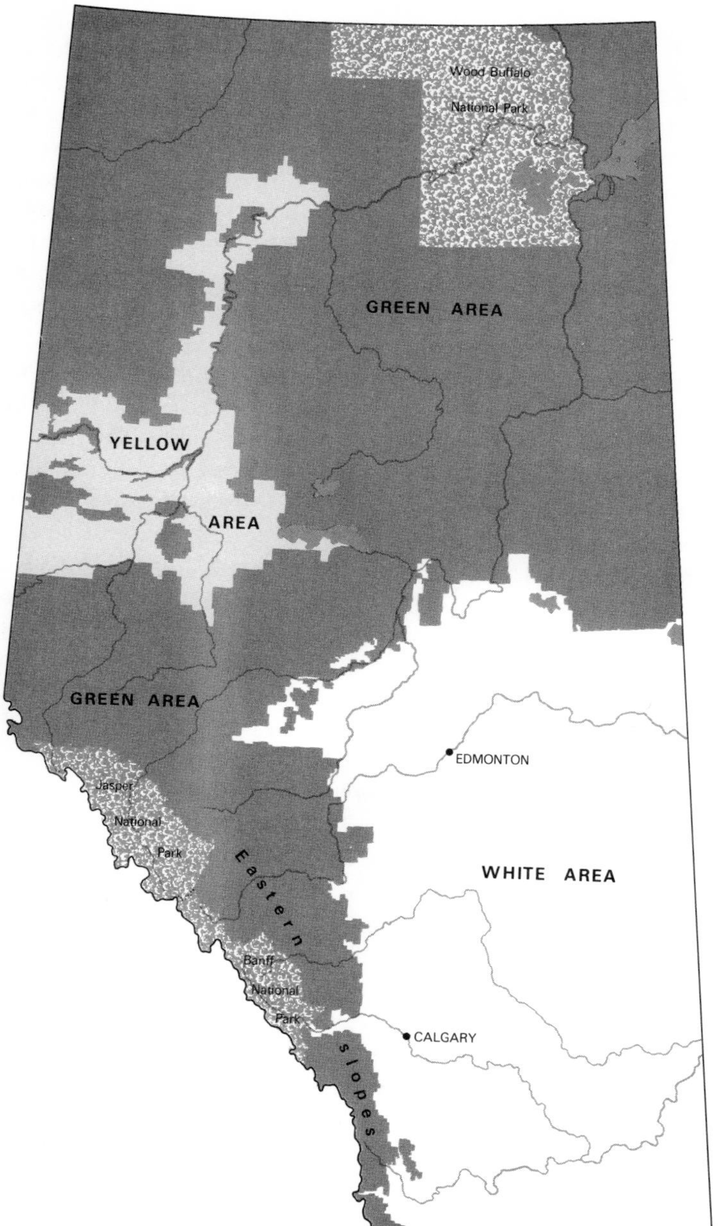

Figure 5–1 Land management zones of Alberta. The "green area" is chiefly Crown land in a wildland state; mining, forestry, recreation, and grazing may be permitted, but the land is not to be broken for farming. The "white" and "yellow" areas are mostly privately owned and agriculture is the most common use. Some homesteading is still possible on Crown land on the fringes of the "yellow area."
Source: Government of Alberta.

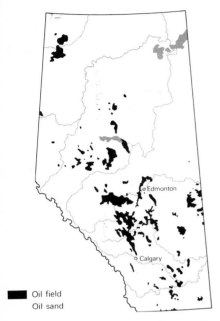

Figure 5–2 Locations of major known oil fields and oil sand deposits in Alberta. Source: Government of Alberta.

stretches far beyond the province's boundaries. The recent constitutional debate, the exigencies of the national and international energy picture, and the perceived necessity on the part of the federal government to achieve a sustainable energy balance, all bear directly on Alberta's role as an energy supplier. Because national goals are to be reached primarily, although not completely, through the continued exploitation of resources to meet anticipated levels of demand, the use of land in Alberta for energy resource exploitation is likely to increase rather than decrease. Environmental impacts are likely to become more pronounced and land use conflicts to increase as development processes and investment decisions outside the province impinge increasingly on Alberta's resources.

Although the history of Alberta's oil industry can be traced to the discovery of the Turner Valley field in 1914, the industry operated at a low level until the modern era began with the discovery of the Leduc field in 1947, followed rapidly by the opening of the nearby Woodbend, Redwater, and Pembina fields. Today, producing oil fields are distributed over much of the province, except for the northern and north-eastern regions and the Eastern Slopes (Figure 5–2). Well over half the conventional crude oil fields, plus one extensive oil sand deposit, are located within the "white area"; the remainder of the oil sands and the conventional oil fields lie mainly within the "green area." At the end of 1981, Alberta's proven remaining recoverable reserves stood at 690 million m³ (with a life-index of 12.2 years at 1981 rates of production) for conventional crude oil and at 3860 million m³ for synthetic crude oil (i.e. heavy oil and oil sands).[2]

Albertan oil strongly affects the pattern of production in Canada (Figure 5–3); national and provincial production both stabilized from 1976 to 1978, following a recognizable decline in the mid-1970s from a peak in 1973. A substantial increase occurred in 1979 as a result of the contribution from the

Figure 5–3 Annual oil production in Canada and Alberta, 1971 to 1981 inclusive. Source: Government of Alberta.

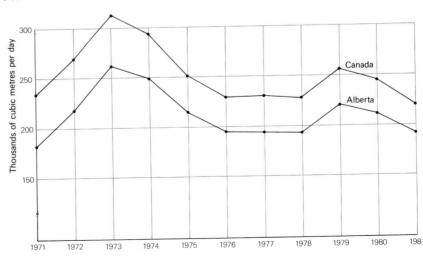

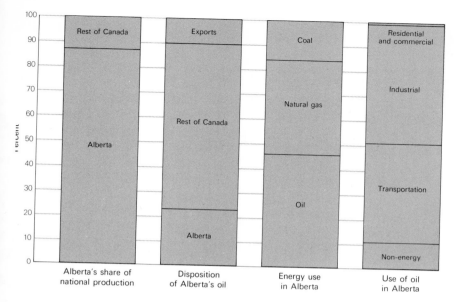

Figure 5–4 Alberta's share of Canadian oil production in 1981; the proportions of Alberta's oil production consumed in Alberta and elsewhere; the relative importance of the three main fossil fuels as sources of energy in Alberta; and the major uses of oil in Alberta. Source: Government of Alberta.

oil sands, but production has subsequently declined, most recently as a response to the National Energy Program of 1980. As a proportion of national production, however, Albertan production increased steadily through the 1970s, from about 77 per cent of the national total in 1971 to 87 per cent in 1981 (Figure 5–4). Alberta's average daily production then was 192,000 m³ per day.

About 77 per cent of Albertan oil is transported to markets outside the province; in 1981, one-tenth was exported to the United States, two-thirds was used elsewhere in Canada, and just under one-quarter was consumed within the province. Oil accounts for 46 per cent of the total consumption of primary energy in Alberta. Industry and transportation are the main users (Figure 5–4).

The history of natural gas exploitation in Alberta is longer than that of oil, dating from the 1885 discoveries near Medicine Hat. Productive gas fields today, like oil fields, are extensively distributed across much of the province, in deposits of varying sizes; only the non-sedimentary north-eastern area is excluded (Figure 5–5). Unlike oil, the majority of gas exploitation is located within the "white area" and results in conflicts with agriculture, when farm operations are disrupted during pipeline construction. There are also growing fears about the possibility of increased soil acidity and health hazards to people and livestock, particularly in the vicinity of sour gas plants. Alberta's remaining reserves of marketable natural gas were estimated at 1,795 billion m³ in 1981, with a life-index of 30 years at 1981 rates of production.

As with oil, Alberta's natural gas production through the 1970s constituted the bulk of Canadian domestic output, varying from 80 per cent of the total

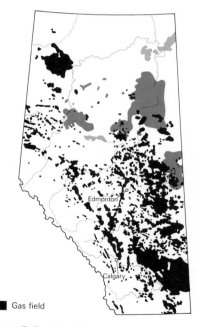

Gas field

Figure 5–5 Locations of known natural gas fields of Alberta.
Source: Government of Alberta.

Figure 5–6 Annual natural gas production in Canada and Alberta, 1971 to 1981 inclusive.
Source: Government of Alberta.

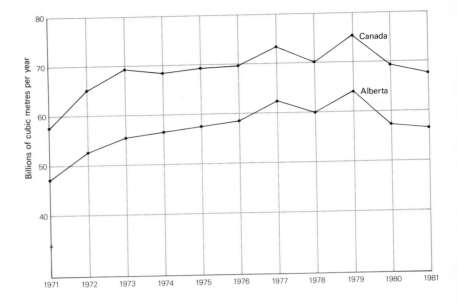

in 1973 to 87 per cent in 1981 (Figure 5–6). In contrast to oil, however, provincial and national production of natural gas increased steadily until 1979. By 1981 there was a slight decline of about 8 per cent. Between 1971 and 1981 Alberta's production increased by 26 per cent, from 47 billion m³ to over 59 billion m³, while Canada's production increased by 18 per cent, from 57 billion m³ to almost 68 billion m³.

About 30 per cent of Alberta's natural gas production is used within the province. This is similar to the pattern of oil consumption, but exports of gas are proportionally greater than those of oil. Most notably, 28 per cent of Alberta's gas was exported to the United States in 1981, which left well under half of the total output to be consumed elsewhere in Canada. Of that gas used within the province, 36 per cent goes to industrial consumers, 14 per cent to commercial, 22 per cent to residential, and 3 per cent to transportation. In addition, 7 per cent is used to generate electricity (one-quarter of Alberta's electricity is generated using natural gas), and the remaining 18 per cent is used as the basic raw material of a complex chain of petrochemical industries.

While oil and gas are the most prominent components of Alberta's energy resources, coal has the greatest potential and longest history of exploitation. Coal mining pre-dates natural gas extraction by 16 years, with the first mine coming into production near Lethbridge in 1869. Over the ensuing 50 years, mines were opened throughout southern Alberta in response to the expansion of the railway network and to the popularity of coal for domestic heating and, subsequently, for the generation of electricity. After the Second World War, the industry declined, not from resource depletion but because coal could not compete with oil and natural gas, the fuels of the new economic era.

For all its relative unattractiveness in recent decades, coal still underlies 46 per cent of the area of the province (Figure 5–7). Most of southern Alberta has extensive and continuous deposits of lignite, sub-bituminous, and bituminous coal of various grades, now worked at four underground and sixteen surface mines. Over 60 per cent of Alberta's production is sub-bituminous coal, a low-grade thermal coal from the plains, important within the province because it generates 61 per cent of Alberta's electricity. The rest is coking-grade bituminous coal from the foothills and mountains, most of which is exported, mainly to Japan. Of the total production, 66 per cent is used within the province (representing about one-sixth of total provincial energy consumption (Figure 5–4), only about 4 per cent is used elsewhere in Canada, and the remainder is exported. The exported coal accounts for 37 per cent of Canada's total coal exports.

Alberta's coal does not appear to play as strong a national role as oil and gas. In 1981, Alberta's production of 18,000 kilotonnes amounted to only 46 per cent of the Canadian total (Figure 5–8). Still, there has been a steady growth in output over the last decade at a rate slightly exceeding that of the national total; between 1971 and 1981 Alberta's coal production increased by 154 per cent, compared with a national increase of 140 per cent. Nor has there been a recent downturn of the kind experienced in the case of oil and gas. Moreover, about 70 per cent of Canada's proven remaining coal reserves lie within the boundaries of Alberta. The most recent estimate, in 1981, was 14.8 billion tonnes with a life-index of 800 years at current levels of production.

Because the continued and increasing exploitation of coal is an important element in national energy policy, and because Alberta's coal production is proportionally less than its share of national production of oil and gas, the

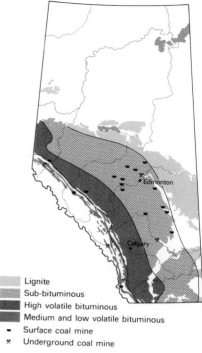

Figure 5–7 Major coal-bearing zones of Alberta.
Source: Government of Alberta.

Legend:
- Lignite
- Sub-bituminous
- High volatile bituminous
- Medium and low volatile bituminous
- ▬ Surface coal mine
- ✕ Underground coal mine

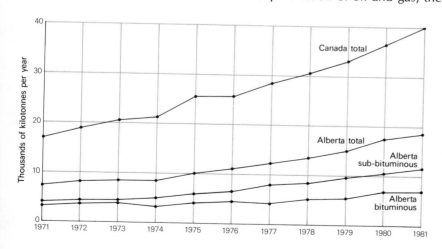

Figure 5–8 Annual coal production in Canada and Alberta, 1971 to 1981 inclusive. Unlike oil and natural gas (Figures 5–3 and 5–6) Alberta does not dominate Canadian coal production but it has been an important contributor to the increase in national coal output since 1971.
Source: Government of Alberta.

*lots of coal
=> production ↑
=> conflicts, because
much is*

province's coal resources will likely grow in national importance. The combination of large reserves and a steady growth of production suggests that given adequate capital for the expansion of production and transportation facilities, Alberta's coal industry will continue to meet any growth in domestic and foreign demand. In the process, though, the problem of negative environmental effects and other types of land use conflict, particularly with agriculture and forestry, will have to be addressed.

Forestry

In contrast to the hydrocarbon resources, Alberta's forests are renewable, if properly managed, and they could provide timber and other benefits indefinitely. While forestry is not as important to Alberta's economy as energy, the industry nevertheless plays a significant role in the economic well-being of the province. Directly and indirectly, it employs 11 per cent of the provincial labour force, and the total value of wood products now exceeds $400 million per annum. This ranks Alberta fourth in Canada in the size of its forest industry. Moreover, most of the wood material produced from Alberta forests is processed within the province. Pulp, lumber, plywood, and other manufactured construction materials constitute 12 per cent of the total value of goods manufactured in Alberta.

Alberta's forests cover more than 400,000 km², but most of the productive forest land is located within the "green area." For management purposes, it is organized into ten major "forests" (Figure 5–9), which have a potential annual coniferous yield of 14.5 million m³ and a deciduous annual yield of 13.5 million m³. As mentioned in Chapter 4, not all of the so-called forest land is actually productive. There are more than 12 million ha of water and muskeg in the "green area" alone, and the productivity of an additional 5 million ha throughout the province is impaired by insufficient reforestation. The initial exploitation of Alberta's forests was uncontrolled, and little incentive was offered for management or regeneration. Only in recent years has the approach of the forest industry changed from the crude clear-felling of wild timber to the harvesting of trees that have been planted and nurtured like an agricultural crop.

Provincial government involvement in forest management has also become more comprehensive during the half century since the transfer of Crown land to provincial ownership. A first major step was taken in 1949 when forest administration was unified under the jurisdiction of the Department of Lands and Forests. Next, the Alberta Forest Service was created in 1953. It was integrated with the Department of Energy and Natural Resources in 1975, and now bears the main responsibility for forest management, including the power to grant forest management agreements, timber quotas, and timber permits to private companies.[3]

Two important management policies are applied by government to Alberta's forests: sustained yield and multiple use. The former implies a balance between cutting and new growth, and incorporates a minimum re-

Potential annual yield

C 1727 Coniferous volume in thousands
of cubic metres per year

D 651 Deciduous volume in thousands
of cubic metres per year

Figure 5–9 The forest management districts of Alberta and the potential annual yield of each forest for coniferous and deciduous timber.
Source: Government of Alberta.

quirement of 80 years for trees to mature. The latter acknowledges that Alberta's forest lands are suitable not only for timber harvesting but also for a variety of other uses, such as recreation and tourism, mineral extraction, and wildlife and watershed management. The forest zone includes the head-waters of most of Alberta's rivers and streams, as well as those of parts of Sas-katchewan, Manitoba, and the Northwest Territories. (See Figure 4–3 in Chapter 4.) Any biophysical changes to these watersheds affect the avail-ability and quality of water downstream, so the value of the forest cover cannot be judged solely in monetary terms or by the volume of timber it produces.

Recreation

Despite Alberta's endowment with all types of recreational lands, there is a paradoxical relationship between supply and demand, in the sense that out-door recreational activities are concentrated in space and time. Certain locations become congested at favoured times. The national parks obviously experience this kind of pressure, although overcrowding is more extreme in the near-urban provincial parks and forest lands, especially west of Calgary, for example, in the Bow Forest, the Canmore Corridor, and Kananaskis Country. Pressures elsewhere are noticeable but less intense.

Like other Canadians, Albertans participate in a wide variety of leisure and recreational activities. Many of them are small-scale and urban-based, and place little if any pressure on the natural environment. Outside the cities, however, Albertans participate in the complete array of outdoor recreational activities: alpine and cross-country skiing, snowmobiling, hiking, trail biking, horseback riding, mountain climbing, picnicking, and sightseeing, as well as the traditional pursuits of hunting, fishing, and camping. The demand for space for all these activities is also increasing.

Five main factors appear responsible for the rapid changes in the demand for recreational resources and the structure of recreational activities. These are population growth; increasing leisure time (between 1940 and 1970 the average work-week declined from 47 to 35 hours, and the four-day work-week became increasingly popular in the 1970s); a great increase in dis-cretionary income; the increase in mobility that comes from high rates of car ownership and greatly improved highways; and urbanization, particularly in the Edmonton-Calgary-Lethbridge axis. This last factor is probably the most important because it entails a physical and mental separation between the majority of Albertans and the natural environment, and a perceived need by city dwellers to relieve the stress of urban life by periodic contact with the outdoors, in an environment relatively untouched by man. Assuming that present trends continue, at least a doubling in recreational demand among Albertans can be anticipated by the turn of the century. The visits by national and international tourists to Alberta can also be expected to increase, especially as environmental resources deteriorate in quality elsewhere.

On the basis of tenure or ownership, four types of land are available for

Figure 5–10 Locations of national parks, provincial parks, and wilderness reserves in Alberta.
Source: Government of Alberta.

recreation in Alberta: federal Crown lands (national parks); provincial Crown lands, including multiple-use forest land and explicitly-designated recreational areas such as provincial parks (Figure 5–10), heritage sites, and wilderness areas; municipal lands, including those administered by rural municipalities for largely urban populations; and private lands. In fact, a considerable amount of Alberta's outdoor recreation takes place on private land, particularly in the form of activities like hunting or snowmobiling for which agricultural land can be used in the off season. There is some evidence, however, that because the supply of private recreational land is limited, the pressures of a rising demand are exacerbated elsewhere, especially on the federal and provincial Crown lands.

Alberta is richly endowed with Crown lands whose unique features, outstanding landscapes and relatively untouched environments, provide unparalleled opportunities for wilderness travel, sightseeing, and vacationing. Under provincial administration four wilderness reserves—Willmore, White Goat, Siffleur, and Ghost River—have been left entirely in their natural state, with no access by motor vehicles and no physical development. Many of the larger provincial parks have also been designated to capitalize on some outstanding feature, for example, the alpine grandeur of the Kananaskis, the fossil beds of the Red Deer River valley, and the beaches of Lesser Slave Lake. Yet, none of these are as well known or as heavily visited as the national parks, and none draw as many visitors from outside Alberta. Albertans also use the national parks in great numbers, but they must share at least the three mountain parks with national and international tourists. The provincial parks, by contrast, are used largely by Albertans.

Alberta contains five national parks: Banff (established in 1885), Waterton Lakes (1895), Jasper (1907), Elk Island (1913), and Wood Buffalo (1922). Together, they encompass more than 54,000 km². This means that about 8 per cent of the province's area is subject to the stringent authority of the National Parks Act, including the absolute ban on natural resource exploitation that is central to national park policy. Yet, various forms of conflict still occur, and the boundaries of the Banff and Jasper parks have fluctuated historically to accommodate resource uses other than environmental preservation and recreation. In addition, although the national parks sustain fewer problems of resource use conflict than other areas of the province, their very restrictiveness has forced recreational and extractive resource users to focus their attention on the provincial Crown lands in the "green area."

Although the effects of human activities are more evident in the "green area" than in the national parks, natural processes are still the dominant agent of landscape change. The basic recreation value of the provincial forests appears to rest on the marked contrast which their landscapes and ambience pose to the rest of Alberta. Recreational uses are not uniformly distributed. Particularly in the northern zone, where topography and other biophysical characteristics are relatively uniform and there are few people, the recreational opportunities and uses are sporadic. Their importance is essentially local. This is in marked contrast to the Eastern Slopes of the Rocky Mountains, which not only offer terrain and scenery that are highly suitable for recreation but are close to the main concentrations of Alberta's population. A survey in the early 1970s showed that 65 per cent of Alberta residents had visited the Eastern Slopes for recreation during the preceding year. Very little of the area is reserved exclusively for recreation, and there is competition with many other uses, including forestry, mineral extraction, watershed and wildlife management, and cattle grazing. Alberta's main problems of conflict between recreational and other land uses occur in the Eastern Slopes.

Resource Conflicts and Environmental Impacts

Resource utilization has brought numerous benefits to the people of Alberta, both tangible and intangible. In their spatial distribution, the different resource uses coincide over much of the province, and conflicts result at many locations.

Some Basic Concepts

Resource-use conflicts may be grouped into at least three basic categories. The first is competition among resource uses. A tract of forest which can serve as a source of timber or as a recreational area may be underlaid by economically exploitable deposits of oil, gas, or coal. Spatial and temporal adjustments to such conflicts, depending on the degree of compatibility, may involve peaceful accommodation, decline in the productivity or quality of at least one use, or exclusion of all but one use. The second category of conflict arises when the environmental effects of one use are deleterious for other uses, while the third stems from the extent or degree of space-utilization associated with each use. Thus, congestion and overcrowding result when one form of recreational activity impinges upon another, as snowmobiling may upon cross-country skiing, for example.

The specific use to which land is put represents the outcome of the way in which the resource is perceived and evaluated. Such deliberate decisions are dictated at least in part by demands for resources and some evaluation of the related productive and ecological capacity of the environment. Resource-use conflicts and depreciative environmental impacts may emerge as the negative consequences of conscious choices.

In the remainder of this chapter, the potential conflicts among energy, forestry, and recreation and their impacts on environment quality are described. First, however, some limitations must be noted. Because the three resource uses coincide in their spatial distribution, the conflicts discussed here are most likely to occur in the "green area," but that does not mean that equally serious conflicts do not occur elsewhere. Agriculture in the "white area," for example, is increasingly experiencing adverse effects from oil and gas activities and from coal mining. There is also the problem that adequate data are rarely available, and that statistics do not fully convey the importance of conflict, especially when intangibles such as quality of wildlife habitat and recreational satisfaction are involved. In addition, while some conflicts are specific to particular uses, others are common to several uses. Thus, to understand certain problems, it may be necessary to unravel the cumulative or aggregate effects of a series of resource use conflicts, rather than to look for the cause in a single action. Finally, the dynamic characteristics of natural ecosystems may initiate chain reactions whose effects are difficult to trace or explain.

Energy: Conflict and Impact

The large scale of energy exploitation in Alberta produces extensive impacts on the environment and on other resource uses. At the local scale, these impacts are commonly intensive, as well. For example, almost all coal is mined by open pit methods that are extremely disruptive, at least in the short term. Even during exploration, large trenches must be dug and vast quantities of earth moved. The use of heavy equipment to disturb the soil and vegetation may cause erosion, damage to wildlife habitat, and a blighted landscape.[4] Coal mining is also alleged to cause particulate air pollution.

The exploitation of oil and gas also requires large tracts of land to be cleared, particularly during exploration. In the "green area" in 1977 there were 378,200 km of seismic lines; at an average width of 6 m, these lines represent a land disturbance of almost a quarter of a million hectares. The length of lines cut varies from year to year, but there was a rapid increase during the exploration boom of the late 1970s. The previous record of about 28,000 km set in 1966–67 was far surpassed in 1978–79, when 110,000 km were cut. Although general regulations require that seismic lines be at least 0.4 km apart, exceptions are made in areas of heavy exploration; and where many of these lines bisect each other, extensive clearings are created.

For development purposes, access roads have to be cut and well sites cleared, and extensive areas of adjacent land are also disturbed. Poorly built access roads may erode and cause siltation, with damage to vegetation, wildlife habitat, water quality, and aquatic life. Wildlife is disturbed by land clearing and by seismic exploration, and may actually migrate to areas with sub-optimal conditions for survival. In areas of intensive development there may be as many as 16 wells on a quarter section; at an average clearing of 1.4 ha per well, development could require 90 ha, nearly one-third of the section. Then there are rights-of-way for pipelines to the well sites, which may be as much as 18 m wide. And when the land requirements of compressor stations, ancillary services, and sulphur extraction plants (whose plumes affect still more land) are added in as well, the impact on the biophysical environment is clearly very great.

The negative effects are felt particularly by the forest industry, which must often co-exist with the primary oil and gas industry and even compete with it. In 1976, the forest industry cleared almost 19,000 ha and the petroleum industry another 14,000 ha. Not all of the latter was in valuable forest, but large volumes of timber are nonetheless wasted. In particular, the loss of merchantable timber, for which the forest industry argues that compensation is insufficient, is one of the major economic impacts of energy exploitation on forestry. The land lost to timber production for the period of one rotation (at least 80 years) is another. There is also the problem that areas frequently disturbed by seismic operations, or containing forest regenerated on seismic lines but out of phase with surrounding timber, are difficult to manage for efficient timber production.

All these problems are exacerbated by the extreme haste displayed by the energy industry, because insufficient time is available for a careful assessment of prospective conflicts and impacts. Although the applications for energy exploration permits in the "green area" are reviewed by Forest Service officers, the large number of applicants and the requirement that a decision be reached in 10 days makes it impossible for thorough impact assessments to be completed. As a consequence, unwarranted restrictions may be placed on the operator in the name of forest protection, or, alternatively, unnecessary damage may be permitted. The oil and gas industry maintains that even 10 days are excessive, and that faster decisions are required to facilitate the sale of drilling rights and to commence operations. The essence of this conflict is that the activities of the energy industry in any given area are short-term but the effects on forest resources are long-term.

The energy industry also affects recreational-resource uses. Land disturbance is a direct impact which at the very least represents a loss of scenic amenity and may prevent an area's use for recreation. Indirect disturbances may take the form of compromised wildlife habitat or sport fishing ruined by water pollution. Conversely, the excessive use of access roads by unrestrained recreationists can induce overhunting, overfishing, and general harassment of wildlife.

Forestry: Conflict and Impact

Forestry operations, like those related to energy, are extensive and entail large-scale land clearance. Clear cutting, as well as being aesthetically displeasing to recreationists and tourists, may accelerate erosion which can lead, in turn, to siltation of streams and pools and damage to fish habitats. The unrestricted use of logging roads by recreational vehicles, like the opening of oil and gas access routes, also introduces the threat of disturbances over wide areas. Stream pollution from sawmills and pulpmills, which is often severe, also impinges upon recreational use, by adversely affecting fish and wildlife and all water-based recreational activities. Although logging can sometimes be beneficial to wildlife, if it allows the establishment of good browse, cutting practices which do not maintain a protective forest cover may be deleterious for animals. On the other hand, techniques that are appropriate for wildlife protection, such as cutting parallel strips in sequence, usually increase logging costs for the operator.

Although forestry has a range of detrimental effects on the biophysical recreational environment, its general degree of incompatibility with other users is less than that of oil, gas, and coal operations. Furthermore, while mineral exploitation poses many direct problems for forestry, logging interferes with the energy industries in a minor way. Some adjustments may be required in management procedures, but the main impact is the forestry industry's desire to be compensated for the reforestation of seismic lines, for the destruction of marketable timber, and for the need to make do with portable equipment in some situations.

Recreation: Conflict and Impact

Recreational land use embraces activities at many scales, from facility-based activities, such as downhill skiing, to those, like hunting and fishing, that are widely dispersed. The former usually have intensive environmental impacts over a limited area, whereas the effects of the latter are diluted and spatially extensive. Like the energy and forestry industries, recreation can have a damaging impact on the natural environment, but most of the conflicts associated with recreation are the result of congestion and the adverse effects of one recreational activity upon another. The pre-emption of large areas for recreation, through the designation of national and provincial parks and wilderness areas, may also conflict with consumptive resource uses. There is also a minor but highly-publicized conflict between recreation and forestry, in the fires that are caused by campers and other recreationists. But while 9.6 per cent of all forest fires in 1978 were started during recreational activities, they accounted for only 0.03 per cent of the area burnt. Indeed the presence of recreationists in forests may actually be beneficial, if they are responsible for the early reporting of fires.

Recreation, particularly tourism, can also lead to urban development which impacts on the natural environment through pollution and the disturbances associated with land clearing, soil compaction, damaged vegetation, and displaced wildlife. This problem may be large-scale, for example, towns such as Banff, or small-scale, supporting ski services such as those at Sunshine Village.

Transportation routes associated with tourism may also harm the environment. If tourists and other recreationists stay close to their cars, however, congestion and environmental damage are confined to areas adjacent to the roads; large peripheral areas remain untouched. Only where limited or insufficient service facilities are provided alongside the access routes is there a serious danger that recreational use may spill over into undesignated areas, and so spread the environmental damage.

The negative effects of recreational land use ultimately detract from human enjoyment of the environment. Sometimes uses impinge on one another, as when incompatible groups attempt to use the same area. This asymmetrical conflict is best exemplified by cross-country skiers and snowmobilers. The presence of snowmobiles is perceived by skiers as interfering with the peace, solitude, and natural environment that is so necessary for them. If controls are then imposed to eliminate the conflict, the most common adjustment is to exclude the interfering activity, as in the case of snowmobile restrictions in Kananaskis Country. Yet, by generating mutual dislike and bitter confrontation between the two groups, this solution exacerbates a conflict that is altogether more complex than mere competition for land. Rather, it is underlaid by deep-seated differences in attitudes towards, and values about, conservation and the natural environment. The general lesson to be learned from this example, and from the other conflicts described above, is that resource-use conflicts and environmental impacts are grounded in the choices and decisions we make about resources, technology, economic growth, lifestyles, and environmental quality.

Conclusion

This chapter has described several resource uses in Alberta and has demonstrated some of their tangible and intangible importance to the province and its people. Obvious benefits have been derived from resource use, but at the cost of adverse environmental impacts and conflicts among resource users. Yet, population growth and increased standards of living in Alberta are predicated upon the consumption of resources. Management of resource-use conflicts thus demands forethought by industry, government, and individual consumers. Improved use of resources requires better information, the development and application of new and environmentally sensitive technologies, a high degree of co-ordination and co-operation among administrative agencies, and new managerial techniques. By themselves, however, such developments will provide only a partial solution, because the conflicts stem from the inherent contradiction between resource exploitation and the maintenance of a high-quality environment.

The resource use and environmental problems facing Alberta are a contemporary manifestation of the debate between economic growth and environmental preservation, the roots of which date from the initiation of the conservation movement. To end the conflict and implement effective management in Alberta will require the people of Alberta to undertake a fundamental re-examination of their values and goals, and of the methods of control that are available to them. Public debate about these issues is likely to be the most effective means of ensuring that future resource use does not generate pernicious levels of conflict.

Notes

1　The responsibility for managing competing demands on a given land resource may be divided among different levels of government and among different departments at any one level. In some cases, the management of one use is fragmented among several jurisdictions; for example, eight agencies in three provincial government departments, Energy and Natural Resources, Recreation and Parks, and Environment share the administration of 38 provincial Acts relating to the use of forest lands.

2　All estimates of reserves of oil, natural gas, and coal are subject to revision. New discoveries are still possible, as in the West Pembina area in 1977 and the major natural gas strikes south-west of Grand Prairie, also in 1977. Price increases have a radical effect on the validity of past estimates, since they stimulate interest in commodities hitherto ignored as uneconomic and enhance the profitability of secondary recovery. Provincial-federal negotiations over oil and gas prices clearly have important implications for the future exploitation of energy resources in Alberta.

3　Forest management agreements apply to several large areas of forest land in the province. Each agreement involves the construction of a large wood-processing facility such as a pulpmill, large sawmill, or plywood mill; and each covers a 20-year span and can be renewed indefinitely. Timber quotas cover considerably smaller areas of land and volumes of standing timber. A quota holder does not have to establish a major wood-processing plant, nor is he responsible for inventory and management planning on the lands under his quota. Quotas generally last 20 years and are renewable if all conditions of the agreement have been met. Timber permits are short term and allow the holder to harvest a specific stand of timber.

4　The environmental impact of exploiting oil sands is comparable, in many respects, to the surface mining of coal. Many of the effects of oil and gas operations described here also apply to the oil sands. To avoid repetition, though, the oil sands are not discussed separately.

Supplemental Readings

Alberta Land Use Forum. *Report and Recommendations*. Edmonton: 1976.

Environment Conservation Authority. *The Impact on the Environment of Surface Mining in Alberta: Report and Recommendations*. Edmonton: 1972.

Environment Conservation Authority. *Land Use and Resource Development in the Eastern Slopes: Report and Recommendations*. Edmonton: 1974.

Environment Council of Alberta. *The Environmental Effects of Forestry Operations in Alberta: Report and Recommendations*. Edmonton: 1979.

Gander, J.E. and Belarre, F.W. *Energy Future for Canadians*. Ottawa: Energy, Mines and Resources Canada, 1978.

Government of Canada. *National Parks Policy*. Ottawa: National Historic Parks Branch, Department of Indian Affairs and Northern Development, 1979.

MacGregor, J.G. "The Impact of the White Man." In *Alberta: A Natural History*, edited by W.G. Hardy, 303–319. Edmonton: Hurtig Publishers, 1967.

Sadler, B. *Forest Recreation in Alberta*. Information Bulletin No. 11, Public Hearings on the Environmental Effects of Forestry Operations in Alberta. Edmonton: Environment Conservation Authority, 1978.

6 Rural Alberta
Elements of Change

R. G. Ironside

Unlike the characteristic features of change so openly displayed within the restricted space of the major cities, the changes in rural Alberta are not always easy to descry. Their physical manifestations are distributed through- out a much larger space, and major structural changes in the agricultural industry are concealed by the apparent immutability of the rural landscape. Even when the environmental effects of natural resource developments are highly concentrated and visible, as they are at so many locations in Alberta, they are set against vast, seemingly timeless expanses of cultivated plains, open rangeland, and forest.

Yet change is no less characteristic of the rural environment of Alberta than it is of the cities. Understanding the processes and consequences of change is no less vital to effective planning and management of our environ- mental resources. Accordingly, the changing face of rural Alberta is treated here from the viewpoint of the particular elements of change, their causes and effects. Specific examples of rural change are identified, including the rural-urban fringe problem, the development of recreational cottages, the impacts of major mineral and forest resource projects, and the more subtle changes affecting the farms and ranches of the province. Activities in both the private and the public sectors, in some ways causing change and in other ways reacting to it, will be reviewed. The implications of these changes, particularly for regional planning will also be discussed.

"Rural" and "agricultural" are by no means synonymous. In the view pre- sented here rural Alberta embraces more than the settled landscape of farms and ranches lying between the city and the wilderness. In fact, that has

Trends in the Agricultural Industry

already been suggested in Chapters 2 and 3, in the classification of rural population into farm and non-farm. Still, given the founding role of agriculture in Alberta's rural economy, and its continuing importance in the Alberta scene, it is appropriate that it should be treated first.

Numbers of Farms

A decrease in the numbers of farms in all the agricultural regions of Alberta is one of the most basic factors associated with the decline in rural population described in Chapters 2 and 3. Migration of farmers has reflected the combined effects of the pull of more attractive, higher-paying employment elsewhere and the push from small, low-income farms. In the peak census year of 1941, there were 100,000 farms in Alberta; by 1976, there were only 57,000, a decrease of 42 per cent over the full 35 years and of 22 per cent in the much shorter period after 1961.

Regional variations in the pattern of decline between 1961 and 1976 can be determined by reading Table 6–1 and Figure 6–1 together. The greatest relative decreases occurred along the forest frontier, in census divisions 9, 12, and 14, although it was only in CD12, in the boreal-parkland transition forest zone, that the absolute loss was also comparatively large. Above average losses were also experienced through most of the mixed grass prairie and central parkland zones (CDs 3, 4, 5, 7, and 10), and into the transition forest zone north of Edmonton (CD13). It was here in the area east and north of Edmonton that the greatest absolute decreases occurred. CD10 was particularly affected, although it still had more farms than any other division in 1976. By contrast, in the dry southeastern corner of the province (CDs 1 and 2) the decrease was slightly below average, perhaps because this was the area most affected by farm abandonment in the 1930s. Irrigation may have had a cushioning effect, as well. A similar pattern of slightly below average losses can be noted in the Edmonton-Calgary region (CDs 6, 8, and 11), perhaps because farmers there have more opportunities to supplement their incomes through off-farm employment.

By far the lowest rate of decrease was experienced in CD15 which occupies most of northwestern Alberta, including the Peace River district. The tradition of off-farm work in this region was supported by substantial resource development in the oil, gas, and forestry industries. Despite harsh physical conditions, there was also some expansion of homestead farms on the fringes of the Peace River parkland zone. In general, however, the declining farm numbers in Alberta reflect a variety of physical and economic limitations on agriculture, and the alternative opportunities afforded by employment in resource development and urban-based activities, particularly in the part of central Alberta between Edmonton and Calgary.

Rural out-migration in Alberta has traditionally been attributed to the lack of facilities for education, vocational training, and the aged. Employment opportunities in agriculture, the main rural industry, have also declined in

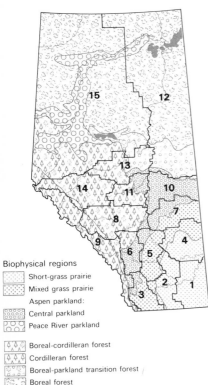

Biophysical regions

Short-grass prairie
Mixed grass prairie
Aspen parkland:
Central parkland
Peace River parkland

Boreal-cordilleran forest
Cordilleran forest
Boreal-parkland transition forest
Boreal forest

14 Census division

Figure 6–1 Census divisions of Alberta overlaid on the map of biophysical regions from Chapter 5.

Table 6-1

Decreases in the numbers of census farms by census divisions, 1961–76

							Census Divisions									
	1	2	3	4	5	6	7	8	9	10	11	12	13	14	15	Alberta
1961	2,165	4,735	2,646	2,126	4,333	4,838	5,199	6,551	175	10,188	8,512	4,494	7,322	973	8,955	73,212
1976	1,759	3,741	1,979	1,556	3,269	4,005	3,916	5,501	54	7,346	6,730	3,144	5,485	697	8,128	57,310
Absolute decrease	406	994	667	570	1,064	833	1,283	1,050	121	2,842	1,782	1,350	1,837	376	827	15,902
Percentage decrease	18.8	21.0	25.2	26.8	24.6	17.2	24.7	16.0	69.1	27.9	20.9	30.0	25.1	28.4	9.2	21.7

Source: Agricultural census, Statistics Canada.

numbers and narrowed in scope. Moreover, the structural changes needed within agriculture to maintain the market competitiveness of farm producers have forced many to quit the family farm or ranch. The out-migrants have usually belonged to age groups below 40 years and have left an imbalance in the age structure of the remaining farmers.

Technological Innovations and Farm Size Adjustments

Since the Second World War, the Alberta farmer has had to become more efficient to offset the increasing costs of farm operation against relatively constant or slowly rising commodity prices. This challenge has been met by investment in new technology and the purchase and lease of more land. Higher-yielding crop varieties, more efficient livestock operations, larger tractors and self-propelled equipment have permitted capital to be substituted for labour. As the need for large families and for hired labour has diminished, the rural farm population has declined.

The modernization of agriculture in Alberta since 1951 is documented by impressive statistics. The average capital value per farm increased more than threefold from $21,225 in 1951 to $83,603 in 1971. Much of this increase was caused by rising land values. Purchased inputs quadrupled from $1,180 to $4,650 over the same period. Farmers have become major consumers of the products of other industries and are the mainstay of the rural economy because of the multiplier effect of the money they spend in rural service centres. Farmers in Alberta spend more than $1 billion annually on fertilizer, weedspray, gasoline, oil, twine, machinery, repairs, processed feed, veterinarian services, transport, and accounting services. They pay substantial taxes to all levels of government and interest charges for mortgages and loans.

Yet, it is the larger amounts of land farmed by individual farmers that affords the most dramatic evidence of the adjustments in Alberta agriculture. The average size of farm increased from 213 ha in 1951, to 320 ha in 1971, and 353 ha in 1976, while the numbers of farms in the larger census size categories have also increased consistently (Table 6–2), despite the general trend to fewer farms. Small farms, defined as having less than 28 ha in 1961–71, and 4 to 97 ha in 1971–76, have become more numerous as well, but that reflects the growing popularity of part-time and hobby farming rather than a major adjustment among the full scale commercial operations.

Table 6-2
Percentage changes in numbers of farms by farm size, 1961–71 and 1971–76

Size of farm (in hectares)	1961–71	1971–76
Less than 1.2	+ 7.1	− 17.9
1.3–3.6	+ 45.0	− 18.6
3.7–27.9	+ 82.9	+ 55.1
28.0–96.7	− 25.0	+ 60.6
96.8–161.5	− 31.8	+ 1.1
161.6–226.3	− 20.8	− 7.0
226.4–307.3	− 3.4	− 6.9
307.4–453.0	+ 13.3	− 1.7
453.1–647.4	+ 21.8	+ 5.1
647.5–906.5	+ 34.8	+ 6.8
906.6–1,165.9	+ 40.6	+ 12.2
1,166 or more	+ 30.8	+ 15.2
All farms	− 9.6	+ 7.7

Note: The 1976 definition of farm used was the same as that of "agricultural holding" for previous census years.

Source: Agricultural census, Statistics Canada.

Because of high land prices, the bulk of additional land acquired by commercial farms is leased rather than purchased. The part-owner/part-tenant farmer is the most common type of commercial operator by land tenure and is usually the larger farmer in terms of acreage, value of production, and farm income. Still, farmers everywhere in Alberta desire to own land. This strong demand is partially reflected in the increase in the average price of land and buildings from $89 per hectare in 1961 to $526 in 1976. Unfortunately, speculators and non-agricultural land developers have also increased their pressure on the land supply. Renting offers younger farmers the opportunity to increase farm income without investing commensurate amounts of capital. Rented land on the prairies usually augments the home quarter section inherited or purchased by the farmers.

Land for agriculture can also be obtained in a variety of ways from the provincial government, particularly along the forest frontier of the Eastern Slopes, northeastern Alberta and, most important of all, the Peace River region. However, land is more commonly leased than purchased these days, partly because a limited amount of Crown land has been posted for sale in recent years and partly because of the high cost of development. In 1976 the Alberta Land Use Forum estimated the average cost of clearing wooded land at $250 per hectare, to that had to be added a capital investment of at least $100,000 to ensure a viable farm operation. Homestead sales are still permitted in the "yellow area" of the Peace. (See Figure 5–1 in Chapter 5.) But no homesteader can acquire more than a single square mile (259 ha) of land, amortized over a maximum period of 20 years. Given the severe physical and economic constraints on agriculture in the northern frontier regions, it is not surprising to find that sales of public lands have dropped sharply (Table 6–3). Indeed, that trend has been underway for the best part of 20 years, as the applications for homestead land declined from a peak of 1,399 in 1965 to no more than 77 in 1979. Today, applications come largely from individual members of such communal groups as the Mennonites in La Crête and Fort Vermilion or from sons of local farm families. In practice, the established farm and the new homestead land are often worked as a single unit.

Over the whole province some 8 million ha of undeveloped land is considered to have potential agricultural capability, giving Alberta the largest

Table 6-3

Public land dispositions in the Peace River region 1978–1982 (in thousands of hectares)

Type of Disposition	1978	1979	1980	1981	1982
Homestead sales	32.0	22.8	17.7	16.6	9.0
Farm development sales	8.7	6.5	8.3	3.4	2.2
Farm development leases	5.2	3.9	4.5	2.4	12.6
Grazing leases	23.6	18.2	22.9	33.5	14.8
Special postings (mostly farm development leases with an option to purchase)	–	–	10.1	1.8	–

Source: Public Lands Division, Alberta Energy and Natural Resources.

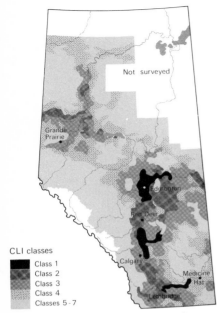

CLI classes

■ Class 1
▨ Class 2
▦ Class 3
▨ Class 4
░ Classes 5 - 7

Figure 6–2 Land quality in Alberta by Canada Land Inventory classes. Class 1 land has the highest natural capability for agriculture; Class 7 land has no capability. Source: Canada Land Inventory.

reserve of agricultural land in Canada. Almost all of it is in the northern bio-physical regions, so its development would be all too likely to bring an increase in the number of marginal farms. This led the Land Use Forum to recommend that homesteading be prohibited (Alberta is the only province in which it is still allowed), and that land brought into production in the near term should have Class 1 and 2 soils on the Canada Land Inventory rating, and be located within settled areas. Land of this kind is seldom encountered within the poor grey-wooded soil (Class 4) districts of the Peace River park-land or of the boreal-parkland transition forest, but is chiefly associated with the brown and dark brown soils of the short-grass and mixed-grass prairie regions of east-central and southeastern Alberta (Figure 6–2). As described in Chapter 4, the grassland zones have pronounced moisture deficits and the cultivation of additional land would require an increase in irrigation. Yet, there is no clear agreement on either the need for more irrigated land or its long-term environmental effects. In 1977, for instance, 80 per cent of the irri-gated land area, then about 375,000 ha, was devoted to crops such as wheat, oats, barley, and tame hay, all of which yield low returns per hectare. Only one-fifth was farmed intensively for sugar beets, potatoes, and other vege-tables, despite the high cost of constructing and maintaining irrigation works. Nonetheless, the provincial government is under considerable pressure to increase its assistance, and a portion of the Heritage Savings Trust Fund has been allocated to the construction of dams and water storage facilities in the Oldman River basin. An advisory committee has also been appointed to examine once again the merits of water transfer from the northern rivers.

The under-utilization of irrigated land is but one example of the unrealized potential that the present area of cultivation is believed to hold. By general consensus, the agricultural output of Alberta could be increased by as much as 50 per cent over the 1971 level, if full advantage were taken of presently-known technology. In 1971, for example, slightly less than one-third of the area under wheat, oats, barley, canola, and tame hay received any fertilizer. Cost was the chief barrier, of course, and fertilizer prices have risen sharply since 1971, which has stimulated interest in other approaches, such as the possibility of changing cropping practices. Some agronomists believe that a reduced use of summer fallow and an increase in planned rotations incorpo-rating legumes would simultaneously protect soil fertility and reduce the danger of salinization. Scientific crop-breeding also continues to hold much promise, as does the development of new techniques of weed and pest con-trol. To the farmer, the benefits of increased output have always been weighed against the increase in the costs of production; any increase in farm income must more than offset the extra investment that is required. But income is affected by many factors which have little or nothing to do with the farmer's skill or efficiency. Market conditions, government subsidies, tariffs, and freight rates can all conspire in patterns of production that fall below the environmental or technological potential.

The majority of Alberta farms by number, area, and capital value are live-stock operations; farms producing wheat and small grains are second in importance. Dairy, poultry, cattle, hog, and sheep operations are concentrated around the cities of Edmonton and Calgary, in the intervening corridor, and between Camrose and Lloydminster. Wheat and small grain farmers are noticeably located in the Peace River region, in the areas immediately around Edmonton, Camrose, and Lloydminster, and in the belt reaching southeast from Red Deer to the international border. Mixed enterprises occupy a crescent extending from Lethbridge through Calgary, Red Deer, Camrose, and Lloydminster to the Saskatchewan boundary; they also characterize the county of Grande Prairie and the area just north of Edmonton. The black and dark brown soils of the mixed grass prairie and central parkland biophysical regions provide the most suitable environment in Alberta, economically as well as physically, for a wide variety of farm types and agricultural products. Away from this fertile crescent, with its dense pattern of settlement and communications, farming is typically more specialized and more extensive. Large-scale ranches or wheat farms are an adaptation to locations that are marginal in either physical or economic terms.

The major agricultural growth sectors in Alberta today are beef, canola, vegetables (potatoes), wheat, and feed grains. But wheat has declined relative to oilseeds, tame hay, and feed grains. Beef cattle and poultry increased steadily in number during the 1970s, but hogs declined.

Alberta farmers export many of their products because of the relatively small Canadian market, but their dependence on external markets and on foreign inputs has squeezed their incomes. Annual product prices fluctuate but costs rise inexorably with inflation. Wheat accounts on the average for one-fifth of Alberta farm income and livestock for one-third, but there are abrupt fluctuations from year to year. Since 1951, grain farmers have increasingly diversified into livestock, feed grains, oilseeds, and pasture to offset income variations. Although future prices for these products will probably rise to much higher levels, the benefit for Alberta farmers will depend on the rate at which farm operating costs also rise.

Nearly half of Alberta's agricultural output is produced by farms on black soils, where 70 per cent of all dairy farms, 52 per cent of livestock farms, 59 per cent of poultry farms, and 47 per cent of mixed farms are located. Yet black soil alone cannot guarantee financial success. Almost two-thirds of the province's farmers produced less than $10,000 worth of commerical commodities in 1971, and 45 per cent of this group were farming in the black soil zone (Table 6–4). Even at the bottom of the scale, among the quarter of all Alberta farmers whose sales in 1971 were less than $2500, 40 per cent were located on black soils; the most logical explanation is the large number of hobby farms near Edmonton and Calgary. At the other extreme, among the 35 per cent of farmers whose sales exceed $10,000, the proportion of black soil farmers rose to 47 per cent. Only 16 per cent of the most productive

Table 6-4

Alberta farms classified by gross farm sales and by physical region

Soil group and biophysical region	Under $2,500	$2,500–9,999	$10,000 and over	Total
Brown				
Short grass prairie	693	2,118	3,503	6,314
Dark brown				
Mixed grass prairie	808	2,422	4,448	7,678
Black				
Aspen parkland (central parkland)	6,673	11,056	10,389	28,118
Dark gray and gray wooded				
Aspen parkland (Peace River parkland)	4,084	5,540	2,513	12,163
Boreal forest, boreal-cordilleran transition forest, boreal-parkland transition forest	3,553	3,301	1,088	7,942
Total	15,811	24,437	21,941	62,189

Source: After Table 6A in Hu Harries and Associates Ltd., *The Future Land Needs for Alberta Agriculture, Technical Report No. 5.* (Edmonton: Alberta Land Use Forum, 1974).

farms were on dark grey and grey-wooded soils, as compared with 47 per cent of the farms which yielded gross incomes of less than $2500.

Many farm operations require additional income to provide an adequate standard of living per family. Non-farm sources of income have become significant since 1951, as opportunities for off-farm employment in towns and natural resource developments increased. The consolidation of school districts and the busing of students to central schools have also provided considerable rural employment. Other work opportunities have been made available by improvements to the rural highway network. In 1945 there were only 115 km of paved roads as compared with 8,750 km in 1971; the length of gravelled roads increased tenfold, from 9,500 km to 95,000 km, over the same period. Today, one-third of farm income is derived from non-farm sources; half comes from salaries or wages, and the other half from dividends, interest, and other investment income. This income has been a valuable supplement to net farm income, which was only $2,800 per census farm in 1961 and $12,000 in 1974. Nevertheless, in its review of agriculture, the Alberta Land Use Forum concluded that such income simply allowed many marginal farmers to remain on the land to the long-term detriment of viable farmers.

The changes in Alberta's agriculture are a response to a variety of economic, social, and demographic factors which ultimately manifest themselves as tangible elements of change in the farming landscape. Tall silage towers, steel wheat bins, feed lots for cattle, bulky automated hog and poultry barns, fields of brilliant yellow canola and blue flaxseed, centre-pivot irrigation systems— these all represent innovations by the farmer. Examples of earlier changes to combat drought in the southern and eastern parts of the province include strip farming, shelter belts, dug-outs, and irrigation canals created by the joint efforts of farmers, the Prairie Farm Rehabilitation Agency and agencies of the Alberta government.

Other changes in rural Alberta have been non-agricultural in character, although they may have their own special implications for agriculture. Two concentrated examples of such change have resulted from the intrusion into the countryside of permanent and temporary residences for metropolitan workers. The first example is the spread of residential subdivisions from the cities and from the dormitory towns within commuting distance of Edmonton and Calgary. The second is the demand for lakeshore cottages at which a growing proportion of urban residents are spending their leisure time, a trend that is particularly evident in the lake zones between Edmonton and Calgary and in northeastern Alberta. Both of these intrusions of urban land uses into rural Alberta have aroused public controversy.

Landscape Change and Land Conversion

Residential Subdivision

Much of Alberta's urban development has occurred on prime farmland (Figure 6–2). Class 1 land is under particular threat, since some 60 per cent of the provincial total (450,000 ha out of 750,000 ha) is concentrated in the Edmonton-Calgary region, which already contains two-thirds of Alberta's population and is forecast to house four-fifths of future population growth. Unfortunately, the rate of conversion of agricultural land to urban use in Alberta is high by national standards. Of all the improved agricultural land converted to urban use in Canada between 1966 and 1971, Edmonton's share was 11.3 per cent, second only to the 20.5 per cent of Toronto. Calgary's share, at 8.05 per cent, came third. In terms of total rural land converted, Edmonton and Calgary ranked third and fourth after Toronto and Montreal.

Rural land once annexed for urban growth is probably lost to agriculture for ever. Some argue that it can be replaced in Alberta by marginal, grey-wooded soils, mainly in the north, but it may be premature and unrealistic to count on enhanced productivity from this land. Apart from the physical limitations, all the alternative ways of increasing future output are costly. The loss of production from 1 ha of black soil requires 2 ha of grey-wooded soils in replacement, and these poorer soils need over four times as much energy and fertilizer and other inputs.

Controversy over the disappearance of prime farm land also extends to the uses which replace agriculture. Nearly half the converted land is subdivided for country residences; the remainder is diverted to other urban purposes, including roads, utility corridors, parks, golf courses, gravel pits, and industrial parks. In the Edmonton planning region alone, 20,000 ha have been subdivided for country residences, while a further 40,000 ha have been allocated to urban uses. Although the Edmonton and Calgary regional planning commissions have recently become more stringent in their examination of subdivision applications, and the rate of subdivision has levelled off, land will still be converted as towns and cities continue to expand. Most of Edmonton's satellites have been permitted to annex rural land in recent years, and the city's territory was doubled on January 1, 1982. Over the next 20 or 30 years, all of that land—some 34,000 ha, much of it of the highest agricultural value—is expected to pass into urban use. Yet the implications of farmland conversion have not been fully investigated in Alberta. Whatever the immediate costs and benefits, the lax application of planning controls on land use, and the absence of a clear land use policy on the part of the provincial government, cause good farm land to be lost unnecessarily to non-agricultural uses. For example, although the Edmonton Metropolitan Regional Planning Commission directs country residents to poor quality lands, 16 per cent have located in Parkland County on class 1 and 2 land— roughly the same proportion as the total area of prime land in the county.

Lakeshore Cottages   The establishment of cottages in rural areas is less controversial, perhaps because it occurs at some distance from the metropolitan centres and leads to temporary rather than permanent occupance. Yet the demand for access to recreation land, especially on lakes, will certainly increase as leisure time expands. Of the 630 lakes in Alberta, only 269 have at least one part of their shoreline suitable for recreational use; much of this land is already committed to lakeshore developments. Cottage subdivisions have nearly saturated the capacity for development around the shallow lakes of the central parkland region in the Edmonton-Calgary corridor. Most remaining lakes with recreational potential are located on Crown land, in the boreal forest biophysical region, at considerable distances from Edmonton and Calgary. Surveys of cottagers report that people prefer to drive fewer than 3 hours to a cottage or a lake, but many lakes in the north are at least this far from Edmonton alone.

About 7,000 cottages were located on Alberta lakes in 1971, and the total has probably increased by at least 1,000 since then. Lac Ste. Anne, Lake Wabamun, and Pigeon Lake each had 1,000 cottages, and Sylvan Lake, Isle Lake, and Elkwater (in the Cypress Hills) together accounted for another 1,000. The balance was distributed among twenty more lakes. Approximately 95 per cent of all cottages are thus located on 5 per cent of the lakes with lakeshore recreation potential. The use of these favoured lakes could also become even more intensive in the future, since only half the approved cottage lots were actually developed in 1971. The main development period for cottages, resorts, institutional camps, and other facilities was between 1955 and 1964. Since then, because of rising costs and more stringent regulation, subdivision for lakeshore land uses has declined. Only the northeastern region has experienced substantial building activity in recent years.

Problems relating to the recreational use of lakes, particularly by cottagers or institutions, led the Alberta Planning Board and the Conservation and Utilization Committeee of the Alberta Department of the Environment to establish a task force in 1972 to examine the subdivision of land adjacent to water bodies. It identified several problems, such as restrictions on public access to lakes as a result of private cottage development and the incorporation of summer villages; the pollution of soil and water by septic tank sewage; and the general congestion of lakes and lakeshore sites caused by vehicles and watercraft. Further studies by the Edmonton and Red Deer regional planning commissions and the Alberta government have determined that algae growth, and the eutrophication of lakes by ground and surface water pollution, is related to cottage subdivisions and summer-weekend visitors. The resultant deterioration in fishing and wildlife habitat is particularly noticeable in the Red Deer area, at Sylvan, Pine, and Burntstick lakes.

Needless to say, all these problems detract from the quality and human experience of the recreational resource. Haphazard control in the past has permitted environmental damage which has now become the concern of government, particularly since the Alberta Land Use Forum completed its hearings. Yet the recommendations of this task force have still not been implemented by legislation, although lake management guidelines have been issued for 15 lakes under the auspices of the Alberta Planning Board and the Land Conservation and Reclamation Act of Alberta. Various municipalities have also adopted area structure plans, as permitted by the Alberta Planning Act, in an attempt to control particular lakeshore developments, which suggests that the need to protect the lake resource by public regulation is now well accepted.

To this point, however, most of the conflict between private and public use objectives has been perceived in terms of access problems, environmental damage, and resource protection. The economic cost-benefit dilemma of recreational cottages and other facilities in rural areas has been overlooked. Since most of the users originate in Edmonton, Red Deer, and Calgary, they comprise a temporary population in the rural municipalities, whereas the cost burden of municipal services falls on the permanent residents of rural areas and resort towns. For example, cottage surveys frequently report on the poor quality of access roads, but rural municipalities, which are responsible for installing and maintaining roads, culverts, and bridges, derive little benefit from cottagers' taxes paid to incorporated summer villages. Even when they are paid to the rural municipality, property taxes are usually insufficient to cover the costs of the services that are demanded. In similar fashion, it was found in one study of Pigeon Lake that the bulk of the cottagers' expenditures on goods and services, the construction or renovation of cottages, and real estate fees accrued to Edmonton, where the majority of the cottagers resided. The economic benefit for rural residents, farmers, shopkeepers, small builders, and the rural government was relatively small. Increased rural taxation of cottagers and some provincial cost assistance to rural municipalities therefore seem to be required. There is also a warning here for those depressed rural regions, such as northeastern Alberta, where recreational developments are often promoted as a means of stimulating the local economy.

Resource Development Impacts and Regional Disparities

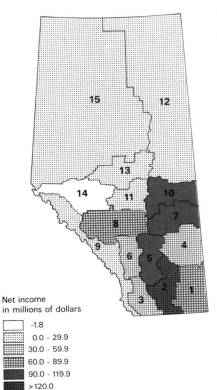

Net income
in millions of dollars

- ☐ -1.8
- 0.0 - 29.9
- 30.0 - 59.9
- 60.0 - 89.9
- 90.0 - 119.9
- >120.0

Figure 6–3 Total net income from farm production for each Alberta census division in 1980.
Source: Government of Alberta.

Just as there are differences in the knowledge and expertise of individuals and the incomes which they earn, so are there differences between places in their resource characteristics and in the quality of life which they provide. These differences are known as "regional disparities," and they can be identified and measured by a wide range of indicators, such as per capita income, unemployment rates, or the proportion of dwellings with piped water supplies and bathrooms.

Within Alberta there tend to be marked disparities between urban and rural areas, particularly between the Edmonton-Calgary core region and the peripheral areas of the province. As mentioned earlier in this chapter, there are also disparities within the agricultural sector of the rural economy in consequence of the broad natural and economic constraints upon farm production (Figure 6–3). When these are overlaid with the spatial variations in economic benefits derived from resource-based industrial development, the potential for disparity is increased still further. It does not even follow that the largest benefits will accrue to the districts in which the resources are located. In particular, exploration activity for oil and natural gas has produced temporary employment in many areas, notably the foothills and northern Alberta, but the greatest concentration of permanent employment is to be found in the Edmonton-Calgary region. Personal incomes also reach their highest per capita levels there (Figure 6–4).

Overall, however, the massive developments of timber, coal, oil sands, and conventional oil and natural gas resources over the past 25 years have had largely positive impacts on the economy of rural Alberta. Many new jobs have been generated, directly and indirectly. For example, the Proctor and Gamble pulp mill, built near Grande Prairie in 1974, employs some 560 persons in the plant and 250 in lumbering and transportation. When those employed in retail and other businesses are included, the project generated nearly 1,000 jobs. Not all forest-product developments have been so successful, though. Near the town of Slave Lake a stud mill and other wood products firms created about 425 direct jobs with assistance from government grants but ultimately failed, for at least three reasons: the American housing market collapsed in the 1974 recession; the costs of training native workers were too high; and an attempt to introduce the use of poplar lumber proved unsuccessful. Yet, Alberta's forests contain a net merchantable timber volume of 1.7 billion m³ with an annual allowable cut of 28 million m³. Since the present harvest totals no more than 4 million m³, the potential for additional production is substantial. Three remaining forest areas could provide resources for pulp and lumber mills like those in operation at Hinton and Grande Prairie, the economic contributions of which are a substantial aid in balancing rural incomes and job opportunities with those available in Alberta's cities.

In northeastern Alberta, a peripheral, traditionally disadvantaged region, the oil sands seem to offer the greatest potential for economic development. The Syncrude processing plant permanently employs 2,800 people, and a further 1,800 work in the longer-established Great Canadian Oil Sands plant. If 10 or more oil sands plants are built in the northeastern region, the population could rise to around 100,000. A new town 70–90 km north of Fort McMurray has already been planned. To meet the problems generated by such a large scale of population growth and construction activity, the provincial government passed the North East Alberta Regional Commission Act in 1974 and appointed a commissioner with powers to coordinate and plan private and public activities.

For all their promise, however, mammoth resource projects mask the stagnation or decline of many small northern communities. In 1978, nearly 30 per cent of Alberta's unemployed workforce was in the two northern census divisions (CDs 12 and 15), and was particularly concentrated on single people and those with grade 8 education or less. Unemployment may be as high as 15 per cent in some communities, and up to 80 or 90 per cent on Indian reserves. Although long term residents have obtained some of the new jobs, most of northern Alberta's new labour force comprises recent in-migrants. Only since the early 1970s has a serious effort been made by government and private companies to train and encourage native people to take advantage of new employment opportunities. The numbers employed do not yet reflect these efforts; culture and environment still present fundamental barriers to the advancement of native people.

Still, future resource projects in northern Alberta can be expected to help reduce regional disparities within Alberta. The government is also attempting to redress these disparities through the decentralization of population to the regional cities and large towns of rural Alberta, and through the diversification of the province's economic base. Processing and manufacturing industries are particularly being encouraged, mainly for petrochemical and agricultural products. Agricultural processing has been particularly assisted

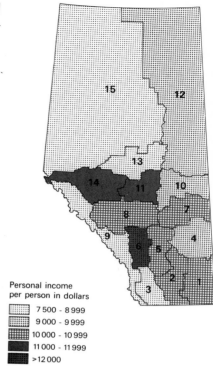

Personal income per person in dollars

7 500 - 8 999
9 000 - 9 999
10 000 - 10 999
11 000 - 11 999
>12 000

Figure 6–4 Average levels of personal income per person for each Alberta census division in 1980.
Source: Government of Alberta.

under the Nutritive Processing Agreement of 1975, a cost-shared incentives program between the federal Department of Regional Economic Expansion and the provincial government.

Community self-help rural resources projects, encouraged and aided by the government since their successful introduction in the Carbon-Drumheller region in 1971, are now active in additional locations: Crows Nest Pass, Lac La Biche, the Elk Island Triangle, High Level, High Prairie, McLennan, and New Norway-Bashaw. Each scheme requires an economic development co-ordinator to be hired by a group of communities which refuse to die and which initiate viable projects to create jobs. Successful examples include an auto-body shop at Carbon, a log house firm at Lac La Biche, a parka manufacturing plant on the Beaver Indian Reserve near Lac La Biche, industrial parks in the Crows Nest Pass, a regional newspaper in the Elk Island Triangle, and time-sharing of heavy equipment by municipalities in the New Norway-Bashaw region.

Rural and Regional Planning

Figure 6–5 The regional planning commissions of Alberta in 1983.

During the last two decades, and especially since 1971, the provincial government has tackled the problems of rural Alberta in a variety of ways. Programs for agriculture, innovative rural resource projects, and guidance of major natural resource developments are examples of public response on many different fronts. It can also be argued that a more integrated regional planning approach should be adopted to ensure that the actions of public agencies are co-ordinated within the framework of a single set of province-wide policies. At this time, there is no such provincial plan. There are ten regional planning commissions with jurisdiction over most of the settled area in Alberta (Figure 6–5), and these commissions were required, by law, to adopt regional plans by the end of 1982. But ten separate plans do not necessarily fit together into one comprehensive plan. Nor do they address the problems of those large areas of the province that lie outside the commission boundaries and in which the major natural resource developments of the future are likely to be located. It is possible that more special area commissions may be created, similar to the Northeast Regional Commission, but this is essentially an ad hoc approach to the needs of particular areas. It fails to allow for the fact that Alberta is a unified settlement system, and that change in any one region, whether it brings development or decline, will have wide-ranging repercussions on other settlements, on other regions, and on the whole province.

The regional planning commissions are limited in another important sense. Their statutory authority extends only to the physical aspects of land use and development, such as subdivision control and land use zoning, and even here they act under considerable constraint. On the one hand, the commission members are appointed as representatives of municipal governments; and most of the real power in the planning control system is vested at the municipal level. On the other hand, the commissions have no jurisdiction over the many agencies of the provincial government which have responsibilities of their own in the regulation of the resource-based industries, in the control of environmental quality, and in the development of new enterprises.

There is an overall lack of co-ordination at several levels: between the regions and the municipalities, on the one hand, and the provincial government on the other; between economic development planning and physical or environmental planning; among the separate regional planning commissions; and even among the separate agencies of the provincial government. Given the anticipated scale of future developments, and the physical and economic effects that are likely to affect rural Alberta, the need for a more co-ordinated approach to regional development and economic planning would seem to be a pressing one. Ad hoc development programs to aid small-town businessmen and agricultural assistance programs of many different kinds, albeit effective in their own right, should be integrated with all other government programs affecting rural life. Ideally, perhaps, the basic economic policies should be administered through a central agency, such as the Alberta Department of Economic Development, and the role of the regional planning commissions could be strengthened to ensure the effective translation of these policies into specific development projects in particular communities. This would certainly permit a more rational approach to the integrated management of Alberta's space-economy and its physical environment.

Conclusion

Rural Alberta has undergone major changes in the composition of its economic activities, the size and location of its population, and the function of its settlements since the Second World War. Growth has been strongly concentrated in the central parkland region of the Edmonton-Calgary corridor, but rural life in the boreal forest, the Peace River parkland, and the boreal-cordilleran biophysical regions has also been stimulated by natural resource exploitation. By the end of the century, these phenomena can be expected to have strengthened still further, and to present yet another new geography of problems and challenges to be met by Albertans. The keys to preserving the quality of life in rural Alberta for future generations should therefore be put in place now, not just through government policy but through the efforts of the farmers and other entrepreneurs whose current practices are so important to the economic and physical landscape.

Supplemental Readings

Alberta Land Use Forum. *Report and Recommendations.* Edmonton: 1967.

Alberta Land Use Forum. *Use of Our Lakes and Lake Shore Lands: Technical Report 12.* Edmonton: 1974.

Hu Harries and Associates Ltd. *The Future Land Needs for Alberta Agriculture: Technical Report No. 5.* Edmonton: Alberta Land Use Forum, 1974.

Ironside, R.G., Proudfoot, V.B., Shannon, E.N. and Tracie, C.J., eds. *Frontier Settlement.* Edmonton: University of Alberta, Studies in Geography, Monograph 1, 1974. Of particular interest are chapter 1, "Frontier Development and Perspectives on the Western Canadian Frontier" by R.G. Ironside, V.B. Proudfoot, E.N. Shannon and C.J. Tracie, 1–45 and chapter 5, "Recent Changes in Population in Northern Saskatchewan and Alberta" by G. Lamont and V.B. Proudfoot, 93–112.

Jankunis, F. and Sadler, B., eds. *The Viability and Livability of Small Urban Centres.* Edmonton: Environment Council of Alberta, 1979.

Lapp, D.M. *The Structure of Alberta Farms, 1941–1974: Technical Report No. 11.* Edmonton: Alberta Land Use Forum, 1974.

Sheehan, P. *Social Change in the Alberta Foothills.* Toronto: McClelland and Stewart, 1975.

Thompson, P.S. *Agricultural Concerns in the Urban Fringe.* Edmonton: Environment Council of Alberta, 1980.

Thompson, P.S. *Urbanization of Agricultural Land.* Edmonton: Environment Council of Alberta, 1981.

The Industrial-Urban Economy

Part 3 is devoted to the urban-based economic activities of Alberta, and the transportation and communication facilities upon which they depend. People working in these activities manufacture, store, and distribute goods, provide retail, personal, commercial, and governmental services, and engage in administration, supervision, research, and economic planning.

In common with advanced industrial economies everywhere, trade is vital to Alberta's prosperity. The desire for trade, in turn, stimulated the development of modern transportation and communications facilities, beginning with the transcontinental railways and continuing on into road, air, energy transmission, and telecommunications services of ever-increasing sophistication. These trends are described by Nigel Waters in Chapter 7, "Transportation and Communications: The Infrastructure of Economic Geography." His central theme, which is summed up in the idea of "infrastructure," is that the transportation and communications systems serve simultaneously to integrate all parts of Alberta into a single functional system and to link Alberta with the world outside. The quality of Alberta's transportation and communications services therefore has a direct bearing on the province's economic performance, just as their spatial structure has a major influence upon the organization of the space-economy.

Most strikingly, the linkages facilitated by the various transport modes have permitted Alberta to become a primary-producing hinterland to national and international communities. Efficient communications are all-important if exported raw materials and primary manufactures are to compete effectively in distant markets. There are unresolved problems, however, especially in rail transportation. The capacities of lines and terminals and freight rates and tariffs are particular sources of concern. As purveyors of bulky, low-value commodities, the producers of Alberta are extremely sensitive to the proportion of transport costs in the delivered value of their goods. They also are concerned about the extent to which transport charges favour the further manufacture of their commodities at the market destinations, since it is cheaper to move unfinished goods than manufactured ones.

Much of Alberta's linkage with other regions and nations has been predicated upon relatively inexpensive energy, and this holds true for the movement of people no less than for the movement of goods. Alberta is distant from world heartlands; many of its residents seek periodic escape in warmer climates, as well as the economic opportunity offered by more profitable environments. Nigel Waters reminds us that the suitability of Alberta for permanent, advanced settlement largely rests with its ability to remain easily connected with outside places of work (the arctic, eastern offshore areas, or overseas), of recreation (milder climates), and of corporate control and investment (central Canada, other industrial nations, and frontier regions).

Many of the processes affecting Alberta's space-economy stem from the province's changing importance in national and international markets and the world's changing access to Alberta. At the same time, the patterns of commodity flows continue to reflect Alberta's peripheral geographical position relative to central Canada, the northeastern United States, western Europe or the Asian Pacific rim. These themes are pursued further in Chapter 8, "The Industrial Economy: Locational Patterns and Spatial Relationships," by Brenton Barr.

Primary activity, especially agriculture, is the most extensive, spatially continuous economic activity in Alberta. Along with its urban-centred support services, or tertiary functions, agriculture sustains an unbroken spread of population and settlement throughout the environmentally suitable areas of southern Alberta. By contrast, settlement and economic activity associated with oil and gas wells, coal mines, and timber harvesting is essentially discontinuous, sporadic, and punctiform. Whether continuous or discontinuous, however, all the primary activity patterns and their associated settlements are facilitated by road, rail and pipeline systems which integrate them into an increasingly mature provincial economic system.

Secondary, quaternary, and quinary industries are basically associated with Alberta's major urban places, especially the two metropolitan centres which dominate Alberta's human geography. Edmonton, the centre of provincial administrative power, has the largest share of civil service employment; Calgary as the head office energy centre is the major location of the province's employment in multi-national energy-related firms. Crown corporations and defence establishments similarly favour these two locations. In addition, the basic components of manufacturing, distribution, wholesaling, medical care, administration, and research are related through the two metropolitan centres to the urban settlement hierarchy and to the rural sector of the space-economy. Edmonton and Calgary also serve as the overwhelming points of connection between external markets and sources of supply, on the one hand, and producers and consumers within Alberta.

More generally, it is useful to interpret the Albertan patterns of human and economic activity through the heartland-hinterland paradigm. Professor Barr suggests that this not only allows the key elements of Alberta's relationship with other regions to be identified, but also permits the internal organization of the province to be better understood. Numerous factors continue to favour centralization in Alberta's economic system, while extensive peripheral areas with declining agricultural opportunities and relatively large indigenous populations remain outside the mainstream of commercial prosperity. These areas are targets of federal and provincial government programs designed to alleviate the more pernicious effects of regional disparity. In combination with a host of regular government activities, these programs make a major contribution to the geography of Alberta's hinterlands. In aggregate they maintain a significant degree of spatial stability in Alberta and offset strong polarization processes.

The influence of government in Alberta's space-economy appears to be even more pervasive than that of either the energy sector or agriculture. The role of government is therefore explored further in Chapter 9, "The Economic Role of Public Employers in the Urban Communities," by Patrick Cadden.

Many services of government, such as education and health care, are labour intensive and so generate large numbers of jobs throughout the settlement hierarchy. Teachers, nurses, and clerks account for the majority of public employees in most communities, but government services also include numerous professional, financial, legal, and technical occupations, as well as municipal administrators and police. The majority of the highly-skilled public service jobs are in the two metropolitan centres, though public sector employment accounts for approximately one-quarter of the employment in all but the smallest categories of urban places. Public sector employees also tend to have higher average incomes than private-sector employees in the same communities. Yet that does not necessarily mean that public sector incomes will bring a larger relative benefit to those places. The impact of government employees on local economies is much more a function of where they choose to live and make their consumer purchases.

In the future, as the province's population continues to grow, a still greater variety of government services is likely to be demanded. If government continues to intervene in routine economic activities by taking greater degrees of equity participation in the economy, then its aggregate influence on the patterns of livelihood and settlement in Alberta will increase. At the same time, as Dr. Cadden points out, deliberate decentralization of government employment has had little effect to date, although it has long been regarded as a valuable strategy for counteracting regional imbalances in the provincial economy. In government, no less than in business, the centripetal pull of the metropolitan centres is exceedingly powerful.

With the maturing of Alberta's energy economy, transactional activities of all kinds have become more prominent. Elizabeth Szplett describes this trend in the final chapter, "The Transactional Environment: Quaternary and Quinary Industry." These industries, she notes, are highly concentrated or localized, not just in the metropolitan centres but in the central areas of these centres. They rely on vast inter-connections and operations ("transactions") which proceed in non-routine personal contact patterns. That, in turn, is a function of the large numbers of tasks that have to be performed and their division among numerous specialist agencies. Hence, transactional activities are chiefly found in offices within central business districts, where the advantages of centralization and inter-function access are at their peak.

Decisions made in the major metropolitan areas affect employment and acitvities in all other regions, but they also produce multiplier effects in the metropolitan economies themselves. These take two forms: immediate connections with information and support services, and the higher disposable incomes of head office employees. Quaternary or knowledge-processing occupations and industries, for example, are concentrated in Alberta's two largest urban places to a much greater extent than their share of provincial population would require. Quinary or knowledge-creating activities, although spatially less constrained because they do not have the same need for immediate response, generally seek central locations as well. The patterns of quinary activity in Alberta also display a concentration in Calgary related to petroleum activities, and another in Edmonton oriented toward the skills and supporting facilities of university and government.

Transactional activities in Alberta clearly demonstrate the strength of the province's core-periphery spatial organization. The disparity between the metropolitan centres and the rest of the province is greater than it is in any other economic sector. If Alberta's economy becomes more associated with the quaternary and quinary sectors in the future, and if managerial and technological activities are intensified, Alberta's patterns of livelihood and population are likely to become even more dependent on Edmonton and Calgary.

7 Transportation and Communications
The Infrastructure of Economic Geography
Nigel M. Waters

"An effective transportation system is vital for Alberta." With this statement, the Transportation Services Branch of Alberta Economic Development has expressed the importance of Alberta's highways and railways, its air service facilities, its pipelines, its power grids, and its telecommunications systems, to the continuing prosperity of this land-locked province. Trade and communication, and the free flow of people, goods, and information, are fundamental needs of any commerical economy. The more advanced and sophisticated the economy, the more elaborate the transportation and communication systems must be. In a very real sense, they form the infrastructure of development, underlying the economic patterns and in large part explaining their geographical organization. It is therefore appropriate that Part 3, dealing with the economic geography of Alberta, should begin with a review of contemporary transportation and communication services.

The general relationship between economic development and the networks of transport facilities, and the implications for the evolving form of the settlement system, have already been discussed in Chapter 2. Here, attention is directed at the major elements of the modern transportation and communication systems, both to convey an appreciation of their variety and functions, and to highlight the special problems that follow from the basic conditions of Alberta's geography—its continental interior location, its peripheral situation in Canada and the world, its small population base, and its resource dominated economy. This chapter concludes with a brief consideration of possible future developments, particularly from the standpoint of public policy and federal-provincial relations.

Railway Systems   The most important rail services in Alberta are provided by the Canadian National (CNR) and Canadian Pacific (CPR) freight systems and the VIA passenger system. In general, CPR trackage and services are concentrated in the southern third of the province, centred on Calgary, while the CNR chiefly serves central and northern Alberta, with Edmonton as its regional headquarters (Figure 7–1).

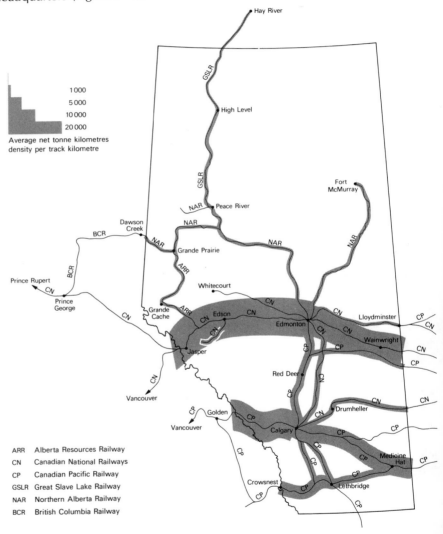

Figure 7–1   Railway systems of Alberta and volumes of freight traffic in 1971. The Northern Alberta Railway was amalgamated with Canadian National in 1981.
Source: *Edmonton-Calgary Corridor Transportation Study.*

ARR   Alberta Resources Railway
CN   Canadian National Railways
CP   Canadian Pacific Railway
GSLR   Great Slave Lake Railway
NAR   Northern Alberta Railway
BCR   British Columbia Railway

Freight Services   The CPR is part of a group of companies which, in 1980, had more than $6 billion worth of assets in land, sea, and air transportation, telecommunications, natural resources, hotels, and real estate. It began as a freight company and is still best known in that role. It now operates some 320 regular freight trains into and out of Calgary every week. The heaviest concentration of traffic is between Calgary and Vancouver, with unit coal trains making up a large part of the total flow (Figure 7–2). The CPR has been a leader in the use of unit trains and now favours them for a variety of bulk commodities.

Considerable amounts of money are being spent by the CPR to increase its freight handling capability in western Canada. The company plans to upgrade its fleet of locomotives at a cost of $200 million over 10 years. It also plans to improve its track between Calgary and Vancouver, by straightening the route, smoothing the grades, and double tracking. The largest single project will cost about $300 million and will require the construction of a 14 km tunnel below the existing Connaught tunnel in the Rogers Pass. This new tunnel has to be in place by 1985 if Canada is to meet a projected 50 per cent increase in grain exports through Vancouver. In addition, the company is upgrading its TOFC (trailer-on-flatcar) and COFC (container-on-flatcar) facilities, and has recently introduced the first general purpose domestic container on a limited transcontinental service.

Similar plans have been announced by the CNR for its Mountain Region, in the face of recent traffic increases which have averaged about 9 per cent per annum (in comparison with an annual increase of about 6 per cent for the entire CNR system). The corporation is also hoping for further substantial increases from industrial development in northern Alberta and the Northwest Territories, as a consequence of its takeover of the Northern Alberta Railway (NAR). This system, which was created in 1929, linked Edmonton to Fort McMurray, Grande Prairie, and Peace River, and provided connections to the CNR's own Great Slave Lake Railway and the Alberta government's Alberta Resources Railway. In 1977, in the report of the Hall Commission, it was recommended that these should be integrated into a single Northern Development Railway under CNR control. A major step to that end was taken in January 1981, when the NAR became the Peace River Division of the Mountain Region.

In the 1980s the CNR has embarked on extensive upgrading of the whole regional system. The line of heaviest traffic, between Edmonton and Red Pass Junction en route to Prince Rupert and Vancouver, will be double tracked by 1985, and so, too, will the section between Red Pass Junction and Valemount. The total cost is estimated at $500 million. A further billion dollars should be spent between 1982 and the early 1990s, to double track the main line between Valemount and Vancouver. Some double tracking of the Winnipeg-Edmonton line and upgrading of the single track from Red Pass Junction to Prince Rupert is also envisaged.

The CNR is aggressively promoting its Super Modal integrated truck and rail services. It is restructuring and expanding its terminals at Vancouver, Prince Rupert, Prince George, and Edmonton, and has introduced innovations such as the supertherm, a specially insulated trailer for temperature sen-

Figure 7–2 Directions in which the major categories of rail freight flow into Alberta, out of Alberta, and within Alberta. Source: *Edmonton-Calgary Corridor Transportation Study.*

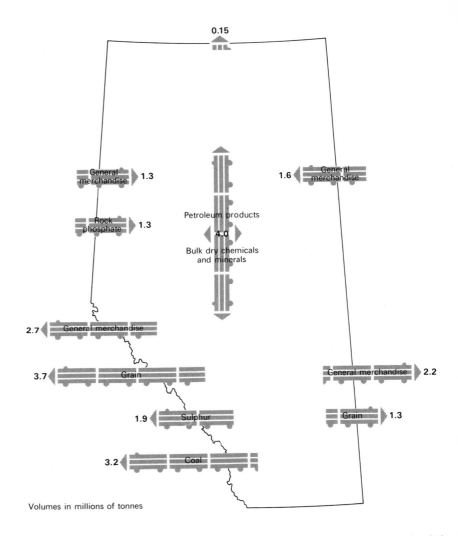

Volumes in millions of tonnes

sitive freight, and the CargoFlo system for hauling small shipments of solids and liquids by train and truck to individual customers. This system takes advantage of the long haul economy of the railroad and the flexibility of truck transportation.

Yet, despite all the improvements projected by the CPR and CNR, the available rail freight capacity may not expand quickly enough. The premiers of the four western provinces have observed that there is likely to be a 66 per cent increase in exports of bulk commodities from western Canada between 1978 and 1990, and that a capital investment of $14 billion will be required to move this and other types of freight. The situation appeared so critical in 1981 that one federal cabinet minister was led to suggest that space for freight on the railways in western Canada might have to be rationed by 1985.

This raises the fear that new export contracts, for example, coal for Japan and grain for the Soviet Union, might go unfilled as they compete for inadequate transportation space.

Throughout their histories, grain has been the most important Albertan commodity carried by either the CNR or the CPR (Figure 7–2), and none better illustrates the difficulty of balancing the desire for a profitable, efficient freight service with the economic needs of a widely-distributed set of producers. Given the continuing importance of agriculture, and particularly grain exports, to the Alberta economy, the ability of the freight system to move huge quantities of grain quickly and at an internationally competitive price is of paramount concern.

Problems of Grain Transportation

The grain transportation system of western Canada has been the subject of considerable research in recent years. Most notably, the Hall report identified those parts of the rail system which should be maintained and those which should be abandoned. It was recommended that the CNR and CPR should exchange ownership of certain portions of their networks, to achieve substantial reductions in maintenance costs and travel distances, and that a Prairie Rail Authority be established to determine the fate of a further 3,750 km of track which were not likely to be needed by the year 2000. Hall was also of the opinion that the Crowsnest Pass rail freight rates should be retained, but that the shortfall between the artificially low rates and the cost of moving the grain should be paid by the railways. Then, in 1981, in the Gilson report, a directly contrary recommendation was advanced. The Crow rate, said Gilson, should be abolished and a subsidy paid to farmers to compensate them for the higher freight rates that would follow. The aim in both cases was to give the railways an economic incentive for providing effective transportation. As the CPR Executive Vice-President has pointed out, 25 per cent of the freight volume in 1979 was handled under the Crow rates which moved grain at approximately one-sixth of the actual transportation cost, making the Crow rate the railway's prime revenue generation problem. In this, at least, the Government of Canada concurred, but the eventual solution was a compromise between the Hall and Gilson positions. The Crow rate was repealed by Parliament in 1983, but the difference between the new rate and the actual haulage costs is to be paid to the railways.

The Hall Commission further recommended that the grain handling facilities at Prince Rupert should be improved, and that, too, is being acted upon. The Government of Alberta and the Prince Rupert Grain Limited consortium have recently reached agreement on the construction of a new terminal with a capacity of 200,000 metric tons. The cost is expected to be well in excess of $200 million, about half of which will come from Alberta's Heritage Savings Trust Fund.

This commitment is concrete evidence of the seriousness with which the Government of Alberta regards the whole grain transportation issue, but it also raises a vital constitutional question. Indeed, grain transportation might well replace energy as the main source of contention between the provincial and federal governments. At present, the export of grain in Canada is controlled by two federal bodies, the Grain Transportation Authority and the Canadian Wheat Board. The former controls grain traffic on the railways and, before the new constitution was adopted, derived its ultimate authority from the British North America Act; the latter has sole control of all wheat, barley, and oats sold outside the country and is governed by the Canada Grains Act. However, the Government of Alberta has now taken independent actions, all of which are intended to increase the efficiency of grain export for Alberta farmers. It has purchased three inland grain terminals from the federal government, it has placed 1,000 newly-manufactured grain hopper cars into service, and it bought a share of the high-throughput Neptune Terminal in Vancouver. Accordingly, the Alberta government seems to be in a position to offer an alternative to the official grain marketing and transportation system. The provincial Minister of Agriculture has stated that a dual system should not hurt anyone, but critics charge that it represents a direct challenge to the Canadian grain marketing system and to the national transportation policy.

VIA Rail   The VIA company was formed to manage the passenger services of the CPR and CNR as a joint undertaking, rather like the Amtrak system in the United States. VIA's main contribution in Alberta has been to operate two daily transcontinental trains, the CPR's Canadian on the southern route through Calgary and the Kicking Horse Pass, and the CNR's Super Continental on the northern route through Edmonton and the Yellowhead Pass. In 1981, however, the Government of Canada announced that all VIA services with a cost recovery of less than 30 per cent were to be eliminated. This included, most controversially, the Winnipeg-Edmonton-Vancouver portion of the Super Continental run, which was to be replaced with some inter-city service between the major centres along the route. The policy was implemented in 1982. Since then, the only transcontinental service has followed the CPR route, and steps have been taken to enhance its market appeal — for example, adjusting the schedule so that the trip through the Rocky Mountains is during the daylight hours.

To be successful in the 1980s, it would appear that rail passenger service will have to be able to generate extremely high volumes of traffic. This means that it will probably be best suited to providing high speed transportation between very large centres. The Alberta government has therefore commissioned a preliminary study into the feasibility of developing a train able to travel at speeds in excess of 200 km/hr on the Calgary-Edmonton route. Such a development would again require federal-provincial co-operation, since the new train might have to use the existing right-of-way operated by VIA, and VIA might wish to operate its own fast train (at speeds of up to 144 km/hr). The possibility of an alternative route for an Alberta train is also being considered, which again raises the prospect of the Government of Alberta setting itself up in direct competition to a federal transport service. At the same time, however, critics charge that Alberta has been slow to consider the possibility of the high speed train, since it would be a major competitor to the airbus service operated by Pacific Western Airlines. Since the Alberta government has sold a major share of the airline, the development of a high speed train appears a more feasible venture.

Highway Transportation

By the end of the 1970s there were over 148,000 km of non-urban highways and roads in Alberta (Figure 7–3), though less than a tenth of this total was paved (13,000 km). The remainder (oiled - 13,000 km, gravelled - 98,000 km, and graded - 24,000 km) served chiefly to provide access to the sparsely populated rural areas. A network of forestry roads also covers some 60 per cent of the province, where it is an essential adjunct to the exploitation of the varied natural resources of the vast frontier region. (See Figure 2–4 in Chapter 2.)

Freight Transportation

As Winnipeg has declined in its traditional role of "Gateway to the West," internal flows between the major centres in western Canada have become increasingly important. Much of this freight is moved by road (Table 7–1), since trucks are highly competitive with trains in both cost and convenience terms, especially when small loads are required or it is necessary to deliver direct to a customer, for example, supermarkets and other city shops. Private commercial trucking now accounts for more than one-quarter of all cargo flow in Alberta, and some 400,000 trucks are registered and in operation. A large demand for general freight carriers has been generated, and numerous firms have emerged in response, usually from modest beginnings. For example, Canadian Freightways began as Chris Transport in 1935, with a single truck on the Lethbridge to Coutts run. The name was changed in 1938 and the company has since grown to have an investment of over $16 million in equipment, terminals, and maintenance shops and a staff of over 640 employees.

Trucks are also competitive for certain types of bulk commodity, as witnessed by the operations of Trimac Transportation System, which has its head office in Calgary. Trimac originated as a trucking company in Saskatchewan in the early 1930s, but it has since become the largest bulk carrier in Canada and one of the ten largest in North America. It is also the only bulk

Figure 7–3 Alberta's primary and secondary highway networks. In 1983 there were more than 13,000 km of primary highways and 14,000 km of secondary roads.
Source: Government of Alberta.

Primary highway ———
Secondary road ———

carrier operating from coast to coast. The company now provides a large variety of services for the energy industry, but transportation still accounts for approximately 40 per cent of its revenue. Trimac's five principal customers are Inland Cement, Gulf Canada, Imperial Oil, Lake Ontario Cement, and Canada Cement. Dry bulk materials, mostly cement, account for 34 per cent of Trimac's hauling revenue, while petroleum products account for 25 per cent and chemicals, paints, and resins 13 per cent. Sixty-nine per cent of the company's revenue comes from western Canada (30 per cent of it from Alberta), 21 per cent from Ontario, and the balance from the rest of Canada and the United States.

An important new influence on freight transportation in Alberta is the Dempster Highway, which was opened in 1979. One study completed for the Yukon government has actually predicted that Edmonton would cease to

Table 7-1

Average weekly commodity flow into and out of Edmonton and Calgary (in metric tons)

Commodity	Inbound		Outbound	
	Truck	Rail	Truck	Rail
General freight	6,323	7,166	6,807	―――
Non-perishable foodstuffs	7,947	4,285	518	2,202
Perishable foodstuffs	1,426	180	3,038	279
Heavy machinery	1,517	1,758	1,293	247
Metal products	3,666	6,217	2,950	112
Petroleum products	450	1,706	3,035	7,855
Bulk liquids and chemicals	549	484	612	2,891
Bulk dry chemicals and minerals	613	3,236	1,350	2,525
Forest products	3,382	12,052	1,535	356
Livestock	200	―――	358	294
Construction materials	926	3,924	2,202	218
Seed, feed, and feed products	202	126	798	2,683
Trailer-mobile homes	120	―――	389	21
Household goods	482	83	459	―――
Other goods	550	3,811	782	2,419
Total	28,354	45,027	26,125	22,100

Source: *Edmonton-Calgary Corridor Transportation Study.*

be the "Gateway to the North" for many shippers, because of the lower cost of hauling goods from Vancouver and other locations in British Columbia to Inuvik, Tuktoyaktuk, and other Mackenzie Delta communities. It is too early to know whether this prediction is correct, or what the ultimate effect of the Dempster Highway will be. But Edmonton is still the most logical service point for most communities in the Mackenzie Valley, particularly for goods originating in the prairie provinces or further east.

Passenger Transportation

In 1980 more than 2,400 commercial buses were registered in Alberta, including those operated by tour and charter companies. With respect to scheduled services, the industry is dominated by Greyhound Bus Lines of Canada, the head office of which is located in Calgary. The company began service in 1929, and its first two routes connected Calgary with Edmonton, and Nelson with Trail, British Columbia. The former is still one of the most lucrative routes in a system that now extends over 22,000 km in Ontario, all four western provinces, the Yukon and Northwest Teritories, and Alaska. Within Alberta, the only competition comes from another local company, Red Arrow Express, which offers regular service on the Edmonton-Calgary and Edmonton-Fort McMurray routes.

Among the Alberta charter companies, the best known is Brewster Gray Line which has been operating for over 70 years and is now a subsidiary of Greyhound of Canada. It operates sightseeing tours in the Canadian Rockies, and a tourist service between Calgary International Airport and Banff.

Ironically, the recession of the early 1980s worked to the advantage of Greyhound and other Alberta bus lines, as many passengers shifted from air travel to cheaper forms of transport. A new union terminal was opened in downtown Edmonton, and late in 1982 construction began on a $450 million project in Calgary, including a new terminal building.

Air Transportation

Air traffic in Alberta has increased dramatically over the past two decades. In 1963 air cargo shipments from the major airports totalled 6,000 tonnes and there were 800,000 passenger movements; by 1979 these volumes had risen to 46,000 and 5.5 million, respectively. The Edmonton-Calgary corridor was then the third busiest air route in Canada, and in the early 1980s it moved ahead of Toronto-Ottawa to become the second busiest route. There are now over 70 licensed airports, 23 heliports, 7 seaplane bases, and approximately 800 unlicensed airports in Alberta. The major facilities and routes are shown in Figure 7–4.

International Airports

Edmonton and Calgary international airports have experienced major increases in traffic in recent years. In particular, their increases in passenger traffic have been the largest among all 50 federally administered airports in Canada. There is also a striking difference in the volume of traffic through the two Alberta airports, with Calgary handling almost twice as many passengers as Edmonton. The explanation is that Edmonton's traffic is split between two airports, Edmonton International and Edmonton Municipal. The latter is limited to domestic service, notably to northern communities and to Calgary, a situation that raises fears about the attractiveness of Edmonton International to foreign carriers. The airbus service between Edmonton Municipal and Calgary International is so convenient, and Edmonton International is so far from the city, that much of the south-bound traffic from Edmonton and the north may be funnelled through Calgary.

The two international airports are served by a number of major Canadian and foreign airlines, including Air Canada, CP Air, Pacific Western Airlines,

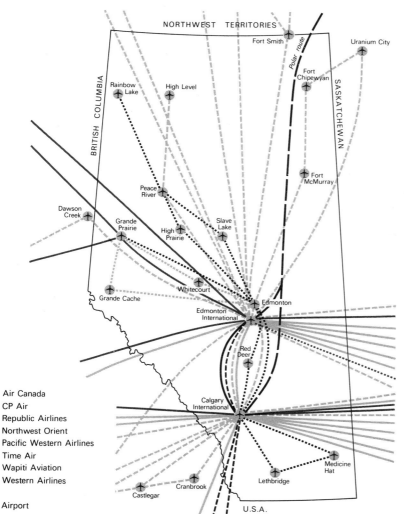

Figure 7–4 Alberta's major airports and the routes flown by scheduled airlines in 1982. Source: Government of Alberta.

Wardair Canada, Republic Airlines, Western Airlines, and Northwest Orient (Figure 7–4). In addition, British Airways and Lufthansa have obtained landing rights for services between Alberta and Europe, although the viability of these extra routes is in doubt, at least in the short term.

Wardair International

Wardair Limited, Canada's largest charter airline, was founded in 1953 by Max Ward of Edmonton. In 1957 the company purchased its first heavy aircraft, a Bristol Freighter, a plane which did much to supply and open up the remote Canadian Arctic islands. In 1961 an International Commercial Charter Licence was obtained and the company began the expansion that brought

Wardair's charter services to every international airport in Canada. It also continued to operate a northern service division out of Yellowknife, until the decline in northern business investment in the late 1970s. The Yellowknife base was closed in 1979.

In July 1980 the Wardair fleet comprised two 455 seat Boeing 747-200s and two 310 seat DC10-30s, and the company had announced its intention to buy six of the A310 European air buses. Yet 1979 had been an extremely difficult year; even the capital realized from the sale of the Northern Division could not save the company from a deficit of $2.5 million. An unhappy combination of factors was to blame, but the important point is that they were all beyond Wardair's control. They illustrate, though admittedly in extreme fashion, the hazards for a modern transportation industry which must function in a global economy. These factors in Wardair's 1979 experience included the compulsory grounding of all DC10 aircraft for safety inspections; a surge of competition from scheduled carriers selling charter class fares on the lucrative North Atlantic run; the Islamic Revolution in Iran which instituted a new round of oil and fuel price increases; severe inflation in the costs of labour, materials, outside services, and government user charges; and finally, the climb in interest rates. In addition, Edmonton's location came to be seen as a handicap for a transportation firm whose business is entirely international. Edmonton is still the head office but the main administrative centre and the principal service facilities are now in Toronto.

Pacific Western Airlines   This company, originally known as Central Columbia Airways Ltd., was started by Russ Baker in 1947. In 1949 he succeeded in obtaining a number of important contracts for the construction of the Kitimat-Kemano aluminum smelting and hydro power complex, followed in 1955 by a contract for the construction of the DEW line. By then, the company was developing into a major enterprise and, under its new name, Pacific Western Airlines, was ready to enter into scheduled passenger service. Further steps were taken in 1959, when PWA took over CP Air's routes from Edmonton to 18 points in the north, and in 1963, when Air Canada gave up the Edmonton-Calgary run and PWA introduced its Chieftain airbus service. This proved to be an overwhelming success, and by September 1980 the original four daily flights had been increased to 19 and the original DC-4s had been replaced by Boeing 737 jets with an intercity flying time of only 35 minutes. In the next phase of development, which began in 1983, the company introduced the new, wide-bodied Boeing 767s, each of which has a capacity of 230 passengers.

The main workhorses of PWA's cargo operations are the huge Hercules aircraft, each of which is capable of carrying 20,000 kg of freight. They are ideal for working in the north, since they can land on semi-prepared runways in the frozen tundra. Like Wardair, PWA has suffered from the downturn in northern development in recent years. It has diversified into other areas, such as tourist charter flights, though its northern service continues to be an important part of its operations.

In 1976 the Government of Alberta acquired a controlling interest in PWA, since it thought that the company had become vitally important to the business life of the province and there was some danger that control might pass to central Canadian investors. The British Columbia government was distressed when it was announced that the company's head office was to be moved from Vancouver to Calgary, but in February 1977 the Canadian Transport Commission ruled in favour of the Alberta government. Then, in May of the same year, PWA acquired Transair Airlines of Winnipeg, a move that extended the company's route network into Manitoba and Winnipeg's northern hinterland. It also consolidated PWA's position as one of Canada's leading regional carriers, and the only one in the western half of the country (Figure 7–5).

Figure 7–5 Scheduled routes flown by Pacific Western Airlines in western Canada in 1983.
Source: Pacific Western Airlines.

Time Air Limited   Since the 1960s, the evolution of the Canadian air transport system has been marked by the emergence of a well-developed hierarchy of scheduled carriers. As the two national airlines, Air Canada and CP Air, have concentrated increasingly on mainline service between the metropolitan centres, the regional carriers, like PWA, have expanded into a comprehensive coverage of the secondary centres, linking them to the regional capitals. That, in turn, has created new opportunities for local carriers offering a third level of service to much more restricted territories. The best Alberta example is Time Air of Lethbridge, a small but aggressive company which has struggled to survive in the face of PWA's domination of the Alberta market. Thus far, it has been able to fend off applications from PWA to provide jet service between Calgary and Lethbridge, the route that provides Time Air with its main revenue. It also expanded into northern Alberta, through the purchase of Gateway Aviation of Edmonton, and introduced the Canadian-built Dash 7 on its Calgary-Edmonton run to provide a downtown to downtown service of 1 hour 35 minutes (including 55 minutes flying time). In its attempt to lure away from the PWA airbus some of the 800,000 passengers who annually fly this route, five daily return flights were provided. The initial response was encouraging, but the future of Time Air as an independent carrier is nonetheless in doubt. In 1983 PWA acted decisively against Time Air's competitiveness by becoming a majority shareholder in the company.

Pipeline Systems   Alberta has over 100,000 km of pipelines, carrying the full range of petroleum products (Figure 7–6). This, in itself, is a major transportation achievement and one that was essential to the productive development of Alberta's energy resources. Within a decade after the Leduc discovery, some 2,150 km of oil trunk lines and a further 1,100 km of field gathering lines were in operation. The trunks included transmission lines for the transport of crude oil to the Alberta refineries, and so were chiefly focused on Edmonton. There were also two main gas pipeline systems serving the most concentrated part of the domestic market, Edmonton and Calgary, as well as a number of smaller systems serving peripheral cities such as Medicine Hat and Grande Prairie.

The second major type of pipeline system in Alberta, again required at an early stage in the growth of the modern petroleum industry, was designed to transport petroleum products to markets outside Alberta. As early as 1950, the Interprovincial Pipe Line Company had completed an oil pipeline from Edmonton to Lake Superior, with various feeder and distributor links to refineries in Saskatchewan, Manitoba, Minnesota, and Wisconsin. The system was extended to Sarnia in 1953, to Toronto in 1957, and to Montreal in 1976. Also in 1953, the Trans Mountain Oil Pipeline Company began to transport oil from Edmonton to the Pacific coast, supplying refineries in Kamloops, Vancouver, and northwestern Washington. In 1954, the Alberta government established the Alberta Gas Trunk Line Company (now Nova An Alberta Corporation) to build pipelines to carry natural gas to the province's boundaries, where it could be delivered into the transcontinental systems. These are the TransCanada Pipe Line system, which serves markets in the Midwest, Ontario, and the St. Lawrence Valley, and is now being extended to Nova Scotia; and the Westcoast Transmission system, which supplies British Columbia and the Pacific coast states, including California. Another major addition to Alberta's export capacity came in 1982, with the completion of the "pre-build" section of the proposed Alaska Highway gas pipeline (Figure 7–7), a project in which Nova was a major participant.

Another significant development in recent years has been the construction of special-product pipelines, as Alberta's petroleum industry diversifies into more sophisticated forms of processing and petrochemical manufacturing. For example, propane has become a valued by-product of natural gas processing. An extensive ethane gathering system has also been built to move this basic feedstock to major processing and chemical plants in Alberta, Sarnia, Ontario, and Green Springs, Ohio. The Alberta Gas Ethylene plant at Joffre is designed to be the heart of this complex transport, processing, and manufacturing system, since ethylene is the most important building block in the chain of petrochemical industries. Much of the ethylene, in its turn, is transported by pipeline to manufacturing plants in the Edmonton area, most notably at Fort Saskatchewan.

Figure 7–6 Systems of main oil and natural gas pipelines in Alberta in 1981. Source: Government of Alberta.

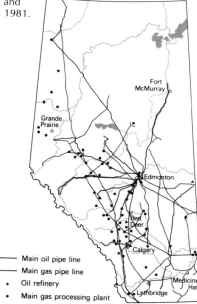

- —— Main oil pipe line
- —— Main gas pipe line
- ▲ Oil refinery
- • Main gas processing plant

- —— Proposed Alaska gas pipeline
- - - - Alternative Mackenzie delta pipeline

Figure 7–7 Proposed Alaska gas pipeline and possible all-Canadian pipeline from the Mackenzie delta. The "pre-build" section in Alberta and British Columbia is indicated by the heavier line. Source: Edmonton *Journal.*

By the late 1970s, Alberta had come to be criss-crossed with an intricate web of pipelines carrying many different commodities. Various public authorities were also showing belated awareness of the potential conflicts and hazards that could arise at the surface, particularly in the Edmonton area, where the greatest concentration of pipelines occurs. The accidental rupture of a propane line during road construction, and the forced evacuation of the Mill Woods community, revealed serious deficiencies in Edmonton's land development procedures. It was a dramatic warning of the danger of allowing the city to expand over pipeline rights-of-way, and led to a renewed interest in the idea of reserving corridors in which all future pipelines would be located. This follows the example of the Northeast Development Corridor, which the government has designated for pipelines and associated petrochemical plants between Edmonton and the oil sands and heavy oil fields of Fort McMurray, Cold Lake, and Lloydminster. The corridor has now been extended into the Strathcona industrial area on Edmonton's eastern outskirts, and the first pipes have been laid. As many as 30 pipelines may eventually be accommodated there.

Also in prospect is the use of pipelines to transport other kinds of commodities. The Alberta Research Council has been pursuing this idea for many years, particularly for the export of coal through west coast ports. The growing trade with Japan has finally made the technique seem more feasible, and the possibility of building a coal slurry pipeline from the Hinton area is under serious investigation.

Electric Power Transmission

Electricity is vital to the modern urban-industrial economy, and the transmission of electric power from generating sites to ultimate consumers is as much part of a modern transport system as the movement of people and goods. Moreover, to try to ensure a secure supply to all consumers at all times, it is now common practice for power production systems to be linked together in a single transmission grid. Alberta is no exception (Figure 7–8). The power plants are widely dispersed and there are three major producers, Transalta Utilities Corporation, Alberta Power Ltd., and Edmonton Power, supplemented by some smaller municipal utilities, but the only communities of any size not connected to the provincial grid are Jasper and Fort Chipewyan.

Alberta is currently ranked fourth among Canadian provinces as a producer of electrical energy. Its net capacity in 1979 was 4,800 MW and the actual production was about 20,000 GWh. Approximately 75 per cent was supplied by coal and 18 per cent by natural gas, making thermal plants by far the major source of Alberta's electricity. The hydro plants, although quite numerous especially in the Bow Valley upstream from Calgary, are all small.

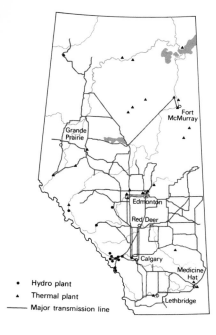

Figure 7–8 Alberta's electric power transmission grid and locations of electricity generating stations in 1981.
Source: Government of Alberta.

In 1979 they accounted for only 7 per cent of Alberta's production. This situation could change as steps are taken to reduce the dependence on non-renewable fuels, particularly by tapping the huge potential of the northern rivers. The controversial Slave River project is but the first to be promoted. The possibility of developing a prairie grid, with power drawn mainly from northern Manitoba, has also been discussed but no agreement has yet been reached. The weakened demand for power during the economic downturn of the early 1980s, added to the Alberta government's preference for developing its own resources before those of other provinces, seems to have pushed this ambitious scheme into a distant future.

Telecommunications

The most important company in the telecommunications field is Alberta Government Telephones (AGT). In 1908 Alberta's first provincial government incurred the first provincial debt by purchasing the Bell Telephone Company operations in the province. Between 1908 and 1922 the new company built telephone lines to 20,000 farms. The venture was a money loser to begin with but it had enormous social impact, since 70 per cent of Albertans were living in rural areas at that time. AGT now provides telephone and related services to all parts of the province, except the city of Edmonton where the local telephone system has always been operated as a

Figure 7-9 Long-range scenarios for the development of transport facilities and for the distribution of urban growth in the Edmonton-Calgary corridor.
Sources: Edmonton-Calgary Corridor Transportation Study and P. J. Smith and Denis B. Johnson, *The Edmonton-Calgary Corridor*, pp. 128–129.

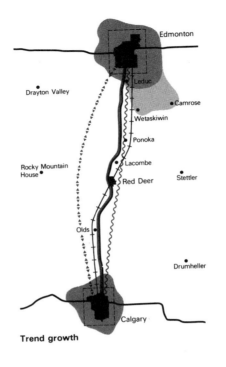

Trend growth

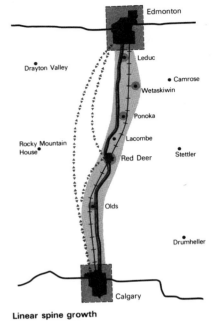

Linear spine growth

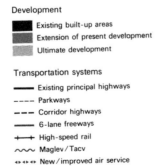

Development

■ Existing built-up areas
▓ Extension of present development
▒ Ultimate development

Transportation systems

——— Existing principal highways
- - - - Parkways
— - — Corridor highways
———— 6-lane freeways
+–+–+ High-speed rail
∿∿∿ Maglev / Tacv
◄►◄►◄► New / improved air service

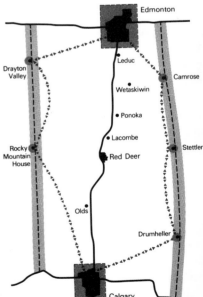

New corridor growth

municipal utility. The possibility of amalgamating the two systems has been discussed from time to time, but it has never won strong support in Edmonton.

Today, AGT is known as a leading innovator in telecommunications technology. It was the first telephone company in North America to make use of the new, highly efficient fibre optics technology. It is also involved in computer communication networks such as DATAPAC, and is a pioneer in the use of the VIDON system for home energy management and security, and for gaining access to Statistics Canada's information source, TELIDON.

Transportation and Development Policy

The most exciting transportation developments are likely to take place in the Edmonton-Calgary corridor, since this is where the greatest increase in demand can be expected to occur. The Edmonton-Calgary Corridor Transportation Study (ECCTS), carried out in 1976, suggested three long-range scenarios (Figure 7–9). In the first, continued and unchecked growth of the two metropolitan centres was allowed for. The implications for transport facility planning included the upgrading of Highway 2 to six lanes; improved air service, probably incorporating STOL (short take-off and landing) and perhaps VTOL (vertical take-off and landing) aircraft; and, especially if the Edmonton Municipal Airport is closed, the introduction of a high speed rail facility such as a MAGLEV (magnetic levitation) or TACV (tracked air cushion vehicle) system. The second scenario called for restricted growth in Edmonton and Calgary and the spread of development into a number of centres within the corridor. This was referred to as the linear spine growth option, and would require facilities appropriate for comparatively short, inter-city trips. Automobile travel would also be favoured over the high-speed, high-technology orientation of a transportation system designed to move large numbers of people between Edmonton and Calgary.

In the third scenario, the option of developing a completely new transportation corridor, to either the east or west of the existing highway, was considered. This would have the advantage of revitalizing settlements which are at present experiencing no growth or a decline in their population, but this plan would also generate negative environmental effects. The western route would entail a loss of recreational land while an eastern corridor would consume agricultural land.

There can be no doubting the central role that the Alberta government sees for transport facilities and services in the provincial economy. In 1973, at the Western Economic Opportunities Conference, the premiers of the four western provinces singled out transportation problems as their primary economic grievance with the federal government. This presumably explains why the Alberta government would like its own independent grain transportation system, why it acquired Pacific Western Airlines, and why it is so interested in technological innovations such as a high-speed Edmonton-Calgary train and a coal slurry pipeline. In a recent interview, the Alberta premier indicated just how seriously transportation difficulties were hindering his government's goal of economic diversification:

> The dilemma we face is we are a small province, far from markets, with no accessibility to an ocean port. . . . We can't be developing products here that have a large transportation component to them. . . . The areas we see for diversification aren't heavy industry areas. Most of the traditional heavy industries won't end up here.

The prime emphasis is therefore being placed on agricultural processing, finance, research, and petrochemical industries. These, along with the electronics, computer, and telecommunication industries, are experiencing high growth rates in all countries with advanced economies, unlike the traditional heavy industries.

As yet, there appears to be no explicit transportation policy which either the federal or the provincial government has promulgated for Alberta, but implicit policies may be discerned. The government of Canada appears to be concerned with: 1) preventing destructive competition (hence the creation of VIA); 2) maintaining the advantages of large scale operations (CN's purchase of the NAR system is an appropriate example); 3) the protection of the consumer from monopolies (in 1980 the Department of Justice initiated court proceedings against 20 western freight carriers for price fixing); 4) fostering national social and economic development; 5) eliminating regional economic disparities. The Alberta government appears to be most concerned with a policy of economic development and diversification within the province. This resulted in its purchase of PWA and its involvement in upgrading the grain transportation system. It can only be hoped that these different policy initiatives will prove, in future, to be complementary and productive.

Supplemental Readings   *Edmonton-Calgary Corridor Transportation Study. Technical Report No. 1: Socio-Economic Background and Growth Patterns.* Edmonton: Transport Canada and Alberta Transportation, ca. 1975.
Edmonton-Calgary Corridor Transportation Study: Transportation Alternatives Report. Edmonton: Transport Canada and Alberta Transportation, ca. 1975.
Gilson, J.C. *Western Grain Transportation.* Ottawa: Supply and Services Canada, 1982.

Hall, E. M. *Grain and Rail in Western Canada. The Report of the Grain Handling and Transportation Commission.* Volumes 1 and 2. Ottawa: Supply and Services Canada, 1977.

Ironside, R. G. and Peterson, D. D. "Edmonton's Wholesale Relationships with Northwest Canada." *The Canadian Geographer* 26 (1982): 207–224.

Smith, P. J. and Johnson, D. B. *The Edmonton-Calgary Corridor.* Edmonton: The University of Alberta, Department of Geography, 1978.

- transportation plays a large role in AB's development; AB is:
    - land-locked
    - resource-based
    - small-pop'n base
    - peripheral

- grain and oil movement are critical to economic development

- grain: 3.7 million tonnes annually, have to collected from distributed producers and moved to a distant port

8 The Industrial Economy
Locational Patterns and Spatial Relationships

B. M. Barr

The purpose of this chapter is to describe the major patterns and functional characteristics of Alberta's space-economy and, in the process, to explore a number of basic themes in Alberta's economic development. Three main topics will be discussed:

1. *The locational patterns and functional relationships of the main elements of Alberta's economic geography.*
2. *Alberta's changing relations with overseas, continental, national, and regional economies.*
3. *The implications for Alberta, today and in the future, of the heartland-hinterland or core-periphery organization of the space-economies of both Canada and Alberta.*

Although many analyses of Alberta's economy focus on the spatial spread of energy production within Alberta, and on the changing nature and importance of its access to world markets, changes in the province's economic geography can also be viewed in terms of the world's changing access to Alberta. This is particularly true of those fundamental physical dimensions of the Alberta economy which support the primary activities that are its mainstays. As agricultural land and energy resources closer to the world's heartland economies and to the core or heartland of the Canadian economic and population system (southern Ontario and Quebec) have been lost or exhausted, the demand for Alberta's resources has increased. As described in previous chapters, this has generated sufficient revenues to overcome a difficult agricultural and forest environment, to probe into the underlying strata, and to offset the long distances over which Alberta's primary commodities must be transported to heartland markets (Figure 8–1). The

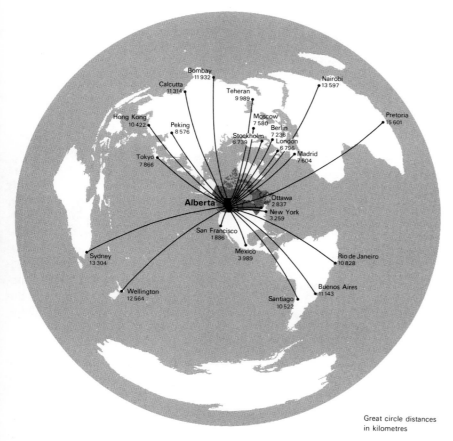

Figure 8–1   Great circle distances from Alberta to selected world cities.
Source: Government of Alberta.

Great circle distances in kilometres

basic themes which characterize Alberta's economic geography in the 1980s thus stem from its experience throughout the twentieth century as a major (but not dominant) agricultural region within Canada, and its recent rapid growth as the nation's key producer of energy. These themes can be itemized as follows:

1. Alberta's persistent role as a hinterland economy.
2. The reduced friction of distance between Alberta and the world's heartlands.
3. The critical importance of the quality of the surface and subsurface physical environments to the province's economic geography.
4. The dominance of primary industry in the provincial economy.

5. Export-led growth of economic activity that is intensive in its dependence on capital and technology.
6. Structural imbalance in all sectors of the industrial economy.
7. Strong market, capital, and technological links with the North American continental economy, but an increasing orientation to the markets and suppliers of the Pacific basin.
8. Vulnerability to economic, corporate, and political forces from outside Alberta.
9. Metropolitan dominance of the location of all economic activity other than primary production.

Alberta's Industrial Economy
Sectoral Components

In the most developed economies of the modern world, industry is customarily considered to comprise four sectors: *primary* (farming, forestry, mining); *secondary* (manufacturing and processing, construction, generation of electricity); *tertiary* (wholesale and retail trade, transportation, and consumer services of all kinds, whether provided by private or by public agencies); and *quaternary* (management, finance, professional services, education, research, government administration, communications, and the arts). Now, given the increasing importance of development planning and forecasting, a fifth sector, *quinary* industry, can be added to the list. All five sectors are present in Alberta, although their importance varies throughout the province and in relation to Canada as a whole (Table 8–1). (Discussed further in Chapter 10.)

The primary and secondary sectors are usually given prominence in regional production accounts because they pertain directly to the production of the wealth that is redistributed, managed, regulated or facilitated by the other sectors. Certainly, Alberta is a highly visible producer of energy and agricultural products, in both raw and processed form. With British Colum-

Table 8-1
Sectoral distribution of labour force in Alberta and Canada* (in percentages)

	Primary	Secondary	Tertiary	Unclassified	Total
Alberta	14.1	19.4	66.5	–––	100.0
Canada	7.1	26.4	65.8	0.7	100.0
Alberta as percentage of Canada	17.7	6.6	9.0	–––	8.9

*Compiled by averaging monthly statistics for December 1978, March 1979, June 1979, and September 1979.

Source: Statistics Canada, catalogue no. 71-0001, *The Labour Force* (Ottawa, 1971).

bia and Saskatchewan, it has been one of the foci of recent economic growth in Canada. In many aspects of its geography and economy, however, Alberta plays a modest role in the Canadian domain (Table 8–2): it produces approximately 11 per cent of the national commodity output; accounts for 11 per cent of national employment; and is home to 8 per cent of the Canadian population. At the same time, it has nearly all of Canada's oil sands and heavy oil, 86 per cent of the proven reserves of conventional crude oil, 78 per cent of the proven natural gas reserves, and almost half of all coal reserves. It is also the fourth most important Canadian province in volume of reserves of merchantable timber and in area of productive forests. By value of production, in 1978, Alberta accounted for nearly one-fifth of Canada's total agricultural output, 100 per cent of its synthetic crude oil, 85 per cent of conventional crude oil, 92 per cent of natural gas, and 33 per cent of coal output.

Table 8-2

Census value added, Alberta and Canada (in percentages)

	Alberta			Canada		Alberta as percentage of Canada	
	1971	1976	1978*	1971	1976	1971	1976
Agriculture	12.4	9.2	8.9	6.7	7.3	17.4	19.2
Mining	39.6	50.7	53.3	9.6	13.8	38.8	56.0
Other natural resource industries	.3	.3	.3	2.3	2.1	1.4	2.0
All primary industries	52.3	60.2	62.5	18.6	23.2	26.5	39.4
Electric power	2.9	1.9	1.9	4.3	3.8	6.4	4.3
Manufacturing	20.9	14.4	15.5	58.1	51.9	3.4	4.2
Construction	23.9	23.5	20.1	19.0	21.1	11.8	17.0
All secondary industries	47.7	39.8	37.5	81.4	76.8	5.5	7.9
Total	100.0	100.0	100.0	100.0	100.0	9.4	15.2

*Alberta Statistical Review 1978 (Edmonton, October 1979), p. 45.
Source: Statistics Canada, Survey of Production, 1976 (Ottawa, 1978).

The spectacular growth of the Alberta economy during the 1970s reflected the growing importance of resource extraction, and the growing demand for energy in Canada, the United States, and the Pacific basin, especially Japan. The continuance of these high levels of demand is far from assured, and the prices at which Alberta's resources enter national and world markets is likely to be the major determinant of the province's future prosperity. Conflicts in petroleum pricing and taxation between the federal and provincial governments have caused uncertainty among investors in the Alberta petroleum in-

Table 8-3
Mineral production in Alberta and Canada, 1978 (in percentages)

	Metals	Non-metals	Fuels	Structural materials	Total	$\$ \times 10^3$
Alberta	–––	1.1	97.6	1.3	100	9,749,382
Canada	28.1	7.9	57.1	6.9	100	19,661,339
Alberta as percentage of Canada	–––	7.3	84.7	9.1	49.6	

Source: Statistics Canada, *Canada's Mineral Production (Preliminary Estimate)* (Ottawa, 1979).

dustry at a time when various jurisdictions in the United States, a major alternative area of opportunity for Alberta capital, are stimulating investment in the expansion of petroleum reserves and coal extraction. The discovery of substantial reserves of oil and natural gas in eastern and northern Canada may also divert development opportunities and income from Alberta.

The long-term significance of oil, gas, and coal to Alberta (Table 8–3) is unlikely to diminish, but periodic fluctuations in world demand and continuous squabbling between the federal and provincial governments, serve as reminders of Alberta's vulnerability to external economic and political forces. They underline the long-felt need to diversify economic activity into products manufactured from petroleum feedstocks and into other productive sectors, including agriculture, which are not subject to the same vicissitudes.

Alberta's manufacturing economy is strongly dependent upon the primary sector. Manufacturers in Alberta chiefly tend to process agricultural, petroleum, wood, or non-metallic mineral commodities, or to engage in custom manufacture and fabrication for the resource development and construction sectors (Table 8–4). "Downstream" benefits from the development of regional resources are only just starting to accrue to Alberta, notably in the ethylene complex centred on Joffre (near Red Deer) and in the Fort Saskatchewan production chain of vinyl chloride monomer, ethylene oxide and glycol, and chlor-alkali. Whether these really portend the emergence of a more sophisticated manufacturing base in Alberta depends on a variety of unpredictable factors: the political and social will of Albertans; changes to a freight rate structure which is biased in favour of raw and semi-processed materials; and the ability of central Canadian interests to prevent their own firms from relocating in Alberta to ensure access to raw materials. In the near future, provincial prosperity seems likely to depend on the continued output of the primary industrial sectors: agriculture, petroleum, coal, and timber.

Each dollar of agricultural production and of petroleum extraction has similar multiplier effects in the provincial economy, but the direct contri-

Table 8-4

Value added by manufacturing in Alberta, 1971 and 1977 (in percentages)

Industrial groups*	1971	1977
Food and beverage	26.5	24.0
Petrochemical, coal, and synthetic textile	16.1	17.5
Non-food and general manufacturing	14.7	14.5
Wood, paper, and allied industries	10.9	12.2
Primary metals, engineering, transportation industries	22.1	22.2
Non-metallic mineral products	9.7	9.6
Total	100.0	100.0

*These groups follow the Standard Industrial Classification, but industries whose production statistics are confidential are not included in the table.

Sources: Statistics Canada, *Manufacturing Industries of Canada: National and Provincial Areas, 1977* (Ottawa: 1979); Statistics Canada, *Manufacturing Industries of Canada: National and Provincial Areas, 1972* (Ottawa, 1975).

bution of agriculture to the net value of provincial commodity production is approximately one-sixth that of mining (chiefly oil and gas extraction). Together, agriculture and mining dominate the primary and secondary sectors, comprising approximately five-eighths of the total value added in 1978 (Table 8–2). Construction accounts for another fifth and exceeds the combined total of manufacturing and the generation of electricity. In Canada as a whole, the share of manufacturing and the production of electricity in the value of commodity production is approximately equal to that of agriculture and mining in Alberta, while primary activity accounts for roughly the same share as manufacturing and construction in Alberta. Thus, the Alberta economy and the national economy are mirror images of each other in respect to these important generators of wealth.

Yet, despite this vital difference, Alberta and Canada are similar in their total structure of employment. Manufacturing employment is not as characteristic of the Alberta goods-producing labour force as it is of Canada as a whole, but, in both cases, manufacturing and primary employment are greatly overshadowed by the service sector. Although Alberta's wealth-generating base differs from that of Canada, the importance of the service sector to each is the same (Table 8–1).

Spatial Structure

Primary activity, especially in agriculture, is the most widely distributed economic activity in Alberta. With its associated consumer-oriented tertiary functions it is responsible for a continuous population distribution throughout the "ecumene," or the settled southern half of the province. Elsewhere the settlement pattern and population distribution are discontinuous, sporadic, and punctiform, characteristics associated with oil and gas wells, coal mines, timber harvesting and processing, access roads, and the basic transportation systems of the frontier zone. Yet, because of the mobility of the related service personnel, the residences of employees in these various activities correspond to the intermediate and higher order places of the provincial settlement and tertiary-industrial systems. (Discussed in detail in Chapter 2.) Together, agriculture and petroleum extraction are the dominant elements supporting the spatially extensive portion of the provincial settlement system.

Table 8-5
Manufacturing in Calgary and Edmonton census metropolitan areas as a percentage of Alberta value added

	1971	1975
Calgary	29.9	32.6
Edmonton	44.2	41.0

Source: Statistics Canada, *Manufacturing Industries of Canada: Geographical Distribution, 1971* (Ottawa, 1975); Statistics Canada, *Manufacturing Industries of Canada: Subprovincial Areas, 1975* (Ottawa, 1979).

Secondary, quaternary, and quinary industries are primarily associated with the two metropolitan areas of Alberta (Table 8–5) although some manufacturing activity, reflecting local markets or localized resources, is to be found in other towns and cities. (Discussed further in Chapter 10.) Some government services have also been decentralized to non-metropolitan locations, and some firms have their headquarters and associated personnel near their production facilities. (This decentralization is examined further in Chapter 9.) Still, metropolitan dominance of these sectors is a predominant and persistent characteristic of Alberta's spatial economy. Edmonton and Calgary simply offer superior locations, due to their broadly-based office and industrial environments, their extensive communication arteries to national and international suppliers and markets, their multifaceted agglomerative economies, and the locational inertia of their existing firms and institutions. The factors affecting the spatial distribution of Alberta's economic sectors therefore lend themselves to a metropolitan/non-metropolitan analysis.

METROPOLITAN CENTRES: Edmonton and Calgary have the largest shares of many provincial activities and are the foci of most higher order functions in their respective regions. Edmonton, as the centre of provincial government, is the chief location of quaternary and quinary employment in the civil service. Calgary, as the head office centre of the province's multi-national, multi-locational petroleum industry, has the largest share of the quaternary and quinary employment generated by that industry. Canadian crown corporations and financial institutions located in Alberta similarly favour these two areas, as does defense employment, despite the importance of such non-metropolitan centres as Cold Lake, Wainwright, and Suffield. For all the publicity to the contrary, neither private nor government employment in the quaternary and quinary sectors has been decentralized to any degree. For many operational and economic reasons it is likely to maintain its concentrated profile in the foreseeable future.

Calgary and Edmonton also are the main manufacturing, distribution, wholesale, and medical centres for Alberta. Ease of communication with national or international industrial heartlands, plus the economies of scale realized by heartland manufacturers, have led Albertans to rely on producers located elsewhere for modern industrial goods. The points of entry to the Alberta settlement system are provided by wholesalers, warehousers, and distributors in the province's two metropolitan centres, which are also the major centres of trucking and rail services in Alberta. In a somewhat similar manner, the location of health care facilities favours a hierarchical system in which the most complex and least frequently required services are located in the two metropolitan centres while routine services are performed by lower level centres. (Discussed in Chapter 9.) Many industrial service and personal-care systems thus appear to require a catchment area comprising at least one metropolitan centre and its associated hinterland in order to function. These systems locate in the metropolitan centres but utilize the provincial highway system to serve a large hinterland, thereby precluding the development of similar facilities in the tributary cities.

In addition to being the transportation foci of Alberta, Calgary and Edmonton are the sites of localized externalities in the form of agglomeration economies. In other words, many economic activities benefit from being located in larger centres, not just because they have their own special links with other firms for materials and information, but because the very concentration of so many different activities in one place, or agglomeration, allows them to find every service they need at the lowest acceptable cost. For many activities, the metropolitan centre provides a large market close at hand with considerable savings in distribution and access costs and the opportunity to profit from the economies of operating on a large scale. Metropolitan firms can therefore expect to have lower average costs of operation and production than non-metropolitan ones. Indeed, for many firms a location outside the metropolitan area is economically unfeasible and psychologically unacceptable. A powerful spatial inertia attaches to the metropolitan centres, all but excluding the smaller urban places from a wide range of economic activities.

NON-METROPOLITAN LOCATIONAL ENVIRONMENTS: The attractions of Edmonton and Calgary notwithstanding, the non-metropolitan centres do have some offsetting advantages. Seven will be reviewed here.

1. Capital-intensive resource processing.

   Timber and some forms of petroleum are highly localized materials; they undergo significant weight loss when processed. In addition, some petroleum commodities, such as sour natural gas, oil sands, and heavy oils, must have harmful properties removed before they can be shipped to market. Capital-intensive, basic processing and primary manufacturing are therefore attracted to areas of resource extraction. They strongly affect the economic bases of many small communities, particularly during construction periods, when labour requirements are high. After start-up, however, when their employment demands have shrunk relative to the construction labour forces, the volume of raw materials consumed, and the value of capital investment in the facilities, their economic effects are concentrated in comparatively few places of medium size. Alberta has over 300 gas processing plants outside the metropolitan areas, but their local labour forces are miniscule. Only a few centres, such as Grande Prairie, Fort McMurray, Red Deer (Joffre), Fort Saskatchewan, Redwater, and Medicine Hat, are noteworthy as locations of capital-intensive, petroleum-based manufacturing. Plants in these centres produce semi-finished commodities which find their ways into the manufacturing processes of yet other plants, most of which are located in communities outside Alberta. But although these commodities have not yet generated much linkage with other industries within Alberta, their potential importance to the economic geography of the province is considerable. With reference to the plastics industry, for example, it was said in *Canada Commerce*, September 1980, that "for every job in primary extraction of oil and gas there are 100 jobs downstream to the final manufacture and sale of the finished product. And while every $24 worth of crude oil becomes $35 worth of gasoline, the same amount of crude oil becomes $3500 worth of plastic widgets."

2. Resource-oriented agricultural processing and related manufactures.

   Many agricultural commodities cannot be moved long distances without processing. Spoilage and weight-loss dictate that processing facilities must be resource-oriented. Many smaller communities in Alberta have substantial local employment related to grain, meat, milk, poultry and eggs, sugar, honey, oil seeds, animal feed, seed cleaning, and vegetable processing. Some of these processors have also attracted packaging and processing equipment manufacturers to their communities, an example of a limited, but significant, backward linkage. (A "backward" linkage is one in which a manufacturer buys some other manufacturer's products; in a "forward" linkage, the same manufacturing firm will sell its products to another manufacturer or to a distributor.)

3. Resource-oriented agricultural implement and oil-field equipment manufacturing.
   Producers in these industries perform custom-service manufacturing for
   the primary industrial sectors. Although initially oriented to local markets,
   some firms have grown into major producers of specialized equipment,
   sometimes serving national and international markets. The advantages of
   non-metropolitan location lie in the proximity of producers and
   consumers, the availability and suitability of local labour, and the basic
   dependence on a diversified (and hence safe) local market comprising
   both service and manufacturing.
4. Government and non-government institutional employment.
   Federal and provincial government employment in penitentiaries and in
   institutions for the disabled and the aged is sporadic in its distribution but
   locally significant, because these facilities are labour intensive. Private
   religious institutions are also important employers in some communities.
   Thus, towns like Drumheller, Bowden, Fort Saskatchewan, Red Deer,
   Peace River, Three Hills, Ponoka, and Claresholm are strongly influenced
   by the contribution of institutional services to their employment structure.
5. Government educational employment.
   As the director of post-secondary education in Alberta, the provincial
   government has been responsible for the establishment and support of
   four community colleges, five special-purpose regional colleges and two
   adult vocational centres in medium-sized centres. The University of Lethbridge, established in 1967, also accounts for considerable employment
   and student residential location in the major centre of southern Alberta;
   and Athabasca University will similarly broaden the economic base of the
   town of Athabasca, when its relocation from Edmonton is complete. The
   consolidation of rural school districts in selected accessible central places
   has been one of the centralizing forces noted in Chapter 2.
6. Government non-metropolitan locational assistance programs.
   The governments of Canada and Alberta have numerous agencies and
   programs to encourage and assist manufacturers and processors to locate
   outside the metropolitan centres. By lending capital at preferred rates and
   under favourable conditions, by providing development grants, by as-
   sisting with infrastructural investment, and by various related schemes,
   both governments attempt to ensure that the backwash effects of metropolitan growth do not denude Edmonton and Calgary's vast hinterland of
   its human resources and economic potential. Although co-operation between the federal and provincial governments is less comprehensive in
   Alberta than in the other nine provinces, federal aid since 1969 has been
   directed into the nutrient processing industry in central and southern
   Alberta and a widely publicized native employment scheme at Lesser
   Slave Lake. The Federal Business Development Bank has been active as
   well, providing loans to entrepreneurs in all parts of Alberta. Yet, as men-

tioned in Chapter 6, it is the provincial government that is most able to influence the economic landscape through its schemes to support agriculture, agricultural processing, and non-metropolitan manufacturing, and through its manipulation of resource production royalty arrangements.

7. Decommissioned military bases.

Numerous military bases, decommissioned after the Second World War, have served as seedbed sites for light industry, particularly for the manufacture of recreational vehicles, relocatable housing, and shelter systems. With their large hangars and concrete aprons available at nominal cost, these bases have served, at various times, as the venue of major manufacturing operations in Grande Prairie, Lethbridge, Fort Macleod, Claresholm, High River, Penhold, Vulcan, and Medicine Hat. They have helped to demonstrate that labour-intensive light manufacturing is indeed one of the viable options for non-metropolitan economic activity in Alberta, particularly if the start-up costs can be kept low.

Dominance and Dependence: Heartland/Hinterland or Core/Periphery Perspectives on Alberta's Economic Geography

The division of Alberta's locational environments into metropolitan and non-metropolitan sectors can also be interpreted as a manifestation, at the provincial scale, of the value of the heartland/hinterland paradigm for the explanation of spatial patterns of economic development. This paradigm postulates that core or developed regions and nations dominate the economic and political structure of peripheral or relatively undeveloped regions. Thus, in the Alberta case, the metropolitan centres are the obvious foci of the space-economy, and the Edmonton-Calgary region dominates the urban system, the distribution of population, and the location of secondary, tertiary, quaternary, and quinary industry. Furthermore, the heartland/hinterland model is a useful means by which to evaluate the overseas, continental, and national economic relations of Alberta.

Alberta and Overseas Regions

Alberta is an important contributor of basic food and industrial materials to countries in Europe and the Pacific Basin, particularly Japan. Grain and coal (Figure 8–2) are the leading overseas exports, though in the past two decades Alberta's international trade has diversified into sulphur, processed agricultural commodities and specialized livestock products, relocatable housing, oilfield and specialized transportation equipment, petroleum expertise, and agricultural implements. Yet the profile of the province's economic relations with offshore areas is still narrowly developed in comparison with the myriad industrial and consumer products, and the volumes of capital and technology, which enter Alberta to sustain the primary sector and the high standard of consumption of its residents. Alberta's dependence on overseas

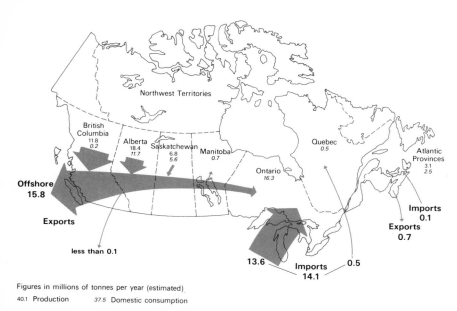

Figure 8–2 Coal production, consumption, and direction of trade for the Canadian provinces, in 1981. The arrows are proportional to the net volume of coal movements (i.e. the difference between the total amounts of coal shipped in and out of a province).
Source: Government of Alberta.

suppliers is especially pronounced in automobiles, electronics, clothing and general consumer goods, specialty foods and beverages, and in the origins of capital investment, real estate funds and equity capital.

Alberta's trade with overseas regions does not generally reflect strong bilateral arrangements between the province and foreign nations, but should be seen as part of the larger pattern of Canadian trade. Nevertheless, Alberta's increasing orientation towards Japanese markets and manufactured goods dominates the overseas economic relations of the province and demonstrates its high degree of dependence on the world's third largest industrial economy. By contrast, our shipments of grain and oilfield transportation equipment to the world's second largest economy, the USSR, do not result in a noticeable reciprocal movement of consumer or capital goods to Alberta.

Alberta and the Continental Economy

Alberta's dominant economic relations are within North America. The province's integration into continental production systems reflects strong international relations with parts of the United States (the world's largest industrial economy) and Mexico, and important, although often contrived, national relations with central Canada.

ALBERTA AND NON-CANADIAN NORTH AMERICA: Alberta's economic relations with North American countries south of Canada are dominated by the flow of oil, natural gas (Figures 8–3 and 8–4), and tourists to the United States, and

Figure 8–3 Oil production, consumption, and direction of trade for the Canadian provinces in 1981.
Source: Government of Alberta.

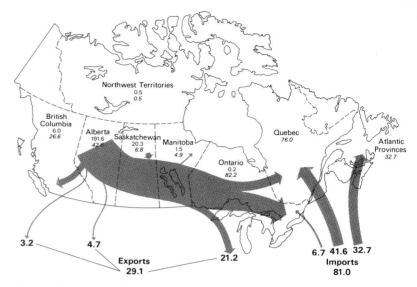

Figures in thousands of cubic metres per day

220.1 Production   272.3 Domestic consumption

Figure 8–4 Natural gas production, consumption, and direction of trade for the Canadian provinces in 1981.
Source: Government of Alberta.

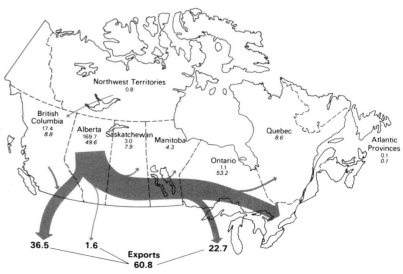

Figures in millions of cubic metres per day

192.1 Production   132.5 Domestic consumption

by the movement in the opposite direction of investment capital, technology, expertise, corporate control, consumer durables, agricultural machinery, food, and tourists. Alberta's relations with Mexico are much weaker but also demonstrate the importance of raw materials, food, and tourists in the pattern of economic relations.

Given the spatial progression of the search for petroleum in North America throughout the twentieth century, and the importance of American firms in that search, Alberta has been, in many ways, a northward extension of areas dominated by financial and corporate controls exercised through New York, Houston, Dallas/Fort Worth, and Denver. Direct American influence on Alberta's petroleum industry has been manifested in two ways: in the contribution that American firms have made to the discovery, development, processing, and marketing of the petroleum resource; and in the deliveries of Alberta natural gas and oil (albeit in patterns subject to fluctuations in protective legislation and policy) to markets in the Midwestern and Pacific coast states. Indirectly, the American influence has been reflected in the movement of American entrepreneurs into Alberta, where they have established small manufacturing and petroleum service firms, and in the purchase of American engineering expertise and production technology for Alberta's energy industries.

Alberta's role as a primary-producing appendage to the continental economy dominated by the United States displays the classic properties of the heartland/hinterland paradigm, but it also shows that the paradigm takes on spatially multilateral forms. While Alberta is a producer of raw materials and income for American purchasers and investors, the reciprocal flow of high value commodities from the United States to Alberta has diverse origins. The energy shipped from Alberta enters the industrial economies of the Midwest, California, and the Pacific Northwest, part of which in turn include Alberta in their extensive markets for high value-added, often sophisticated capital and consumer goods. These range from pocket calculators and household gadgets to the most comprehensive forms of electronic, aeronautical, and production technology available in the world. Alberta also relies on American manufacturing expertise in developed petroleum-extraction regions for oilfield equipment ranging from drilling technology through development and extraction systems to the compressing and monitoring equipment required to move oil and gas through their gathering, processing, and marketing systems. As well, New York acts as arbiter for the host of financial transactions required to develop and sustain the complex petroleum and service economy which has developed in Alberta. Many areas of the American southwest and California, not associated with either corporate or technological dominance, are essential suppliers of food to Alberta.

ALBERTA AND CANADA: The issues, problems, and characteristics of Alberta's spatial and functional relationships with Canada are well-documented and widely, although variously, understood. As in its relations with the United States, Alberta's relations with Canada display classic traits of the heartland/hinterland paradigm. Alberta is the prime domestic supplier of energy to the national economy. (Alberta's energy industry is reviewed in Chapter 5.) It is also a major contributor of basic foodstuffs, and a substantial market for Canadian manufacturers, especially those producing agricultural, engineering, and transportation equipment. Increasingly, too, it is a market for the great variety of capital goods and final-demand goods that are deemed essential to a developing producer economy which is also a sophisticated consumer economy.

The basic products of Alberta's commerce with both Canada and the United States depend on forces operating in the markets and political arenas beyond its boundaries. The cost of capital, the prices for energy, food, and manufactured goods, the size and extent of customs and transportation tariffs, and corporate and governmental policies regarding regional investment and paths of economic development—these are largely beyond its ability to control. Yet all are crucial to the operation of Alberta's economic system, and to the viability of its diverse spatial components.

The 1970s brought the first signs of a shift in the balance of economic and political power between Alberta and Canada. Quantum changes in the prices of crude oil and natural gas, and in the availability of these commodities, placed Alberta in a crucial position within the national economy after 1973. These changes allowed Alberta to play a role never played before, and unlikely to persist in the 1980s in the face of petroleum discoveries elsewhere in Canada and a reassertion of central authority by the federal government. This interlude brought much prosperity to Alberta, and witnessed important shifts in the location of corporate control and financial decision-making within Canada in favour of Alberta. Economic and population growth threatened, for the first time, to dislocate the traditional dominance of central Canada over its periphery. Calgary, in particular matured as a comprehensive head office energy centre, capable of administering vast petroleum operations throughout Alberta, Canada, and much of the world. Although crude oil production peaked in 1973 and the discovery of new reserves has failed to keep pace with the growth of demand, the province gained significantly in its proven reserves of natural gas and in the value of its coal reserves. A second oil sands plant came on stream and several others, including those processing heavy oil, were on the verge of development as the 1980s began. Alberta, and particularly Calgary, played a leading role in charting and implementing the search for petroleum in western Canada, the Beaufort Sea, the Arctic archipelago, and eastern Canadian offshore areas. Many of these new reserves underlie lands controlled by the federal government or other provinces, but much of the employment and economic benefit associated with their discovery accrued to companies based in Alberta.

The 1970s also witnessed another development which has considerable importance to Alberta's economic geography. With the unprecedented increase of revenue obtained by the provincial government from the rise of oil prices, the Government of Alberta in 1974 established the Heritage Savings Trust Fund to direct a large part of its revenues into projects intended to diversify the provincial economy and to reduce its vulnerability to the possible exhaustion of its energy base. By creating this financial lever, the provincial government has demonstrated the extent to which the redistribution of wealth can begin to change the locus of financial power in Canada and, thus, to redress the economic grievances which have plagued the region since long before Alberta became a province in 1905. (Discussed in Chapter 1.) The relocation by Canada's chartered banks of their petroleum investment and financial sections to Calgary in the 1970s complemented the growth in financial power symbolized by the Heritage Fund.

Unfortunately for Alberta, the shift of capital and economic growth to the west occurred simultaneously with the growing improverishment of the central government and with a decline in the fortunes of Canada's manufacturing economy based in southern Ontario and Quebec. While both problems may have been induced by defective economic policies on the part of the central government, their effect has been to create a need in the minds of many Canadians for an adjustment in the growing financial economic disparity between the west, particularly Alberta, and the six provinces east of Manitoba. The economic development of Alberta in the 1980s is more likely to be constrained by, and subject to, political and economic policies enunciated by the federal government than it was through most of the 1970s. Alberta's future relations with the rest of Canada may therefore be more in keeping with those that existed prior to the 1970s, when the traditional interests of central Canada dominated the west and Alberta. Although this historic dominance is traditionally interpreted as reflecting the economic interests of central Canadian business sectors, the reassertion of central authority in the 1980s appears to be more a function of the political goals of the central government than of the central Canadian business community.

trend back toward east

Conclusion

This brief assessment of Alberta's economic geography has emphasized Alberta's persistent, although sectorally maturing, role as a hinterland economy dependent on and vulnerable to changes in overseas, continental, and national heartlands. Core/periphery relationships also exist within the province and are displayed in the economic disparity between the two metropolitan centres and their vast hinterlands. Fundamentally, however, the entire province relies on capital-intensive primary industry. It is still the inherent wealth of the surface and subsurface natural environments that sustains Alberta's prosperity. That wealth is enhanced, on the one hand, by a diminishing friction of distance, as access is improved to outside markets for energy, and curtailed, on the other, by the institutionalized friction imposed by disadvantageous freight rates for the movement of agricultural and processed or manufactured commodities.

Production and consumption in Alberta is chiefly associated with either the initial or the final ends of major production chains extending into the world's heartlands and other markets. Downstream benefits from the application of technology to energy and agricultural commodities occur after these primary materials have been shipped out of Alberta; most manufactured goods consumed in the province have undergone numerous additions of value in processes located elsewhere. While this relationship did not prevent a surge of prosperity during the 1970s, most of Alberta's history and most scenarios for its future demonstrate the vulnerability inherent in the province's economic structure and economic geography. They suggest that the present interlude of prosperity must be managed effectively by all concerned to ensure that the characteristics of the province's economic base, its major markets and suppliers, and its corporate and governmental relationships do not adversely affect the well-being of all Albertans.

Within the province, the uneven distribution of economic activity has increasingly come to be seen as a source of weakness. It is even feared in some quarters that the unrestrained growth of Edmonton and Calgary could simply drain whatever remains of the viability of large hinterland areas. Whether that fear is warranted or not, regional disparity is indisputable, and the governments of Alberta and Canada have taken various steps to mitigate the social and economic consequences. (Chapter 6 looks at this problem.) Singly or in cooperation, they have extended aid for agricultural production and nutritive processing, provided support for small and local businesses in lower-order population centres and rural areas, assessed mineral resources, developed water resources, assisted indigenous populations in northern Alberta and slow-growth regions such as northern Alberta, and offered guidance to those requiring detailed sub-provincial spatial information. Many other programmed actions by government indirectly enhance the non-metropolitan locational environments of Alberta by maintaining significant levels of service and administrative employment, by improving sub-regional transportation services, infrastructure, and publicity, and by providing services to facilitate site selection. Ad hoc actions by government, such as the decentralization of some administrative and service functions, strengthen the employment bases of particular places. (Discussed further in Chapter 9.) Thus, as development arbiter and large employer, government has come to play a major role in the economic geography of Alberta.

Alberta Business Development and Tourism. *Industry and Resources*. Edmonton: 1980.

Barr, B.M., ed. *Calgary: Metropolitan Structure and Influence*. Western Geographical Series, Vol. 11. Victoria: University of Victoria, Department of Geography, 1975.

Barr, B.M. and Lehr, J.C. "The Western Interior: The Transformation of a Hinterland Region." In *A Geography of Canada: Heartland and Hinterland*, edited by L. D. McCann, 251–293. Scarborough: Prentice-Hall Canada, 1982.

Caldarola, C., ed. *Society and Politics in Alberta: Research Papers*. Toronto: Methuen, 1979.

Hall, E.M. *Grain and Rail in Western Canada. The Report of the Grain Handling and Transportation Commission*. Volumes 1 and 2. Ottawa: Supply and Services Canada, 1977.

Smith, P.J., ed. *Edmonton: The Emerging Metropolitan Pattern*. Western Geographical Series, Vol. 15. Victoria: University of Victoria, Department of Geography, 1978.

Smith, P.J., ed. *The Prairie Provinces*. Toronto: University of Toronto Press, 1972.

Smith, P.J. and Johnson, D.B. *The Edmonton-Calgary Corridor*. Edmonton: University of Alberta, Department of Geography, 1978.

Supplemental Readings

9 The Economic Role of Public Employers in the Urban Communities

Patrick G. Cadden

For the greater part of its history, Alberta has been governed by political parties of a conservative persuasion. The public sector of the provincial economy might therefore be expected to be small. In reality, however, a seeming paradox exists: expenditures on public education, health services, and administration are sizeable; public sector employees are numerous. Indeed, the portion of an urban economy occupied by the public sector can be estimated visually; the size and number of schools, hospitals, and government offices merely have to be compared with the size and number of all non-residential buildings.

The paradox can be explained partly by the abundant resources of the Alberta government. Post-war royalties from oil and gas production have provided the means for developing infrastructure and delivering a wide range of high quality public services, including education and health care. They are also labour-intensive services, so the number of public employees in Alberta has grown, and public employment is a major factor in the economic bases of urban communities all across the province.

The public sector influences local economic conditions in several ways. First, government policies for the management of national and provincial economies affect business activity and public expenditures generally. Second, a large part of the salaries of employees of educational establishments, hospitals, and government agencies (federal, provincial, and municipal) will be spent in the local community, as goods and services are purchased from local businesses. Third, public employees and employers alike contribute towards the cost of municipally-provided services, by paying taxes and user fees.

In this chapter some of the direct effects of having public offices and estab-

lishments in Alberta's urban communities will be reviewed. The relative size of the public labour force and its income is examined and explained. The spatial expenditure patterns of public employees and public employers are described. Past changes in the relative magnitude of the public workforce are analysed, as are the effects of the recent decentralization of government agencies. The findings are then used as a basis for speculating on the future importance of the public sector to the urban communities of Alberta.

Teachers, nurses, and clerks probably account for the majority of public employees in most communities but the scope of public employment includes many professional, financial, legal and technical occupations, municipal administration, and police. However, the majority of the most highly skilled jobs for the federal and provincial governments are located in Edmonton and Calgary, as are most university teaching positions and specialized hospital appointments. In most urban places, the variety of occupations in the public sector is relatively small.

The numerical importance of public sector employment can be assessed by counting the number of communities where public employees work and by calculating the number of jobs in the public sector as a percentage of a place's total labour force. Education employees are located in all the incorporated centres in Alberta, except some of under 500 population. When average percentages of the labour force are calculated for groups of places defined by population (Table 9–1), education employees account for shares between 6 per cent and 18 per cent. Moreover, the shares appear to increase, the smaller the community. The average for the group of smallest places (less than 250 population) deviates from this pattern because the absence of education employees from half the places—some of which are summer villages—pulls the average down.

Hospital and public administration and defence (PAD) employees are located in the larger communities but in only a few of the communities of less than 2500 population. As a consequence, their average labour force shares vary among the size-groups but do not increase or decrease consistently. The hospital employees' average shares lie between 1 per cent and 10 per cent, while the average shares of PAD employees lie between 2 per cent and 10 per cent.

When the employees in liquor stores, urban transit systems, telephone systems, and the post office are added to the total, it can be seen that public sector employees are ubiquitous among communities of over 250 population but not among smaller places. Their average share of the labour force in the latter communities is 18 per cent, which contrasts with averages between 24 per cent and 26 per cent in the higher size-groups. In round figures, the

Public Employment in Alberta's Communities in 1971

[handwritten margin note:] most urban places cntued excluding Ed. and Calg. have a small variety of gov't emp.; tends to fall in the lower-wage categories relative to other gov't jobs (teachers, nurses, clerks).

Table 9-1
Public employees in the urban labor force of incorporated communities, by population group, 1971

| Population group | Education and related services | | Hospitals | | Public administration and defence | | Total public sector* | | |
	Average share (%)	No. of employment locations	Average share (%)	No. of employment locations	Average share (%)	No. of employment locations	Average share (%)	No. of employment locations	No. of communities in the group
≥ 50,000	8.5	2	4.9	2	8.6	2	24.8	2	2
10,000–49,999	6.9	4	7.7	4	7.6	4	24.8	4	4
5,000–9,999	7.5	6	6.6	6	9.5	6	25.4	6	6
2,500–4,999	9.7	30	7.0	29	7.0	30	24.9	30	30
1,000–2,499	11.3	42	5.4	28	8.5	41	25.6	43	43
750–999	10.6	18	9.4	13	4.6	15	24.0	18	18
500–749	14.7	21	5.2	8	4.5	15	25.2	21	21
250–499	17.9	53	2.2	9	5.1	25	25.9	56	58
< 250	14.6	46	1.9	6	2.2	11	18.2	51	88
All groups	13.7	222	4.1	105	5.0	149	23.0	231	270

* "Public Sector" is comprised of education and related services, hospitals, public administration and defence, urban transit systems, highway and bridge maintenance, telephone systems, post office, water systems, and liquor, wine, and beer stores.

Source: *Census of Canada, 1971.*

public sector contributes—on average—a quarter of the employment in larger communities and about one-fifth in the smallest communities.

Average values do not imply that public employers, individually or collectively, provide the same percentage of local jobs in all the places in a group; the actual percentages differ from place to place. Moreover, statistical tests show that the population size of a community (a proxy for market size) cannot be used to predict the size of the public employers' percentages of the labour force in that place. The explanation for the variation among communities lies primarily with past organizational and locational decisions.

In the case of education, variables such as student numbers, accessibility, efficient operating size, range and quality of services, and the availability of funds have had to be considered by school boards when deciding whether or not to build new schools and where to locate them. Moreover, country schools have been consolidated in response to rural population changes over the last 40 to 50 years. The provincial government, for its part, has located universities, colleges, and technical institutes in Edmonton, Calgary, Grande Prairie, Fairview, Lac la Biche, Vermilion, Red Deer, Olds, Lethbridge, and Medicine Hat. The relative magnitude of the total educational employment in most of these places is correspondingly inflated.

The provincial government has also decided the location of most hospitals opened in the post-war period. According to longtime former premier of Alberta, E. C. Manning (1943–1968), hard and fast population or distance standards were not applied by his government. Rather, the selection process merely "took account" of the number of people in an area and the distance to an existing hospital in a neighbouring community. The locations of the province's mental hospitals were chosen with two needs in mind: regional accessibility and the maintenance of upper limits on the size of individual facilities. Such hospitals are located at Edmonton, Camrose, Red Deer, Ponoka, Calgary, Claresholm, and Raymond, with attendant effects on the share of the labour force in hospital employment. In Ponoka, for example, the mental hospital employs about 35 per cent of the urban labour force, which makes it by far the single largest contributor to the town's economic base.

extreme example of a discretionary facility's impact

The administrative and geographic organization of government departments and agencies varies from the simple to the complex. The government of an urban municipality will obviously be located in the city, town, or village it administers. Similarly, the government of a county or municipal district is located in one of the urban communities within its jurisdiction. Furthermore, nearly half the federal and provincial departments in Alberta are organized in a simple geographic manner, being represented in only one or two locations in the province, typically Edmonton or Calgary. The functions performed by these highly centralized agencies include specialized economic, fiscal and legal work, scientific research, and services related to the operation of the public service and the legislature. They account for only one-tenth of the federal and provincial employment in Alberta.

Most of the remaining federal and provincial agencies perform their responsibilities through field offices located in several urban centres, as well as through offices in Edmonton and Calgary. Their functions include the provision of services to selected areas with a particular socio-economic or resource character (for example, Indian reserves, national and provincial parks, agricultural regions and forests), as well as services to all of the province's population (for example the administration of educational, health and welfare services, and the operation of law courts and prisons). The agencies providing services to selected areas maintain offices in communities in the respective areas. The province-wide services are delivered from accessible locations in the administrative regions independently delimited by the various agencies, which do not maintain the same number of offices or share an identical set of field locations. Only four agencies with a regional organization are present in over 50 places: the Alberta Liquor Control Board, Alberta Treasury Branches, the Post Office, and the Royal Canadian Mounted Police. Most agencies have located in 25 or fewer communities, the majority of which happen to have a population of over 1000.

Other things being equal, a community will contain a relatively large proportion of government employees if several federal and/or provincial agencies have located there. Alternatively, a single facility located in or adjacent to the community may be large enough to account for an exceptionally high proportion of the labour force in PAD employment. Examples of such facilities are the national parks at Banff and Jasper, the Canadian Forces bases near Wainwright and Grand Centre, the Prairie Farm Rehabilitation Administration at Vauxhall, and the federal penitentiary at Drumheller. These locations have been chosen for environmental, strategic, or political reasons.

The Relative Size and Impact of Public Employees' Incomes

When Alberta's communities are grouped as in Table 9–1, the average incomes of education and PAD employees in each group of places are found to exceed the average income of the labour force as a whole. By contrast, the average income of hospital employees in each group falls below the labour force average. These relationships, while not holding in *all* the communities in each group, probably result from the relative bargaining strength of public employees. Teachers and civil servants are highly unionized and are paid according to provincial pay scales. By contrast, most private employees in Alberta communities are in retail and service occupations which tend to be low-paying. Moreover, relatively few private sector employees in smaller communities are unionized. Most hospital employees, while they may be unionized, bargain locally. Their below-average incomes may be due to a weakness in their negotiating power, or they may simply reflect the degree to which teachers' and civil servants' salaries pull up the average income levels of the communities.

Despite the inferior incomes of hospital employees, the average income of public sector employees as a whole exceeds that of private employees in every group of communities. On the average, and other things being equal, a public employee therefore possesses a greater potential for affecting the local economy than a private employee. However, public employees—like private employees—may distribute their expenditures among several centres. As consumers, they may be unable to obtain some goods and services locally or may prefer, for various reasons, to shop elsewhere. In addition, payments for some services may be mailed to out-of-town businesses (e.g., credit and finance companies), or they may be transferred to out-of-town head offices as soon as accounts are settled at local branch offices (as in the case of utility services).

Table 9-2

Geographical distribution of personal expenditures by public employees in 23 Alberta communities

| | Expenditures made in the home community | AVERAGE DISTRIBUTION OF EXPENDITURE BY A COMMUNITY'S PUBLIC WORKFORCE | | | | | | |
| | | Expenditures in other communities, by service centre rank of community | | | | | | |
Rank of workplace community in the Alberta hierarchy of service centres	(%)	First-order places (%)	Second-order places (%)	Third-order places (%)	Fourth-order places (%)	Fifth-order places (%)	Unidenti-fied places (%)	Total commun-ities (%)
Second-order	67.4	5.4	0.2	3.1	0.7	0.6	22.6	100.0
Third-order	54.7	9.6	10.1	1.1	0.3	1.0	23.2	100.0
Fourth-order	50.7	11.4	6.6	3.8	0.6	3.1	23.8	100.0
Fifth-order	31.4	14.9	7.3	9.7	11.3	2.7	22.7	100.0

Note: The questionnaire surveys on which this table is based were not administered to public employees in Edmonton and Calgary, the only first-order communities in Alberta. Between 75 and 85 percent of their expenditures are estimated to be local.

Questionnaire surveys in 23 Alberta communities confirm that on average public employees spend progressively more of their budget locally as the community's rank in the hierarchy of service centres increases (Table 9–2). For example, the employees in the second-highest rank of communities spend two-thirds locally, while employees in the fifth and lowest rank of places spend less than one-third locally. Irrespective of the community's rank, most out-of-town expenditures occur in relatively accessible places drawn from just one or two, but not necessarily all, of the higher ranks. The single most important external spending location is commonly one of the two first-order places, Edmonton and Calgary, whatever the distance from the place of work.

In view of these expenditure patterns, the local economic importance of public employees who earn exactly the same income but who work in different communities need not be identical. By the same token, the external economic impact of public employees will vary. If public sector jobs are partly intended to stimulate urban economies, employees' expenditure patterns should clearly be considered when the locations of the positions are being decided. An objective of maximizing the impact on a single community would be achieved by locating the positions in a high-ranking place, where a wide range of goods and services is available. Conversely, if several communities are intended to benefit from the employees' expenditures, the positions might be better located in a lower-ranking place. The limited range of goods and services available locally would encourage a high degree of patronage of other urban centres.

Expenditures by Public Employers

In theory, several kinds of non-salary expenditures can be made locally by public offices and facilities. Goods and services can be obtained from local businesses, premises may be leased from local property-owners, and payments for municipal services can be made to the local government. In practice, the total impact on the most urban economies is small.

Most Alberta communities are service centres which supply some of the needs of the residents of the locality and its hinterland. (Chapters 2 and 8 further study this pattern.) The manufacturing sector in these communities is extremely limited in size and diversity. Most of the costlier supplies required by schools, hospitals, and government offices are therefore unavailable. Even if items can be purchased from local sources, official purchasing regulations and the uncompetitiveness of locally quoted prices may work to the disadvantage of local firms. The federal and provincial governments, for example, are both likely to require their departments to purchase goods and services through a centralized purchasing agency. Moreover, the scale of government purchasing gives large suppliers and manufacturers a competitive advantage, since quantity discounts can be applied. Because the larger firms are concentrated in Edmonton and Calgary, and perhaps a few other places, firms in Alberta's small towns can rarely supply the local offices of federal and provincial departments with more than minor items.

Schools, hospitals, and municipal governments may try actively to support local businesses for reasons of policy. Materials such as stationery and foodstuffs may be available locally, but the suppliers of specialized needs are absent from most communities; some external purchasing is unavoidable.

It therefore has to be concluded that the business expenditures of public employers are secondary to the consumer expenditures of public employees in all communities except the very largest. One possible exception to this pattern occurs when office space is leased from a local property-owner. Not only does this generate revenue for the private sector, it is of benefit to the municipality as well, since publicly-owned buildings are exempt from local property taxes. Grants-in-lieu of taxation are commonly used to compensate municipal governments, but the public employers are obliged neither to make grants in respect of all their buildings nor to equate the grants with the municipalities' calculations of the tax owed.

[handwritten margin note: local purchasing minimal: - specialized goods unavailable, or uneconomical - central purchasing - publicly owned buildings exempt from taxes, grants don't make up for it]

The Changing Importance of Public Employment

Public employment has not always been as important economically as it was in 1971. The situation in that year was the product of continued growth in the number of employees in education, health and welfare services, and PAD in Alberta since the end of the Second World War. The needs arising from the post-war population boom, the demands of an increasingly affluent population for a higher quality of public services, and the acceptance by government of the need to regulate an increasingly complex economy were the main reasons. In Alberta, where oil and gas royalties provided the funds to support a large public workforce, the growth in public employment has been quite dramatic. Between 1961 and 1971, for example, the percentage of the urban labour force in education, health and welfare services, and PAD rose from 19 to 25 per cent.

This growth of public employment was not confined to just a few communities. Between 1961 and 1971 (the only census years for which compar-

Table 9-3

Public employees in the urban labour force of incorporated communities, by population group, 1961 and 1971 (based on place of residence)

1961 population group		Education and related services		Health and welfare services		Public administration and defence		Total		No. of communities in the group
		Average share (%)	No. of employment locations	Average share (%)	No. of employment locations	Average share (%)	No. of employment locations	Average share (%)	No. of employment locations	
≥ 50,000	1961	4.4	2	5.6	2	10.8	2	20.8	2	2
	1971	8.5	2	7.2	2	9.5	2	25.2	2	2
10,000–49,999	1961	4.3	3	9.9	3	8.7	3	22.9	3	3
	1971	7.3	3	11.4	3	8.9	3	27.6	3	3
5,000–9,999	1961	4.6	3	11.0	3	5.6	3	21.2	3	3
	1971	8.3	3	11.5	3	7.5	3	27.3	3	3
2,500–4,999	1961	5.7	19	8.1	19	8.4	19	22.2	19	19
	1971	8.4	19	9.5	19	8.8	19	26.7	19	19
1,000–2,499	1961	7.1	44	6.7	42	8.1	44	22.0	44	44
	1971	9.5	44	9.1	42	9.4	44	28.0	44	44
750–999	1961	7.4	15	5.4	10	6.6	15	19.4	15	15
	1971	10.5	15	7.8	15	8.8	15	27.1	15	15
500–749	1961	8.7	31	6.2	20	4.8	29	19.6	31	31
	1971	11.9	31	7.7	23	5.6	28	25.2	31	31
250–499	1961	9.7	71	3.0	30	6.2	59	18.9	71	71
	1971	13.6	68	4.8	42	8.1	57	26.5	71	71
<250	1961	10.6	44	2.4	10	3.2	20	16.2	49	55
	1971	8.9	35	4.8	16	6.5	23	20.2	44	55
Total	1961	8.7		4.7		6.0		19.4		
	1971	10.8		6.7		7.8		25.3		

Source: *Census of Canada,* 1961 and 1971.

able data are available), public employment increased as a percentage of the local labour force in three-quarters of Alberta's urban places. Moreover, the average percentage of public sector employment increased in every community size-group (Table 9–3), further indicating that the growth was not an isolated phenomenon. In 1961, the averages ranged from 16 to 23 per cent but by 1971 had risen to between 20 and 28 per cent. (Because of differences in the data base, these percentages for 1971 are different from those quoted earlier.) The increases were due largely to the job opportunities created in newly-constructed or expanded schools and hospitals in all sizes of communities. However, among the places of less than 250 population, the relative importance and number of locations of education employees decreased, a possible result of school consolidation. The relative importance of PAD employees generally grew less than that of education and health employees. Indeed, the PAD employees in places over 50,000 population (i.e. Edmonton and Calgary) increased numerically but experienced a decrease in their share of the labour force. Employment in other white-collar and service industries, including education and health, increased more rapidly.

Since 1971, the relative importance of public sector employment has probably increased. Certainly, the Government of Alberta has initiated programs that will increase the number of public employees in centres other than Edmonton and Calgary, most notably through the decentralization of provincial agencies and the construction of new hospitals in small centres. As the latter program was announced only in 1981, the community impacts remain to be seen. By contrast, the decentralization programs became government policy in 1971, so some of these effects can be assessed.

In the first five years, 11 offices and workshops were decentralized to 10 medium-sized or small communities. The donor communities in the majority of cases were Edmonton or Calgary. How the recipient communities were selected is unclear, but relevant considerations included a community's ability to accommodate new growth and the strength of the local lobby. The total number of positions which were moved or created by the relocated agencies was 287; the number of positions added to a single community ranged from 13 to 68 (Table 9–4). However, in 9 of the 10 communities the PAD employees' share of the local labour force was increased by only 3 per cent or less, and the one exception (16 per cent at Airdrie) is misleading. Four-fifths of the employees in the relocated agency live out-of-town, primarily in Calgary, only 30 km to the south. In this first phase of the decentralization program, the relative magnitude of government employees in the host communities was only marginally increased.

In other respects, the employees appear to have a similar economic impact to other Alberta government employees. The average salaries of the staff of the decentralized agencies are believed by some officials to be higher than local averages, and the employees generally conform to the spending pat-

impact increasing due to government decentralization and hospital building

Table 9-4

Alberta government decentralization, 1971–1976: selected employment statistics

Recipient place by urban size-group in 1971	Donor place and year of relocation	Relocated or newly created positions	Additional positions as percentage of 1971 labour force	Employees residing in recipient place	Resident employees as percentage of total agency employment
Group two					
Camrose	Edmonton, 1973	68	1.9	59	86.8
Group three					
Barrhead	Edmonton, 1974	16	1.4	15	93.8
Ponoka	Edmonton, 1974	38	1.9	38	100.0
Wetaskiwin	Edmonton, 1974 and 1975 (2 agencies)	34	1.3	28	82.4
Group four					
Airdrie	Calgary, 1975	47	15.9	9	19.1
Lac La Biche	1975*	15	1.5	12	80.0
Rimbey	1975*	19	2.9	16	84.2
Stettler	Edmonton, 1975	13	.7	5	38.5
Valleyview	1974*	23	3.0	15	65.2
Group five					
Vulcan	1974*	14	2.6	11	78.6

Sources: Progressive Conservative Association of Alberta, *A New Vitality for Alberta's Smaller Communities* (Edmonton, 1975); *Census of Canada,* 1971 (Unpublished data); senior officials in the decentralized agencies.
* No single donor place; the positions were drawn from Edmonton and various field offices existing prior to the administrative reorganization of the relevant agency.

terns of public employees as a whole. However, most of the recipient places are reasonably accessible to places ranked high (first or second order) in the Alberta urban hierarchy, which may encourage relatively more out-of-town shopping than if they were further away.

The relocated agencies resemble other government agencies in their local economic effects. Local purchasing of goods and services is negligible due to government purchasing regulations or the unavailability of the items required. Utility payments usually have little local impact; rental payments for accommodation are small; and custom-designed buildings are to be substituted for rental premises in several places. The municipal governments may therefore be eligible to receive grants-in-lieu of taxation, but not necessarily in fair reflection of the value of the property.

If the decentralization program had continued on the same scale as was practised between 1971 and 1976, the local importance of public employment would not have changed very much. Since 1976, however, some larger agencies have been included. An environmental research centre with an ultimate work force of 250 has been established in Vegreville to house various laboratory activities previously performed in Edmonton. Athabasca

University (150 employees) is to be moved from Edmonton to Athabasca, the Alberta Correspondence School (140 employees) has moved from Edmonton to Barrhead, and selected programs of the Northern Alberta Institute of Technology are being transferred from Edmonton to a new institute at Stony Plain.

The public sector's share of the labour force in the new host communities seems likely to increase more dramatically than in the places receiving agencies prior to 1976. Yet, in other respects, the impact may be quite limited. The facilities will not obtain goods and services locally and are not obliged to make grants-in-lieu of taxation. The employees, for their part, will stimulate the local retail economies, although not as much as if the communities were further from Edmonton. Since Edmonton is the closest centre and since it provides appreciably more purchasing opportunities, items which could be obtained locally may be purchased in the course of multi-purpose trips to the capital. Furthermore, the position of Stony Plain relative to Edmonton is similar to that of Airdrie with respect to Calgary. Those employees of the new institute who live in Stony Plain will be able to travel quickly to regional shopping centres in west Edmonton; employees who commute from Edmonton will have little reason to shop anywhere but in Edmonton.

If the local importance of public agencies and their workforces is to be increased significantly by decentralization, two key matters should be considered at greater length: the distance between host communities and larger service centres, and the lack of a local preference policy in official purchasing regulations.

The Future

As employment is the dimension of the public sector which is most significant to Alberta's urban economies, it is appropriate to consider how important public sector employment will be in the future. In the first place, if the province's population continues to grow, the demand for government services will increase, necessitating the hiring of more public servants. Yet, for organizational reasons, additional federal and provincial jobs may be located in the headquarters and field offices which already exist; not all communities may be affected. In addition, although the number of employees may increase, their relative importance will not grow if the workforces in other industries grow faster.

The future demand for educational and hospital services will be determined by the behaviour of specific components of population change. (See Chapter 3.) At present, the fertility rate and the death rate in Alberta are falling, and the rate of natural increase, until recently, was exceeded by large-scale immigration from other provinces. Although the total population will grow, the percentage of school-age people (5 through 19 years) in the population is projected to fall slightly by the end of the century. If any new education jobs are created, they would seem likely to be located in Edmonton and Calgary, the centres receiving the bulk of the additional families. As the percentage of senior citizens (65 years and over) in the population is projected to grow slightly, the demand for hospital services may increase. However, the facilities are likely to be spread between the larger communities, where the greatest numbers of senior citizens are likely to be concentrated, and the smaller communities, in which senior citizens already comprise a large proportion of the local population. The percentage of hospital employees in the labour force may grow more in the smaller communities, which seem unlikely to receive large infusions of private sector jobs and in which education employees may become economically less important.

Judging by experience to date, decentralization of provincial government agencies generally has little effect on the economies of the host communities. However, the workforces of the agencies being relocated in the early 1980s are larger than those of the agencies moved previously. Since the magnitude of the local economic effects will be increased proportionately, the relative importance of education and PAD employees may be increased in a few medium-sized or small communities. Moreover, the revival of hospital construction is likely to increase the relative magnitude of hospital employees in rather more of the smaller communities.

Two unknown factors are the future level of revenues from resource industries and the extent of opposition to "big government." Since the royalties paid by energy and mineral producers account for half the provincial government's revenues, any changes in output will directly affect the amount of funds available for education, hospital care, and provincial administration. Even if funds are available, the provincial government may be constrained by popular sentiment against further increases in the size of the public sector. In this event, the public employment shares of local labour forces would likely stabilize or fall. Indeed, that result may be achieved without a policy shift, since the comprehensiveness of the present social, economic, educational, and health care programs limits the scope for further increases in public employment throughout the urban system.

In short, the future magnitude of public employment is unpredictable. If past trends provide any key to the future, the public sector *will* become even more important as a source of employment and income in the majority of communities. However, the limited industrial and commercial base of most communities, and the omission of local preference from official purchasing regulations, will continue to prevent the public sector from broadening its economic importance to other than the very largest communities.

Supplemental Readings

Bird, R. M., Bucovetsky, M. W. and Foot, D. K. *The Growth of Public Employment in Canada.* Montreal: Institute of Research on Public Policy, 1979.

Bowland, J. G. "Geographical Decentralization in the Canadian Federal Public Service." *Canadian Public Administration* 10 (1964): 323–364.

Dale, E. H. "The General Problems of Western Canada's Small Rural Towns." In *Saskatchewan Rural Themes, Regina Geographical Studies,* edited by J. E. Spencer, 1: 87–100. Regina: University of Regina, Department of Geography, 1977.

Fairbairn, K. J. and Ironside, R. G. "An Appraisal of the Public Components of the Peace River Region." In *Frontier Settlement,* edited by R. G. Ironside, V. B. Proudfoot, E. N. Shannon and C. J. Tracie, 113–129. Edmonton: University of Alberta, Studies in Geography, Monograph 1, 1974.

Stabler, J. C. "The Future of Small Communities in the Canadian Prairie Region." *Contact* 9, No. 1 (1977): 145–173.

10 The Transactional Environment
Quaternary and Quinary Industry

Elizabeth S. Szplett

The transactional aspects of economic activity comprise the quaternary (knowledge-processing) and quinary (knowledge-creating) sectors. Together, they occupy a special place in the evolution of advanced economies. As modernization proceeds, and the industrial age gives way to the post-industrial one, there are pronounced shifts in the contributions which the various industrial sectors make to the gross national product. The share produced by the primary sector declines as the growth impulse shifts, in turn, to the secondary and tertiary sectors. Each expands rapidly, then stabilizes, and in the case of the secondary sector, may eventually experience a relative decline. In this general sequence, the transactional sectors expand late, but explosively. Many individual firms—even whole industries—of advanced economies come to engage almost exclusively in transactional activities, and they may eventually account for more than one quarter of the total labour force.

The purpose of this chapter is to identify the quaternary and quinary activities of Alberta, to assess their locational characteristics, and then to compare Alberta's transactional industry with that of Canada as a whole. Since the contribution of the public sector has been discussed in Chapter 9 (and government is a major transactional employer) the emphasis here is upon transactional activities in the private sector. The basic themes of Alberta's economic geography, as described in Chapter 8, will also be emphasized again. The importance of the physical environment particularly stands out, because of the dominant place that the petroleum industry holds in Alberta's transactional activities. Most notably, quaternary activities in Calgary, Canada's oil administrative city, are a profound reflection of important recent changes in Alberta's role as a hinterland to distant metropolitan centres.

Quinary activities are less developed in Alberta as yet, but they still serve to indicate the increasing complexity of economic activity and supporting services in a hinterland region. They are chiefly concentrated in Calgary and Edmonton, and are supported by the interest of government and business in research into the more effective use of environmental resources.

Quaternary Activities

Quaternary activities include the collection, receipt, recoding, arranging, storage, retrieval, exchange, dissemination, and interpretation of information and ideas. This information is used to control, coordinate, integrate, and plan corporate activities. Although entire industries engage in quaternary pursuits, every firm and industry devotes a substantial proportion of its activity and personnel to quaternary functions. Within a firm, the functions of many departments—general finance, accounting, office services, administration, advertising, public relations, personnel, records, legal, and data processing—are primarily quaternary. More generally, for the purposes of this chapter, the quaternary sector of the economy is taken to include those firms and organizations (or the relevant parts of firms and organizations) associated with commodity exchanges, securities, banking, insurance, legal services, accounting, advertising, the media, publishing, real estate, data processing, religion, libraries, education, medical services, and governments (including regulatory and development agencies).

At all levels—global, national, and metropolitan—quaternary activities are highly concentrated. They are drawn to the central areas of large metropolitan communities because attempts to reach non-routine decisions and to carry out strategic planning create a need for specialized information that cannot normally be satisfied in any but the largest urban complexes. The highly interdependent nature of business necessitates face-to-face meetings with similar businesses (whether a purchaser, supplier, project partner or competitor), with government agencies (which may act as purchasers, regulators, partners or financiers), and with specialized information-generating business services (which are themselves dependent upon high information access).

Accessibility to decision-makers and business services in other urban areas is also crucial, and the larger the city the better its access to other large cities is likely to be. Thus, the rapid rise in quaternary employment and its accelerated concentration in large cities has affected regional economies and exacerbated inequalities that existed already. Even decentralization of office employment does not necessarily offset this effect, since it is normally only the lower level, routine jobs that are relocated. This simply increases the relative concentration of the most highly skilled employees in the head office, where they make decisions that affect the employment trends and structure of all other regions. The greatest economic benefits therefore accrue to the major cities, because head office employees have higher disposable incomes and, relative to employees at other levels and in smaller places, they require more specialized information and services. The firms providing these services and information are themselves most likely to be located in the same cities.

Alberta's Quaternary Industry

As the western provinces comprise a hinterland to the Ontario-Quebec heartland, it might be expected that Alberta would enjoy proportionately less quaternary employment than Canada as a whole. Yet Alberta's early and persistent hinterland status is revealed most strikingly in its high employment in primary activities and its low employment in manufacturing; the difference between Alberta and Canada in the employment structure of their tertiary and quaternary industries has never been great. Indeed, industries with a high proportion of quaternary activity—public administration, finance, insurance, real estate, services (especially business services), transportation, communication, and utilities—are well represented in Alberta.

GENERAL QUATERNARY EMPLOYMENT STRUCTURE: Alberta's employment in managerial occupations is average for Canada (Table 10–1). Although an un-

Table 10-1
Managerial employment in Canada and Alberta, 1971

Sector	Managerial employment as a percentage of total employment in each sector		Distribution of total managerial employment by sector (%)	
	Canada	Alberta	Canada	Alberta
Primary, except mining	0.3	0.1	0.4	0.4
Petroleum	4	11	2	10
Manufacturing	4	4	19	8
Construction	3	3	4	6
Transport/communications/ utilities	4	4	7	7
Trade	3	2	10	9
Finance/insurance/ real estate	13	14	13	12
Services	5	5	26	29
Public administration	11	8	18	16
All sectors	4	4	(100)	(100)

Source: Statistics Canada, catalogue no. 71-001, *The Labour Force* (Ottawa, 1971).

usually high proportion of Alberta's total labour force is in non-petroleum primary industries which have low ratios of quaternary activity (in both Alberta and the entire country), Alberta has the same proportion of managers and administrators in the labour force as Canada as a whole. The difference, of course, is made up by the petroleum industry. Relative to Canada, Alberta has: (1) an abnormally high proportion of managers in the petroleum industry; (2) a slightly high percentage of managers in construction and services (reflecting the high percentage of employment in those industries); and (3) a very low proportion of managers in manufacturing.

Within Alberta, quaternary activities of all kinds are disproportionately concentrated in the major urban centres. Four-fifths of the managers in manufacturing, finance, insurance, and real estate, almost 70 per cent of those in communications, and two-thirds of those in health, transportation, education, business services, and public administration work in Edmonton and Calgary alone (Table 10–2). The proportion of employment in managerial, professional, and clerical fields has also risen steadily in these cities. Both have disproportionately large labour forces in manufacturing, trade, transportation, communication, utilities, and services, all of which generate substantial quaternary employment. In addition, Calgary exhibits greater

Table 10-2
Percentage of each sector's managerial employment in major groups of urban places, 1971

	Edmonton	Calgary	Lethbridge, Red Deer, Medicine Hat	All other towns
Percentage of total urban population	32	26	6	35
Percentage of managerial employment in:				
mining	16	43	2	39
manufacturing	44	35	9	12
trade	31	24	6	39
transportation/ communications/ utilities	40	31	7	22
finance/insurance/ real estate	40	40	6	14
business services	38	31	8	23
public administration	42	23	6	29
Total	36	32	6	25

Sources: Alberta Bureau of Statistics, *Alberta Statistical Review*, 1980, and Statistics Canada, catalogue no. 71-001, *The Labour Force* (Ottawa, 1971).

than average participation in mining (petroleum) and business services, while Edmonton exhibits greater than average participation rates in education, health, and public administration.

In the group of second-order cities (Lethbridge, Red Deer, and Medicine Hat), where the shares of managerial employment tend to be in proportion with population (Table 10–2), the only sectors in which all three cities have an over-representation of total quaternary employment are trade and services (especially health services). Some other sectors also show higher than expected quaternary employment in individual cities (e.g. transportation in Medicine Hat, manufacturing in Lethbridge and Medicine Hat), but in the smaller towns of Alberta the proportions of managerial and administrative personnel are comparatively low. Thus, only in Edmonton and Calgary is there indisputable evidence of high-level quaternary activity.

BUSINESS SERVICE COMPONENT: Business services may be quaternary activities in their own right or facilitators of decision-making in other industries. They grow with the overall level of quaternary activity, and may therefore be used as a general measure of quaternary functions.

Alberta's business services are concentrated in Calgary (48 per cent) and Edmonton (35 per cent), although some types of service are more concentrated than others (Table 10–3). Architects, electronic data processing firms, employment agencies, and management consultants are highly concentrated; advertising agencies, engineers, security firms, and lawyers are somewhat concentrated; accountants are dispersed. Calgary also has a

Table 10-3

Distribution of selected business services in Alberta, 1980

| | Percentage of firms | | |
	Edmonton	Calgary	All other places
Architects	49	45	6
Data processing	17	73	10
Management consultants	45	45	10
Employment agencies	48	40	12
Engineers	28	57	15
Advertising agencies	43	41	16
Security firms	37	46	17
Lawyers	42	39	19
Accountants	32	40	28

Sources: Alberta Government Telephones, *Calgary Yellow Pages*, 1980, and Edmonton Telephones, *Edmonton Yellow Pages*, 1980.

higher business service profile than Edmonton, and more of its labour force is engaged in services demanded by the oil industry including electronic data processing, engineering, security, and accounting. Relative to Calgary, Edmonton offers more employment agencies and legal services.

CORPORATE HEAD OFFICE COMPONENT: The ranking by *Canadian Business* of the largest businesses in Canada indicates the relative concentration of quaternary activity in Canada, as measured by the locations of head offices (Table 10–4). It also supports the notion that quaternary functions congregate in the largest urban areas. Almost 54 per cent of the top 500 head offices are located in Canada's two largest cities. Of the 47 Alberta firms which made the list for 1980, 39 (83 per cent) have head offices in Calgary, seven (15 per cent) have head offices in Edmonton and one has a head office in Lethbridge. Nearly half—eighteen petroleum companies and four industrials—are oil and gas firms, confirming the petroleum industry's importance to Alberta's quaternary structure.

Calgary is outstanding as Canada's oil and gas administrative centre. From 1950 to the present, Calgary has been the location of over half of the country's head offices for both oil-operational and oil-administrative firms. Edmonton, a distant second, has approximately one-eighth of the nation's oil business head offices.

But while Calgary dominates the administrative side of the industry, financial affairs are controlled from Toronto. Calgary is the Canadian oil industry's

Table 10-4

Head office location of major Canadian corporations

	Percentage of total population	Percentage of top 200 firms (by sales)		Percentage of top 500 firms (by sales)
		1971	1980	1980
Montreal	12.7	17.0	22.0	18.0
Toronto	10.9	36.0	53.0	36.0
Vancouver	5.0	7.5	12.0	9.0
Ottawa	2.8	0.5	3.0	2.0
Winnipeg	2.5	0.5	4.0	2.2
Hamilton	2.3	3.0	1.5	0.8
Edmonton	2.3	1.0	2.5	1.8
Quebec City	2.2	0	0	0.2
Calgary	1.9	9.0	9.5	7.2

Source: *Canadian Business*, July 1980.

head office location for almost seven-eighths of the producers, explorers, and developers, three-fourths of the lease brokers, land services, and consultants, and two-thirds of the data processors, but only 30 per cent of the finance and investment firms. On the other hand, in addition to being Alberta's financial centre, Calgary is Canada's fourth largest city in terms of the value of stocks traded. The city grew as a financial centre during the 1970s when Canada's chartered banks began to relocate their petroleum finance and investment sections, and many international financial institutions established Canadian offices in Calgary.

Although control of petroleum operations is dispersed, Calgary also dominates operational head offices. Over half the geophysical, exploration drilling, oil well drilling contracting, pipeline and power distribution head offices in Canada are located in Calgary. It is also the major head office location for service and supply, engineering, design, construction and fabrication, and refining, marketing and processing firms. Only the head offices of firms in transportation and oil well servicing are not highly concentrated in Calgary, which has been consolidating its position of control in all other aspects of the oil industry over the past thirty years. Edmonton, meanwhile, has declined in all respects as a petroleum quaternary centre.

Calgary has developed as Canada's permanent quaternary petroleum centre on the basis of accessibility, skilled labour, superior transportation connections, specialized services, and comprehensive amenities. As the closest major city to Turner Valley, where oil and gas were first discovered in 1914, Calgary became the headquarters for oil exploration and related services companies. Alberta's first refinery, emphasizing proximity to the oil fields, was also located in Calgary. Social and business clubs dedicated to communications among oilmen, and the establishment of government agencies such as the Petroleum and Natural Gas Conservation Board (now the Energy Resources Conservation Board), affirmed the city's importance as an oil centre.

Few firms relocated in Edmonton after the Leduc discovery in 1947 because contact networks were strong in Calgary and head office locations had become independent from oil fields. Calgary's access to the south (Texas and Oklahoma) and east (New York) was superior to Edmonton's, and oil developers from the western United States were at home with Calgary's "stampede city" atmosphere. The petroleum clubs also helped these developers to maintain their network of contacts with the American industry. In addition, Calgary businesses were more oriented to the oil industry, and the city's business community appears to have reacted more quickly than Edmonton's to the industry's special needs. During the several oil booms, for example, the growth of office space in Calgary has outsupplied that of Edmonton.

Although Calgary-based firms are active in oil fields throughout the world—at least one firm with a head office in Calgary operates only in

Labrador—inertia is likely to maintain Calgary's petroleum quaternary status in the near future. Oil industry decision-makers must locate near other producers, explorers, and developers; the high costs and high risks of exploration and government regulations concerning the joint management of pools force them into a web of complex transactions which require close relationships.

Quinary Activities

Quinary activities emphasize the creation, assembly, rearrangement, and interpretation of new and old information and ideas. They also focus on innovation in methods of data interpretation, and on the derivation, implementation and evaluation of new techniques. Firms and organizations in this category include colleges, universities, "think tanks," institutes of basic and applied research, planning agencies, and various consultants (managerial, socio-economic, engineering, scientific, and environmental).

Because the benefits of basic research are not usually immediate (i.e. profitable), government dominates quinary industry. The federal government, for example, funds 43 per cent and performs 28 per cent of all research and research-related activities in Canada. Over sixty government agencies and departments spent over $668 million on scientific activities during the 1978–79 fiscal year. Provincial governments fund and perform an additional 6 per cent per year, while universities account for a further 15 per cent and 28 per cent, respectively. Finally, private business funds and performs about one-third of all research activity, though it prefers to concentrate on applied research; consultants in engineering, socio-economic, geological, and environmental fields and computer software companies are examples. Many firms, particularly large, multi-locational corporations, contain quinary components like research laboratories and corporate planning departments. All the large oil companies in Calgary, for example, have corporate planning departments, engaged in the preparation of economic forecasts. Some have developed their own petrological, geophysical, or micro-paleontological laboratories as well, and many of them participate in collaborative petroleum-related research.

In some respects, quinary activities are less constrained in their choice of location than high-order quaternary functions. Nevertheless, research and development activities also tend to agglomerate in large urban areas, where federal government facilities, universities, manufacturing activities, and corporate headquarters are most likely to be found.

Alberta's Quinary Industry

Alberta's quinary sector, like its quaternary sector, is not out of proportion with that of Canada as a whole. In 1971, 28 per cent of the total federal expenditure for extramural research (grants and contracts to non-federal government agencies) went to support research in institutions and firms in Alberta. Likewise, over one-third of all extramural research and development expenditures by provincial governments in 1971 were spent by Albertan government research trusts, departments, and agencies.

GENERAL QUINARY EMPLOYMENT STRUCTURE: The location of quinary industry is difficult to determine from census employment statistics, because separate classifications are not provided for research. Natural and social scientists can be used as surrogate measures for quinary employment, just as managers and administrators are indicators of quaternary employment. Overall, Alberta has the same proportion of natural scientists and social scientists as Canada, but it has more natural scientists in mining (petroleum) and services and more social scientists in public administration (Table 10–5). The obverse, once again, is proportionately fewer natural scientists in manufacturing and fewer social scientists in either services or manufacturing.

Table 10-5
Scientific personnel in Canada and Alberta, 1971

| | SCIENTISTS AS A PERCENTAGE OF EMPLOYMENT IN EACH SECTOR | | | | PERCENTAGE DISTRIBUTION OF SCIENTIFIC PERSONNEL BY SECTOR | | | |
| | Natural | | Social | | Natural | | Social | |
	Canada	Alberta	Canada	Alberta	Canada	Alberta	Canada	Alberta
Primary, except mining	0.6	0.3	––	––	1	2	––	––
Petroleum	10.0	17.4	0.2	0.6	6	23	––	3
Manufacturing	3.8	3.3	0.1	0.1	28	10	3	1
Construction	2.2	2.2	––	––	5	6	––	––
Transportation/communications/utilities	3.9	3.8	0.2	0.1	11	10	2	1
Trade	0.5	0.4	––	––	3	2	1	1
Finance/insurance/real estate	1.5	0.7	0.4	0.1	2	1	2	1
Services	2.8	3.4	2.6	2.1	25	29	68	60
Public administration	6.7	6.4	3.0	3.6	18	17	24	33
Total	2.7	3.0	0.9	0.8	100	100	100	100

Source: Statistics Canada, catalogue no. 94-792, *Occupation by Industry* (Ottawa, 1971).

FEDERALLY FUNDED RESEARCH: Because of the role of government agencies in research in Canada, the location of federal research institutions is particularly important to quinary industry. The major Albertan research branches of the Department of Energy, Mines and Resources (EMR) are the Western Research Laboratory in Edmonton, the Institute of Sedimentary and Petroleum Geology in Calgary, a mining research laboratory in Calgary and the Coal Mining Research Centre at Devon. One of the Department of Environment's (ENV) six national centres is also located in Edmonton, and the Department of Agriculture has a northern research station at Beaverlodge. The Department of National Defence has a laboratory at Suffield to investigate countermeasures against chemical and biological warfare.

The same pattern is revealed in the research which various federal departments and ministries contract to private industry and universities. Of the 106 contracts awarded to Alberta during the 1979–80 fiscal year, 46 per cent went to Edmonton and 43 per cent to Calgary. The average value of contracts awarded to Calgary researchers was substantially greater, however, so that the distribution of expenditures was 64 per cent to Calgary and 28 per cent to Edmonton (Table 10–6). The remaining contracts were awarded chiefly to southern Albertan business for agricultural and petroleum-related research.

Calgary and Edmonton are notably different in terms of funding agency and performer. Forty-three per cent of the contracts and 20 per cent of the

Table 10-6
Federal government funding of research in Alberta in 1979–80
(in percentage of funds)

Funding Agencies	Edmonton	Calgary	Other
To universities			
Energy, Mines and Resources	1.4	1.5	0
Agriculture	1.6	0	0
Other	2.6	0.9	0
Total	5.6	2.4	0
To private firms and individuals			
Energy, Mines and Resources	8.7	23.2	0.7
Environment	2.4	15.7	0.2
National Research Council	7.5	16.9	0
Agriculture	1.8	3.5	2.4
National Defence	0	0.4	2.6
Other	2.1	2.3	1.8
Total	22.4	62.0	7.7
Grand totals	28.0	64.3	7.7

Source: Canada Supply and Services, *Research and Development Bulletin,* April 1980.

funds were awarded to university researchers in Edmonton, as compared with 7 per cent and 4 per cent, respectively, in Calgary. Half of the Edmonton EMR contracts, for example, were awarded to university researchers, in contrast to 5 per cent in Calgary. There was also a distinction in the chief sources of funds, with Calgary receiving more EMR contracts and fewer ENV contracts than Edmonton. These patterns strongly emphasize the petroleum orientation of Calgary's quinary industry, and the orientation toward university and government in Edmonton.

PROVINCIALLY FUNDED RESEARCH: In comparison with the nation as a whole, provincial funding of research in Alberta is above average. For example, the Alberta Research Council (ARC), which focuses on resource evaluation, environmental problems, primary industry, industrial development, and transportation, funds 28 per cent of all research supported by the eight provincial industrial research institutes in Canada. Research is also supported by provincial departments and agencies, some of which have established separate research agencies (such as AOSTRA, the Alberta Oil Sands Technology and Research Authority, the Alberta/Canada Energy Resources Research Fund, and the Reclamation Research Program). In addition, the province has established research trusts (Alberta Agricultural Research Trust, Alberta Environmental Research Trust, Alberta Heritage Foundation for Medical Research, Alberta Mental Health Research Fund, and Alberta Forest Development Research Trust) to support research in areas of critical importance. These government agencies both conduct their own research and sponsor the research efforts of universities, industries, and private persons.

Nearly two-thirds of the funding of research at the University of Alberta and the University of Calgary originates from the government of Alberta (Table 10–7); and over half of that share is directed into medical research. In addition, the University of Alberta is a major recipient of grants for agricultural and forestry research, while grants to the University of Calgary tend to focus on energy technology and natural resources.

PRIVATELY FUNDED RESEARCH: Private research support at the two universities also displays Calgary's emphasis on petroleum activity; relative to the University of Alberta, the University of Calgary receives twice as much funding from resource-related private associations and foundations (Table 10–7). In addition, over four-fifths of the University of Calgary's industrial donors are energy firms.

This difference between Calgary and Edmonton is also seen in the number of resource-related consultant firms (geological, geophysical, biological, and environmental) in the two cities: 279 in Calgary, only 59 in Edmonton. On the other hand, the number of economic research and analysis companies is

Table 10-7
Sources of funds for sponsoring research, 1981–82 (in percentages)

	University of Calgary	University of Alberta
Federal Government	43.3	44.8
Natural Sciences and Engineering Research Council	25.8	27.3
Medical Research Council	11.4	12.6
Total Medical	12.2	12.8
Total Agriculture	0.04	0.4
Total Natural Resources	1.5	2.1
Provincial Government	40.6	37.1
Alberta Heritage Foundation for Medical Research	26.3	20.3
Alberta Oil Sands Technology and Research Authority	5.4	3.0
Alberta Agriculture	0.1	4.7
Total Agriculture and Forestry	0.1	6.3
Total Natural Resources	9.3	5.7
Total Medical	30.8	23.8
Private	14.4	16.2
Associations	9.4	12.3
National Cancer Institute of Canada	0	3.9
Total Medical	7.1	7.0
Total Natural Resources	0.7	0.3
Total Environment	0.5	0.7
Business and Industry	4.8	3.7
Canada energy firms	3.4	*
International energy firms	0.9	*

* Data not available.
Sources: Comptrollers' Offices of the University of Calgary and the University of Alberta.

about equal (Calgary 12, Edmonton 10), while Edmonton has more research and development bureaus than Calgary does (18 and 10 respectively).

Summary and Conclusion

Quaternary and quinary activities favour large urban areas, by virtue of their need for contact with other businesses, corporate head offices, specialized information-generating business services, money markets, universities, and government agencies. In Alberta's case, the available evidence on sectoral employment, management, business services, head offices, scientific personnel, government research agencies, and government and private funding of research suggests the upward transitional nature of the province's hinterland role. The location of these activities confirms the intense concentration of quaternary and quinary activities in the two metropolitan centres—Calgary and Edmonton. Those few activities that are found in peripheral areas of the province are related mainly to primary industry.

Between the two principal quaternary centres, Calgary is the more prominent. A foundation of accessibility and labour supply, enhanced by the development of specialized services, comprehensive amenities, and a "stampede" spirit, enabled Calgary to become Canada's quaternary oil centre. Since the 1950s, centripetal forces have consolidated the industry's head offices in Calgary, and have also pulled related quaternary functions, notably financial and computing services, to the city. Edmonton's quaternary role, on the other hand, rests on its function as the provincial seat of government. Thus, Edmonton's business services and managerial expertise, although heavily resource-oriented, are more diverse.

Similar differences are found in the quinary activities of the two metropolitan areas. In Calgary's case, research and development activities are attracted by the concentration of petroleum and other head offices, by the availability of several institutions of advanced education, and by the presence of federal and provincial government agencies. Quinary firms choose Edmonton because of its concentration of federal and provincial agencies, and its educational institutions. Moreover, Edmonton's research is predominantly performed by government agencies (including universities), while that of Calgary is split between private industries and public universities. Thus, Calgary's transactional activity is dominated by petroleum, Edmonton's by government.

In conclusion, Alberta's high primary-sector employment and low manufacturing employment still signify a hinterland Canadian economy, although its relatively strong quaternary and quinary sectors are a mark of economic advancement. In its mix of transactional employment, however, Alberta continues to be unbalanced: primary petroleum and agriculture are still heavily favoured and underline, for the final time in this book, the continuing importance of the natural environment to the provincial economy. It also follows that transactional industries are vulnerable to external influences on their underlying primary industries. Yet, they also offer the brightest hope for a prosperous future. As Alberta's quaternary and quinary economic base is strengthened, and generates its own locational inertia, the transactional industries can be expected to offset the probable decreases in employment in primary oil and gas extraction. They will thus help to ensure that the employment bases of the metropolitan centres will remain viable and dynamic, maintaining a prosperous economic climate from which Alberta's smaller cities should also be expected to benefit.

Supplemental Readings

Britton, J. N. H. and Gilmour, J. M. *The Weakest Link: A Technological Perspective on Canadian Industrial Underdevelopment.* Ottawa: Science Council of Canada, Background Study 43, 1978.

Malecki, J. "Locational Trends in R & D by Large U.S. Corporations, 1965–1977," *Economic Geography* 55, no. 4 (1979): 309–323.

Pederson, E. O. *Office Location: An International Bibliography.* Monticello, Ill.: Council of Planning Librarians, Exchange Bibliography, No. 1278, 1974.

Pred, A. R. *Major Job-Providing Organizations and Systems of Cities.* Washington, D. C.: Association of American Geographers, Commission on College Geography, Resource Paper 27, 1974.

Robbins, S. M. and Terleikyi, N. E. *Money Metropolis.* Cambridge, Mass.: Harvard University Press, 1960.

Semple, R. K. *Trends in the Geographical Concentration of Corporate Headquarters in Canada.* Columbus: Ohio State University, Department of Geography, Discussion Paper No. 44, 1974.

Zieber, G. H. "Calgary as an Oil Administrative and Oil Operations Centre." In *Calgary: Metropolitan Structure and Influence,* edited by B. M. Barr, 77–121. Western Geographical Series, Vol. 11. Victoria: University of Victoria, Department of Geography, 1975.